IMAGES
of America

BANGOR
VOLUME II
THE TWENTIETH CENTURY

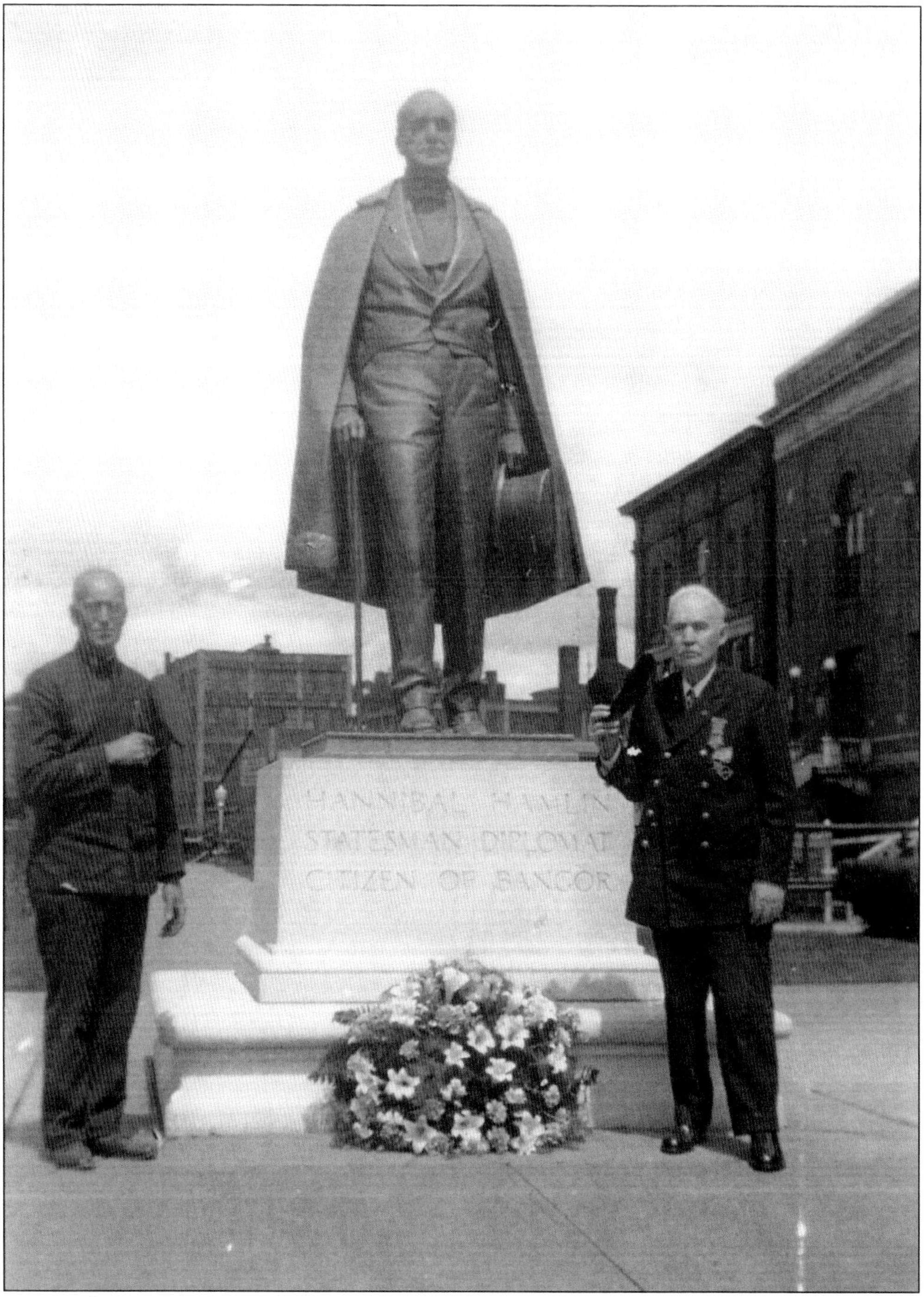

Bangor's last two surviving Civil War veterans stand by the Hannibal Hamlin statue downtown on Memorial Day, May 30, 1933. George S. Smith is pictured on the right; the other man is Daniel W. Warren. In 1868, just three years after the war ended, local men organized a chapter of the Grand Army of the Republic. They formed a second chapter in 1891. Ryan King, a Civil War re-enactor, made this photograph available for publication.

IMAGES
of America

BANGOR
VOLUME II
THE TWENTIETH CENTURY

Richard R. Shaw

ARCADIA
PUBLISHING

ISBN 978-0-7385-3703-0

Published by Arcadia Publishing,
Charleston, South Carolina

Printed in the United States of America

Library of Congress Catalog Card Number: 2004111105

For all general information, contact Arcadia Publishing:
Telephone 843-853-2070
Fax 843-853-0044
E-mail sales@arcadiapublishing.com
For customer service and orders:
Toll-free 1-888-313-2665

Visit us on the Internet at www.arcadiapublishing.com

Affectionately dedicated to my fellow airport greeters who, in 1991, gave a hometown welcome to untold thousands of returning Gulf War troops. I believe we made a difference.

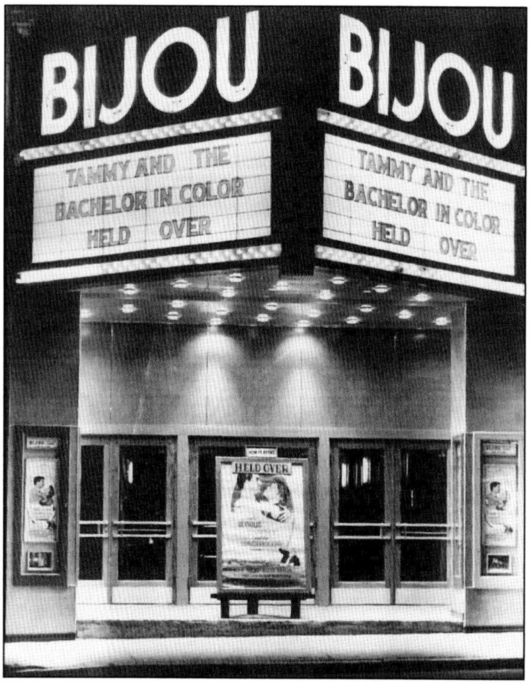

The marquee of the Bijou Theater illuminates the exterior of the Exchange Street movie house in 1957. Opened in 1912 as a vaudeville theater, the Bijou later mixed live and filmed entertainment, but eventually showed only motion pictures. The building was razed in 1973 and the property is now the site of a bank building.

Contents

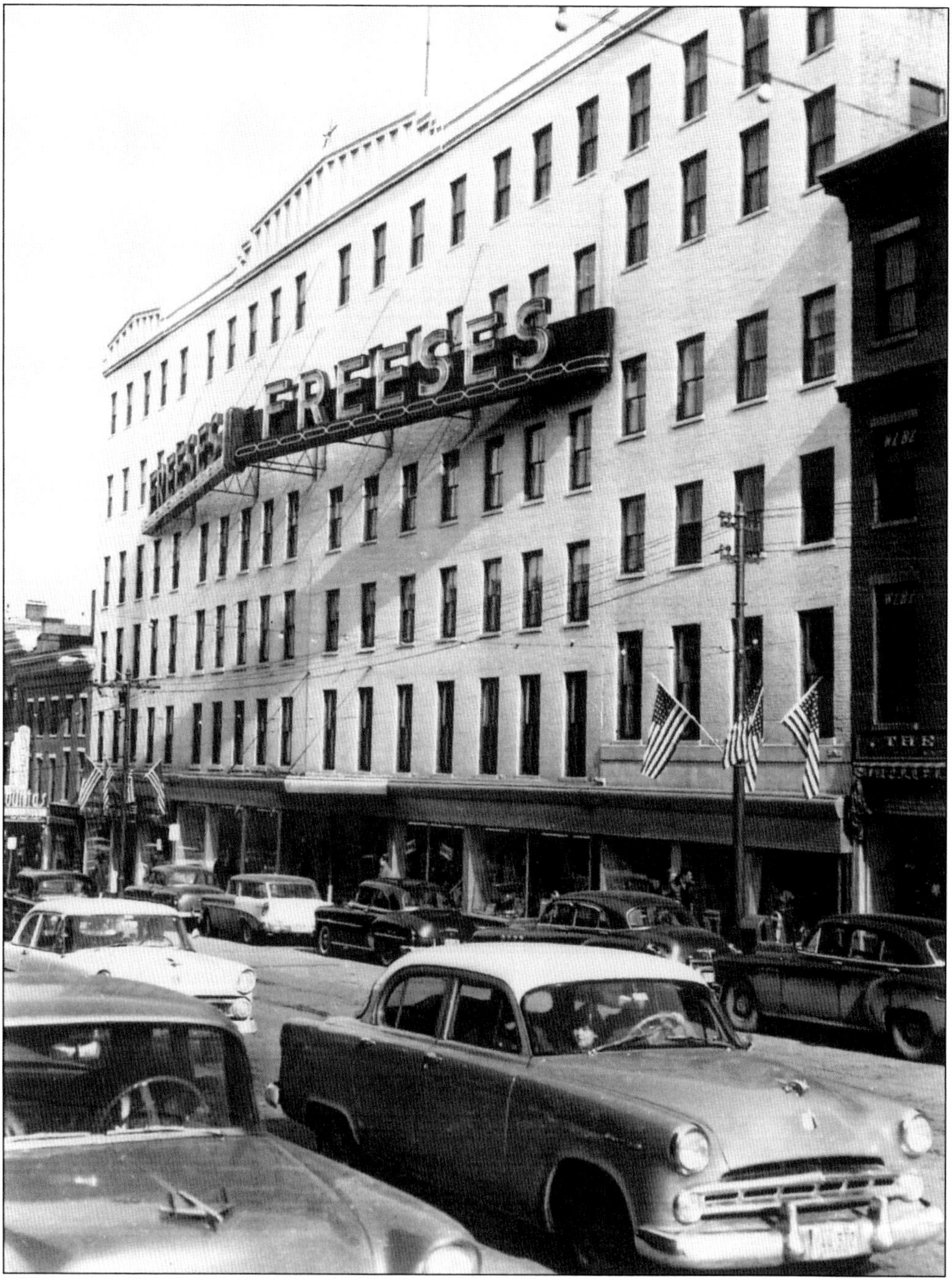

Downtown Bangor and Freese's Department Store were synonymous from 1892, when A. Langdon Freese opened a small business on Main Street, until 1985, when it closed its doors forever. Renovation projects eventually expanded the store to seven stories, where shoppers' purchases ranged from Boy Scout uniforms to wedding dresses. The business was nicknamed "Fifth Avenue in Maine" because of its popularity and the variety of merchandise.

Introduction

When I was invited by Arcadia editors to compile a second volume of vintage Bangor photographs, it didn't take long for me to decide what those images would show. With the millennium just around the corner, and a myriad of television shows, books, and magazine articles soon to chronicle life in the twentieth century, I settled on an informal portrait of my hometown featuring pictures from the last one hundred years. My work was cut out for me. The postcard collections that I had access to were chock full of pictures of the Great Fire of 1911, the spring flood of 1923, airport activities, and other pivotal events from this century. Others showed Bangor's downtown when it was the hub of eastern Maine, along with those of everyday people working at the city's many industries or, in contrast, sitting on a park bench soaking up the Sunday sun. The files of the *Bangor Daily News*, where I have worked for two decades, also produced some wonderful photographs that haven't been published in years, if at all. With a little digging, head librarian Charles Campo and his staff unearthed pictures of John F. Kennedy delivering a 1960 stump speech (pp. 14–15), Richard M. Nixon's disastrous airport visit in 1971 (pp. 16–17), and a photograph that brought tears to my eyes, the dynamiting of Union Station tower in 1961 (p. 126). Many happy and sad moments are recalled in this book. As a baby boomer well into his fifth decade as a "Bangorean," I can conjure up a few myself. But tattered clippings and eager historians tell the real story of what happened to us in this century. Turn-of-the-century celebrants at downtown ballrooms could only have guessed what the next ten decades held in store as they raised a toast to the strange-sounding 1900s and bid goodbye to the nineteenth century on New Year's Day 1900. If a local Nostradamus had stood up and told them their city would burn flat and miraculously be rebuilt, that people would fly anywhere in the world from their hometown, or that Pickering and Haymarket Squares would one day cease to exist as marketplaces, a skeptic surely would have shouted him down. But that's just what happened to the "Queen City" in the twentieth century. The highs and the lows, perhaps as any small city of its size, have been remarkable. Looking only at the highs for a moment, imagine that during the Great Depression, the Bangor and Aroostook Railroad Company was one of the few railways in the nation to turn a profit. Or that the city's trolley system, which ran into the 1940s, was one of America's first. And think of this: when many predicted Bangor, and certainly its airport, would wither up and die when Dow Air Force Base folded its tent and left town in the late 1960s, farsighted civic leaders believed the city geographically was suited to build an international airport, which is just what it did in 1968. But how to represent the lows in a book designed to have nostalgic value? Well, some images were just never included. Many I considered were either too gruesome, too depressing, or too redundant. After all, how many photographs of building demolitions must we see to know that Bangor lost many treasures during the Urban Renewal era? I think the point was made with the handful I decided to publish. Fires, floods, even gangster shootings, don't have to be negative images. They have become a part of our community heritage and need to be seen again and again. There is a kind of twisted beauty in the 1911 view of the burning of the First Congregational Parish steeple (p. 69), and pathos in the 1923 picture (p. 70) of a local businessman standing knee-deep in flood waters getting on with the business of the day. Which brings me to another point. What makes a good picture? People do. Few photographs here don't contain at least one man, woman, or child doing something reflective of his or her community. The picture on p. 59 would just be an Opera House movie screen without the Hitchcock-like silhouettes of the two men standing in profile. And the image on p. 65 of the hapless Alfred Brady, Public Enemy Number One, was greatly enhanced when the photographer invited a doctor and a cop to stand behind the thug's bullet-ridden body. You can almost read Officer Connelly's mind as he gazes down into Brady's inert features: Just a boy of twenty-six. Too young to die. Think of this collection, then, as a walk through a century about to pass into history. I hope these scenes of our little city—or big town, take your pick—explain why its past continues to fascinate people who appreciate what made Bangor tick. The former lumbering capital of the world had some tough times maintaining its dignity in the twentieth century, but, as these pictures prove, I think it found a way to define and diversify. A century from now, I trust my future counterpart will have positive images today's generation will have left behind. But today, only Nostradamus could tell us what they'll show.

Richard R. Shaw
Bangor, Maine
August 1996

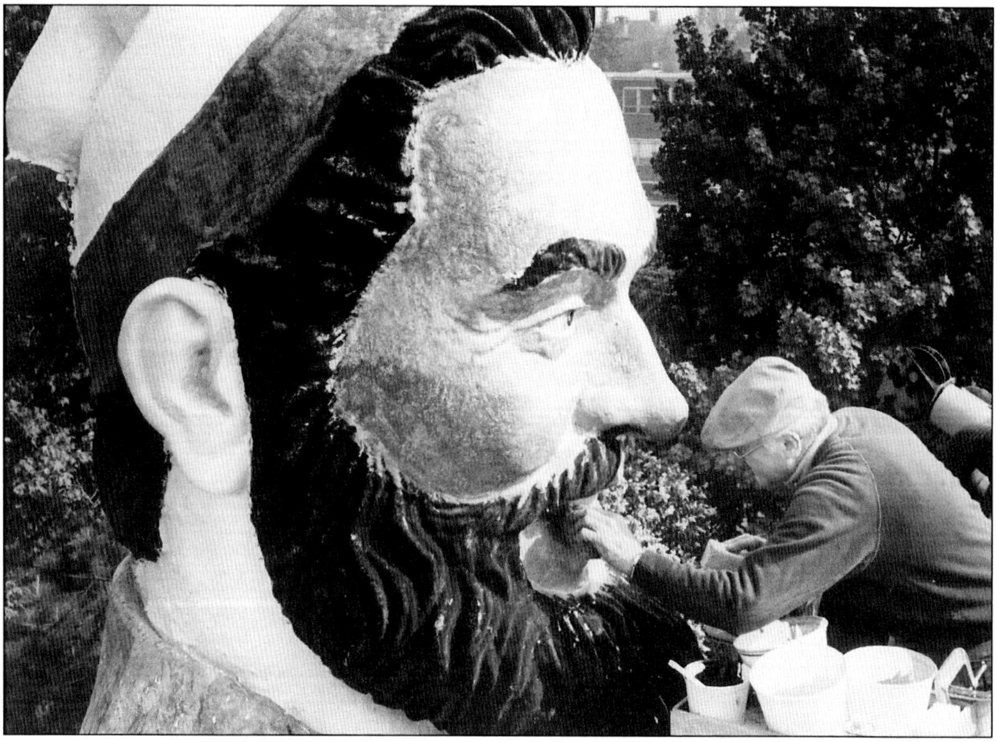

Normand Martin gives the Paul Bunyan statue a facelift in 1986. With inspiration from Connie Bronson, Martin designed the 37-foot-tall statue in 1959 to help publicize the city's 125th anniversary celebration. Martin and fellow artist Wallace McQuarrie climb into a cherry picker and donate their time to repaint the tourist attraction whenever it starts to peel.

One

Jimmy Carter Slept Here

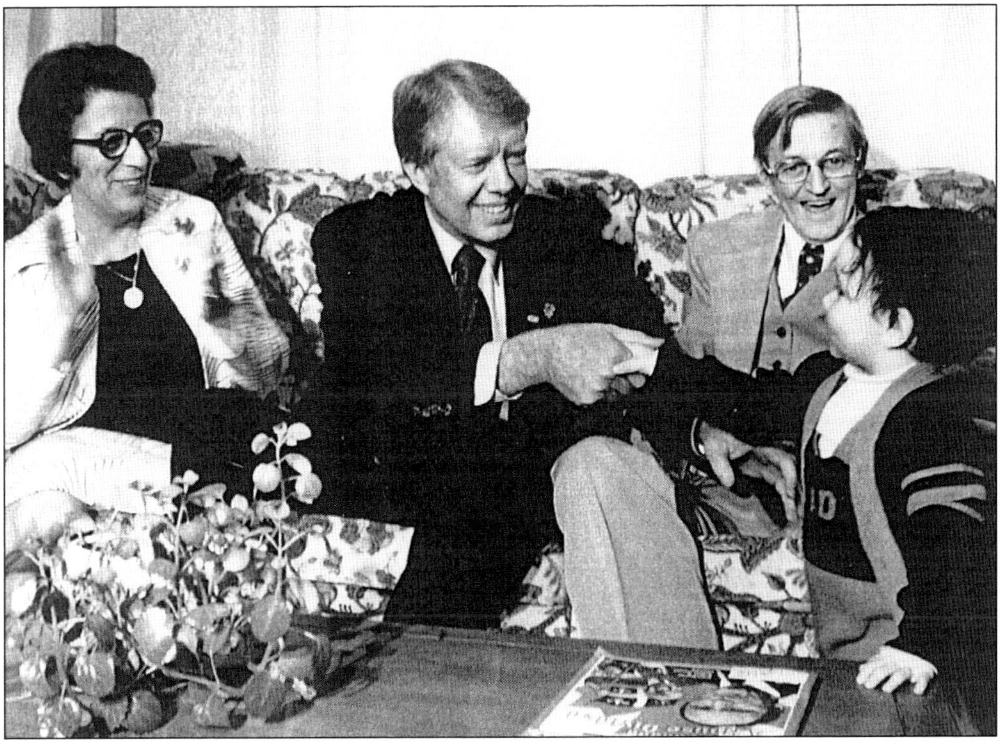

Typical of his simple Georgia heritage, President Jimmy Carter spent the night of February 17, 1978, in the private home of Robert Murray at 215 Maple Street. After hosting a town meeting at the Bangor Auditorium, Carter was driven to the East Side residence, where he chatted with Robert and Laura Murray and their young grandson, Emmett Beliveau. Carter slept in the bedroom of the Murrays' eighteen-year-old son Buddy, a student at Boston College. Only one other chief executive, Ulysses S. Grant, a visitor in 1871, spent the night in the city. All the others visited for the day.

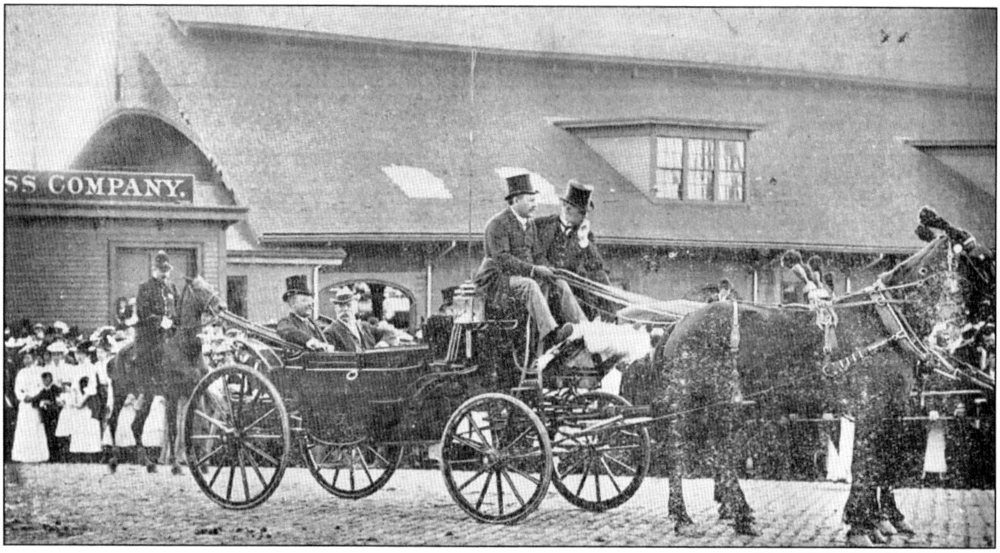

Teddy Roosevelt stopped in Bangor on August 27, 1902, as part of a speech-making tour throughout Maine. He is pictured leaving the train depot on Railroad Street seated in an open carriage with former mayor Flavius O. Beal (see p. 82). After a tour of the city, TR spoke from the front portico of the Bangor House and at the fairgrounds, Maplewood Park.

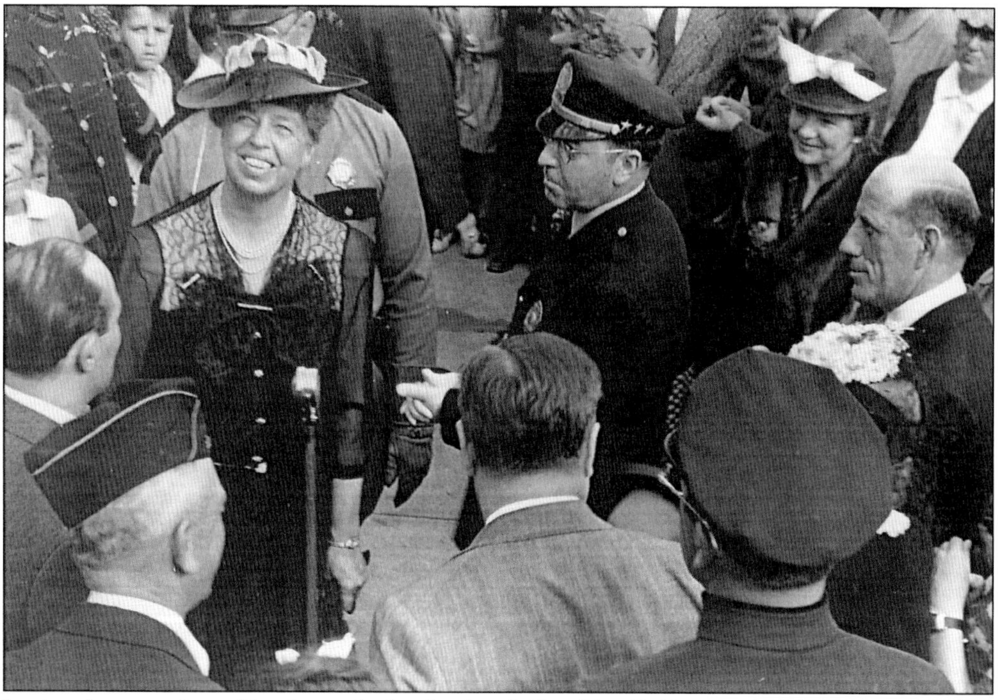

In the absence of an official visit by her husband, Franklin D. Roosevelt, Eleanor appeared in Bangor on May 20, 1941, the first formal visit by a first lady to the city. She is shown here in a photograph from the Fred Bryant collection, surrounded by police officers and spectators while speaking at a downtown park. After dining at the Bangor House, Mrs. Roosevelt delivered an address at the old Bangor Auditorium following a brief concert by the Bangor Symphony Orchestra and a speech by Maine Governor Sumner Sewall.

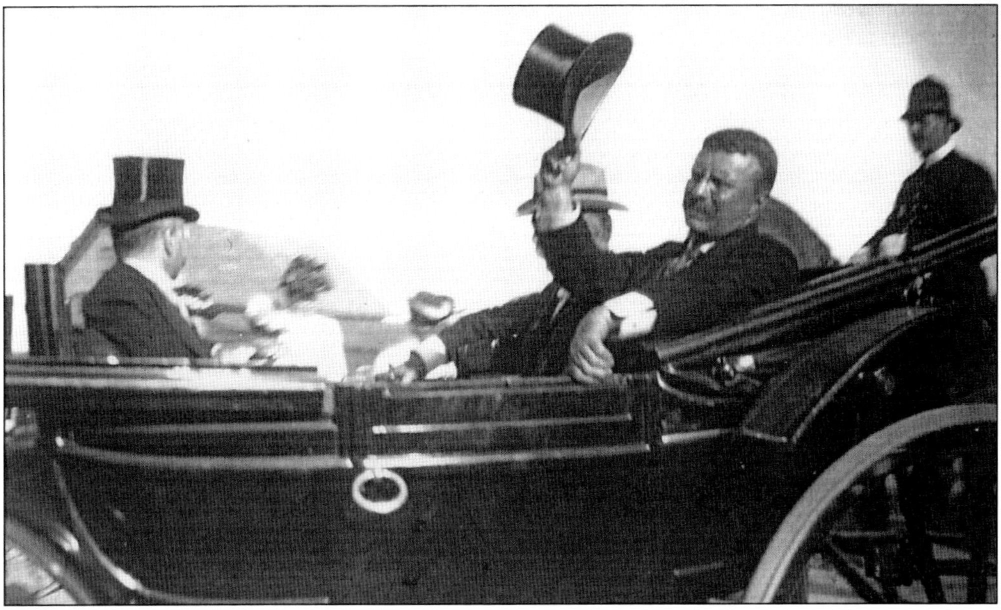

President Roosevelt toured the Bangor State Fair, as the guest of fair president Flavius O. Beal. "It was the first time in the history of the world," remarked local resident Lawrence Smyth, "that a country fair exhibited a president of the United States as its prize attraction and charged 50 cents a head admission." TR spoke from the judges' stand, toured the horse stands and cattle sheds, and was reputed to have remarked, "I've had a bully good time!"

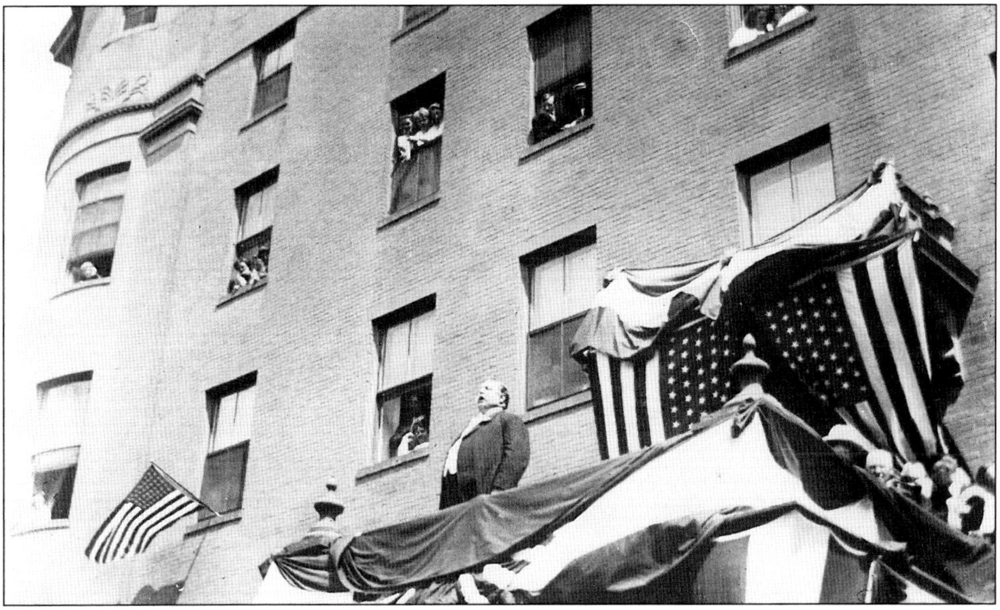

Standing at the front of the Bangor House as Teddy Roosevelt had done eight years before, President William Howard Taft addressed a crowd of spectators on Main Street on July 23, 1910, speaking on farming and other topics. Newspaper reporter Frank H. Davis recalled a later speech by Taft, who returned to the city as a former president: "He had a deep-down chuckle which cannot be described and a smile which made you feel that life was really worth the living."

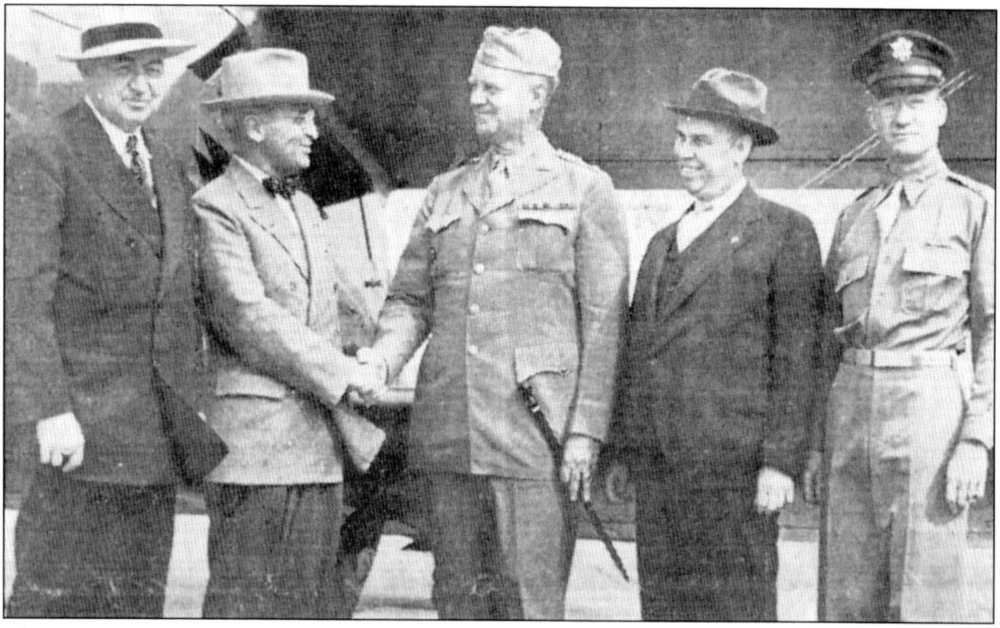

The presidency was three years into the future for Senator Harry S. Truman, but his trademark bow tie, hat, and winning smile were evident while inspecting Dow Field as head of the Senate Truman committee. Joining him on August 20, 1942, are, from left to right, Senator Harley M. Kilgore of West Virginia, Major General Sherman Miles, Maine Senator Ralph O. Brewster, and base commander Colonel George Lovell Jr.

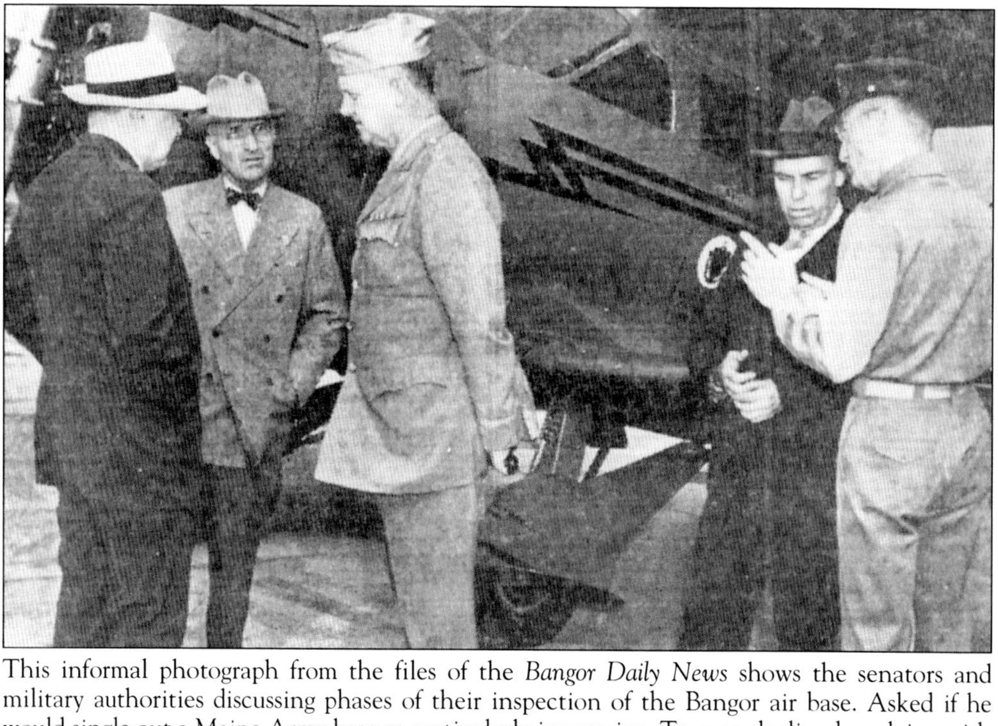

This informal photograph from the files of the *Bangor Daily News* shows the senators and military authorities discussing phases of their inspection of the Bangor air base. Asked if he would single out a Maine Army base as particularly impressive, Truman declined, replying with a smile, "You know diplomacy is a basic qualification of a senator."

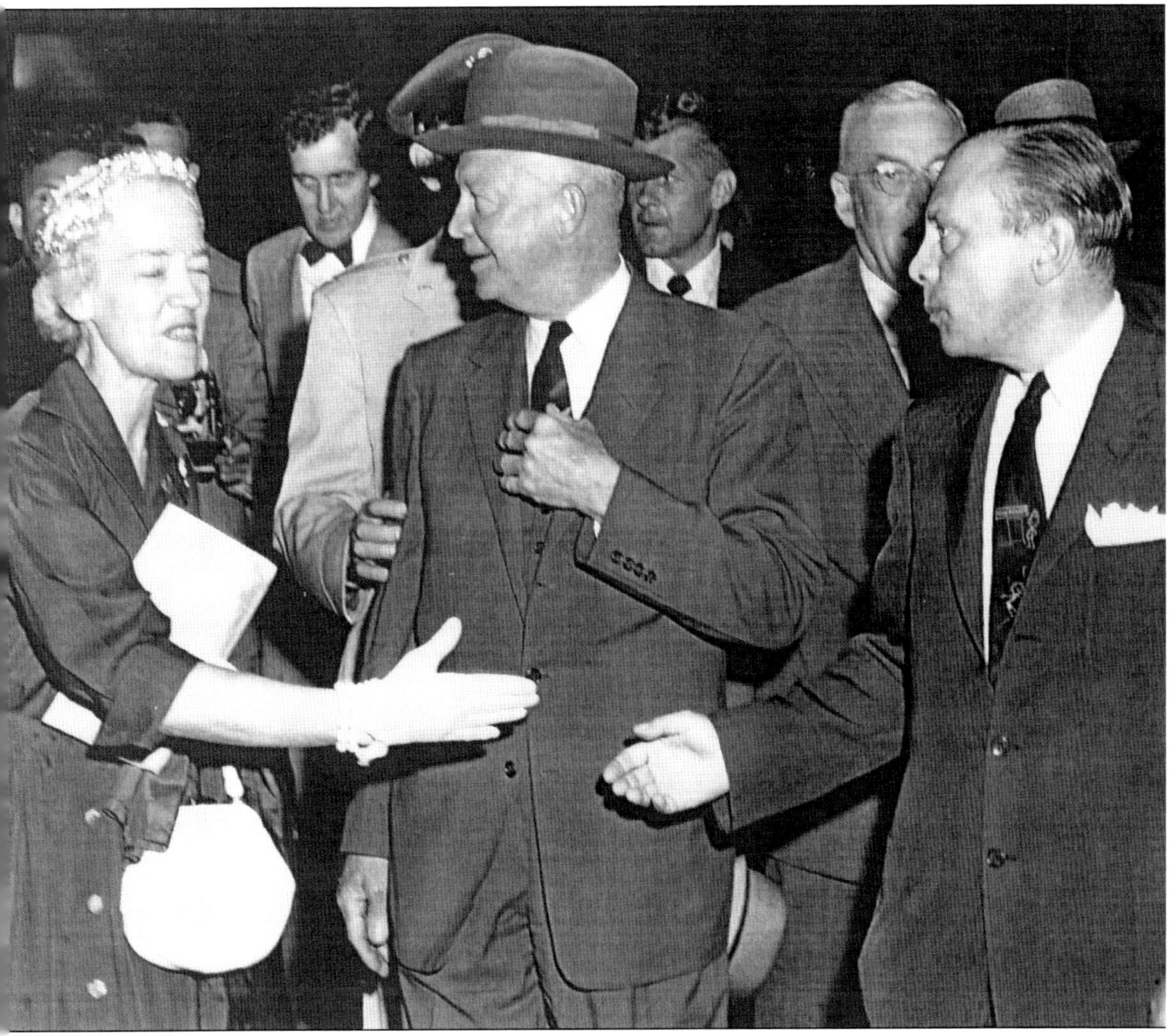

Dwight D. Eisenhower looks somewhat bewildered while Maine Senator Margaret Chase Smith reaches in front of him to shake the hand of Curtis M. Hutchins, general chairman of the committee that oversaw the president's June 27, 1955 visit to Bangor. Ike had spent the weekend on a fishing excursion in western Maine before joining a motorcade that stopped at Senator Smith's Skowhegan home, where he feasted on Maine lobster. This photograph was taken at Dow Air Force Base as the president prepared to fly back to Washington, D.C. In the background are Maine Governor Edmund S. Muskie (left) and John Foster Dulles (right), the secretary of state. Dow was the only military installation Ike had visited up to that point during that year. One other bit of trivia: Eisenhower, the former Supreme Allied Commander during the well-timed D-Day invasion of June 6, 1944, upheld his reputation for punctuality as his automobile arrived at the Bangor air base at exactly the specified time—8:25 pm Monday evening.

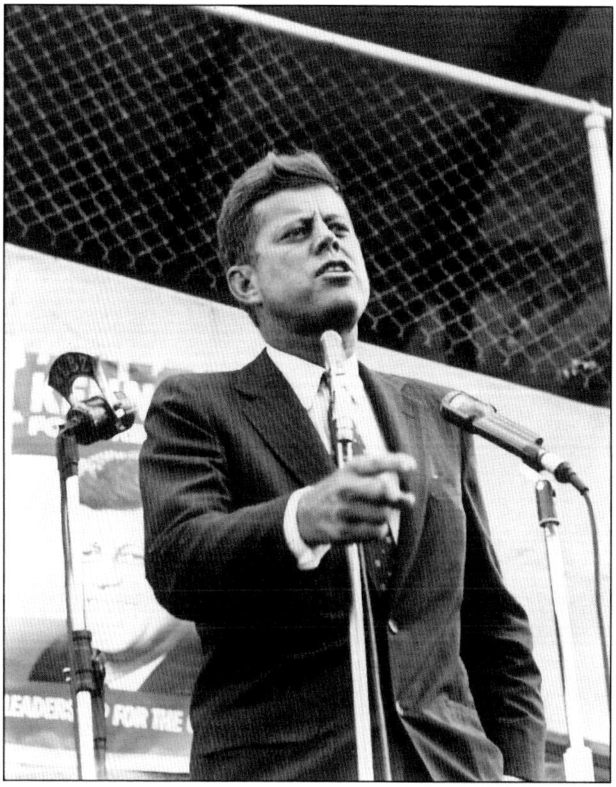

John F. Kennedy delivered a brief campaign speech at Bass Park on September 2, 1960, part of a whirlwind tour of New Hampshire and Maine. The Democratic candidate for president spoke with no prepared text, describing the presidency as "the greatest office within the gift of the free world's people." He also said the state of Maine was typical of the "New Frontier," the slogan of his campaign, and later, of his all too brief term in office.

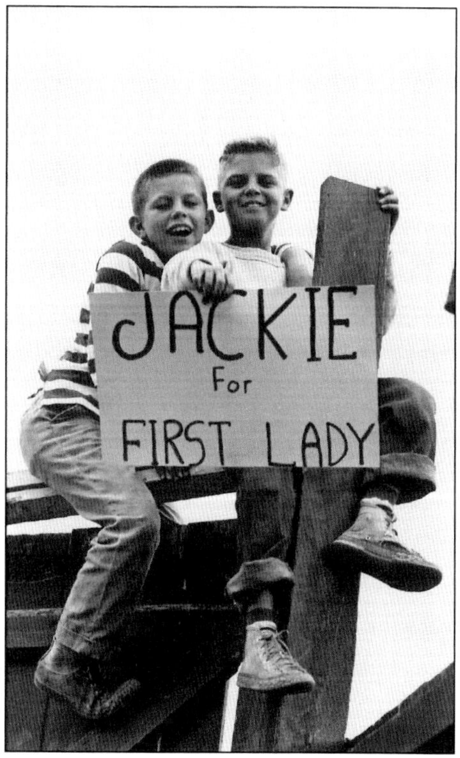

Fans of Jacqueline Kennedy got their wish in November, when JFK was elected president, but she didn't appear with him in Bangor. Mrs. Kennedy, pregnant at the time, became air sick after leaving Boston on the morning of September 2, and had to leave the senator's party in Manchester, New Hampshire. Wrote reporter Nelle Penley, "She apparently was trying to spend a few hours with her husband on the kick-off of his national campaign and turbulent air stepped in to put a stop to it."

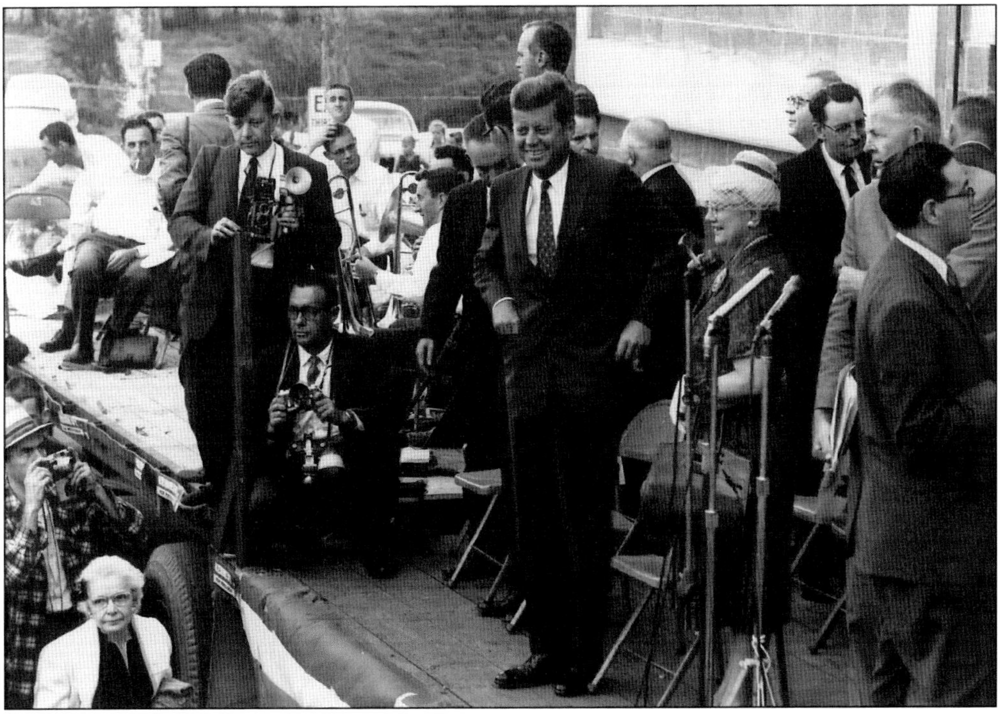

Although he was reported to have slept only ten hours in two days, Jack Kennedy was exuberant as he prepared to shake hands with some of the more than 1,500 supporters in the audience. Among the party names with JFK were Edmund S. Muskie and Frank Coffin, the Maine Democratic candidate for governor. Local reporters Bob Taylor and Nelle Penley (with note pad, lower left) covered the speech, along with such nationally known writers as James Reston of *The New York Times*.

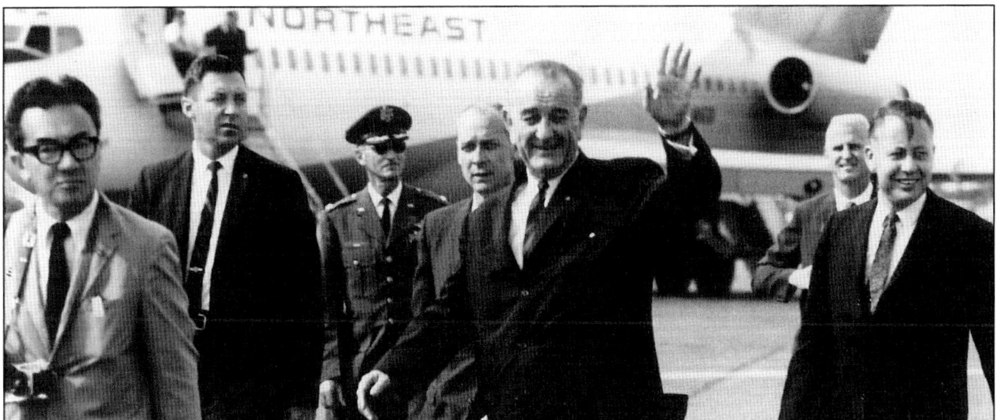

Kennedy successor Lyndon B. Johnson appeared in Bangor on August 21, 1966. The president is pictured waving to a crowd of spectators at Dow Field, after hosting dedication ceremonies at Roosevelt International Park at Campobello, New Brunswick. Maine Senator William Hathaway is at the far right. "There was neither sight nor sound of any anti-LBJ demonstrations," reported the *Bangor Daily News*, referring to protests of Johnson's Vietnam War policies that were an occupational hazard for him and, later, Richard M. Nixon (see pp. 16–17).

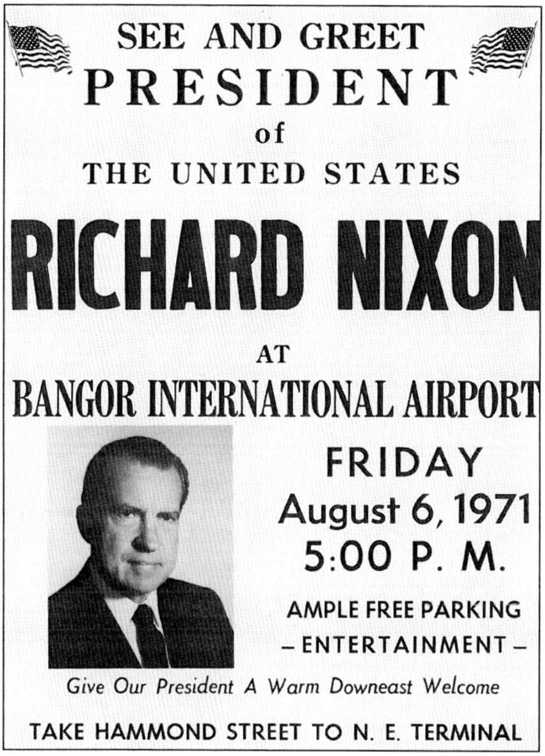

Republican Party organizers posted these handbills around the time President Richard Nixon and his family were to stop in Bangor on the way to a quiet weekend on an island in Penobscot Bay. The weekend was not quiet nor was the "Downeast welcome" entirely hospitable. In the waning years of the Vietnam War, a small group of protesters disrupted the chief executive's speech.

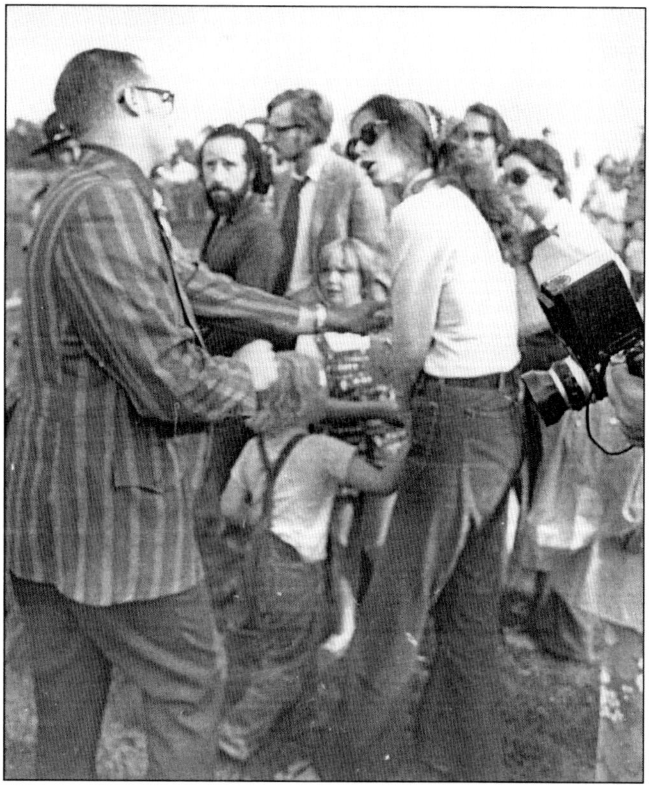

While the president addressed the crowd of seven thousand, anti-war dissidents stood at the rear of the assemblage and were at first peaceful. The mood, however, turned ugly when local police and secret servicemen moved in and began tearing up protest signs on the grounds that the protesters were standing on private property. Later, a federal court ruling upheld the right of the dissidents who were, in fact, on public property owned by the city of Bangor.

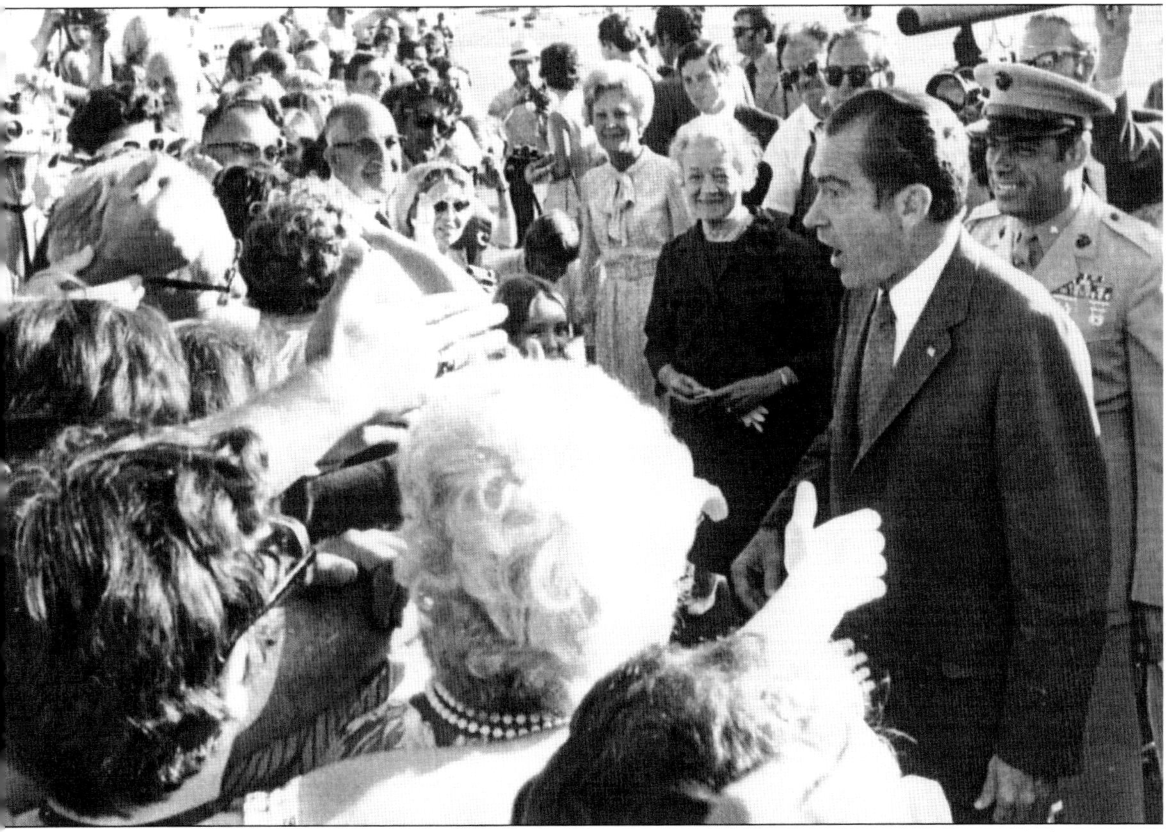

President Nixon later was quoted as saying that he was "disgusted" with the reception accorded him by the group of dissidents in Bangor. He also praised an Orrington woman, Paulette Morin, for confronting the protesters and defending the president. During the course of his brief visit on Minot Island, Nixon heard about the woman's actions and later offered to help her find a job in the Washington, D.C., area when she finished school. The president also was quoted in the press as stating that during his brief Bangor appearance, he chose to ignore the protesters at the rear of the crowd. This photograph shows Nixon greeting his fans while his wife Pat stands to the left. Senator Margaret Chase Smith, who often accompanied dignitaries of both parties to her native state, is between them. Nixon never returned to Bangor, either as president or during his years as a private citizen. He campaigned in the city as Dwight Eisenhower's vice presidential candidate in 1952, returning as the GOP's candidate for president in 1960.

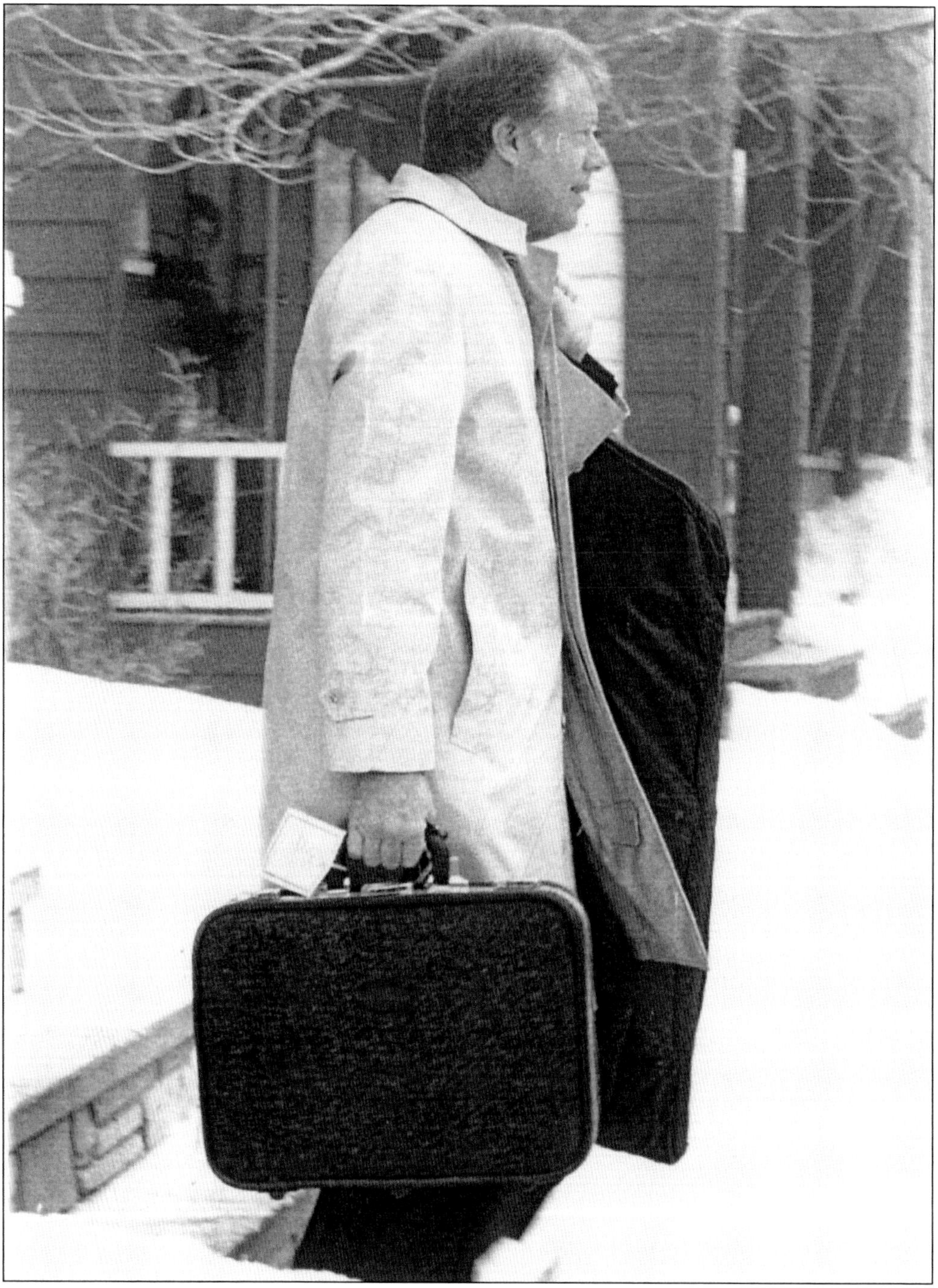

Jimmy Carter carried his own bags as he trudged through the snow at the Robert Murray home on Maple Street on the morning of February 18, 1978. The president hosted a town meeting at the Bangor Auditorium and spent the night at the residence of Murray, the chairman of the county Democratic organization. Inside, photographers were given precisely two minutes to take their pictures before being ushered out. Carter left the house by 8 am the following morning to attend a $10-a-plate Democratic Party fund-raiser at Husson College.

During a ninety-minute town meeting, Carter was spared the bluntness of reporters' questions since ordinary citizens questioned him instead. A member of the Penobscot Indian Nation asked him about the Indian land claims settlement. The president answered, "I could have washed my hands of it and let the people of Maine sweat it out. But I felt there was a need for us to resolve it fairly quickly."

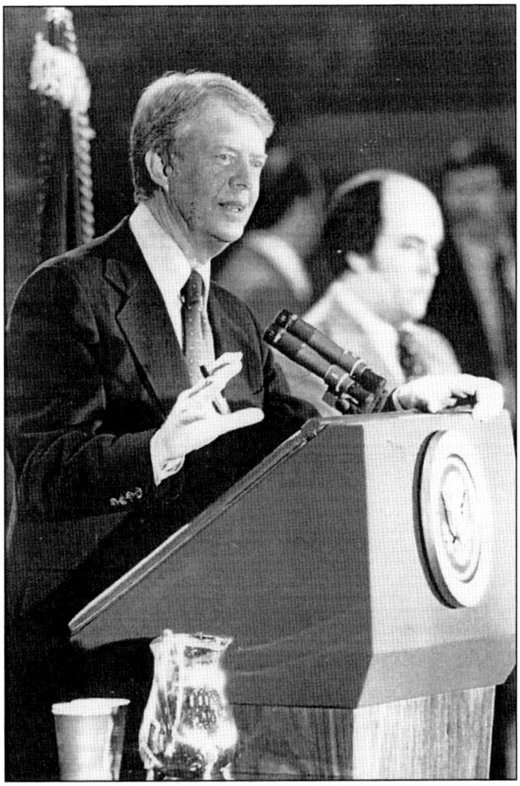

Facing a banner that welcomed him to Maine's Queen City, President Carter continued on the topic of Indian land claims: "I think I've done my job as well as I could, and we have not imposed the will of the Executive branch on the state of Maine at all. The governor of Maine is still free to do anything he chooses." Carter's visit lasted a total of fifteen hours, including a fund-raiser in Orono for Democratic Senate candidate William Hathaway.

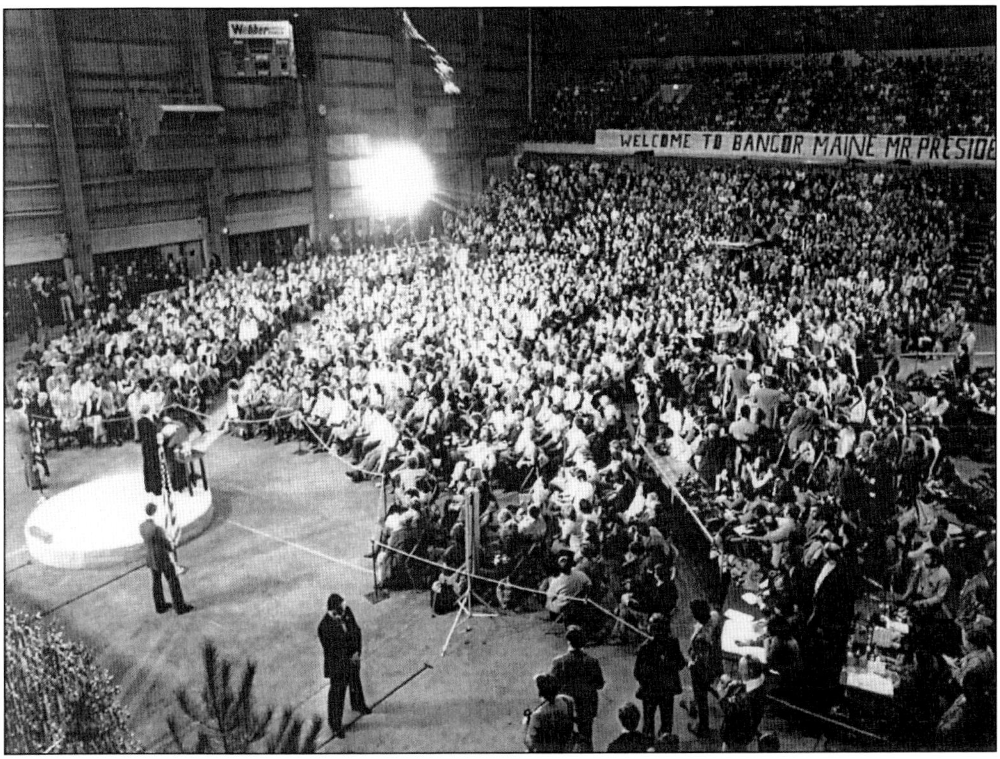

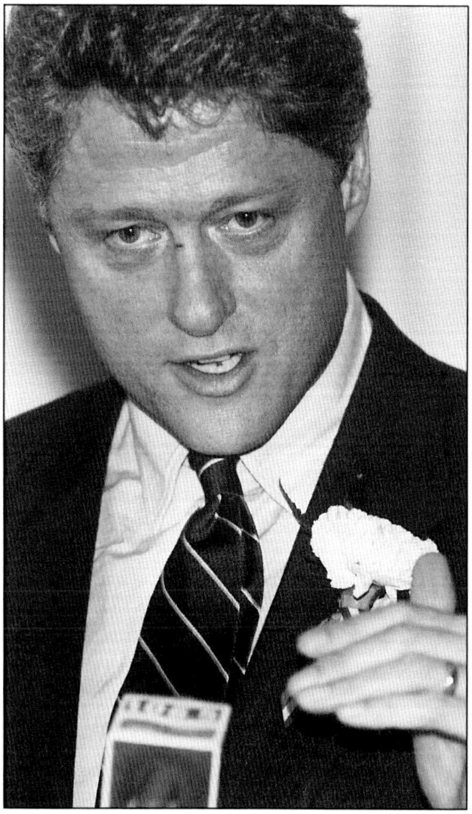

Candidate Bill Clinton, still a long way from the Democratic Party's nomination, campaigned at the Bangor Airport Hilton in early 1992. There were many other candidates in the field at the time, some of whom also visited the city. The former Arkansas governor answered questions for newspaper, television, and radio reporters. The scar on the bridge of the future president's nose is not a photographic defect; Clinton had recently undergone minor surgery. He returned as president in November 1996.

Republican George Bush, also a candidate in search of a nomination, visited the same airport hotel in January 1980. He had just won the Iowa presidential caucuses and was focusing on New England since the New Hampshire primary was only a month away. Newspaper photographer Carroll Hall took this picture of Bush, but it was not explained why both arms were extended. Perhaps he was telling a fish story, or better yet, how big his lead would be over Ronald Reagan. Reagan went on to win the Republican nomination and the presidency with Bush as his running mate. Bush would be elected president in 1988.

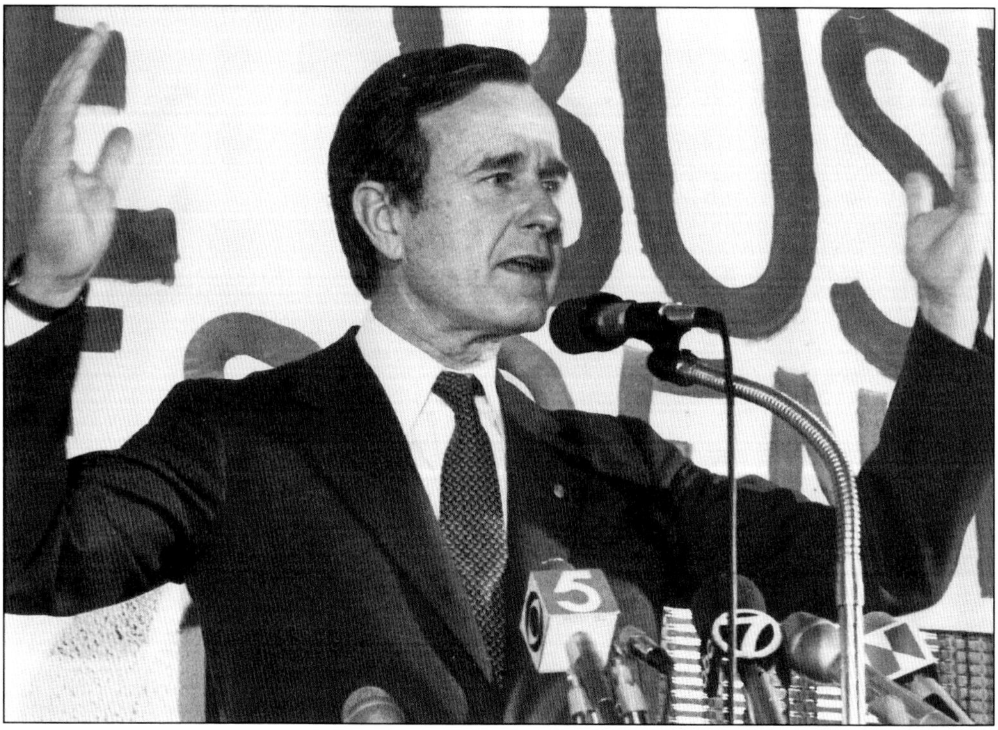

Two

Bangor from on High

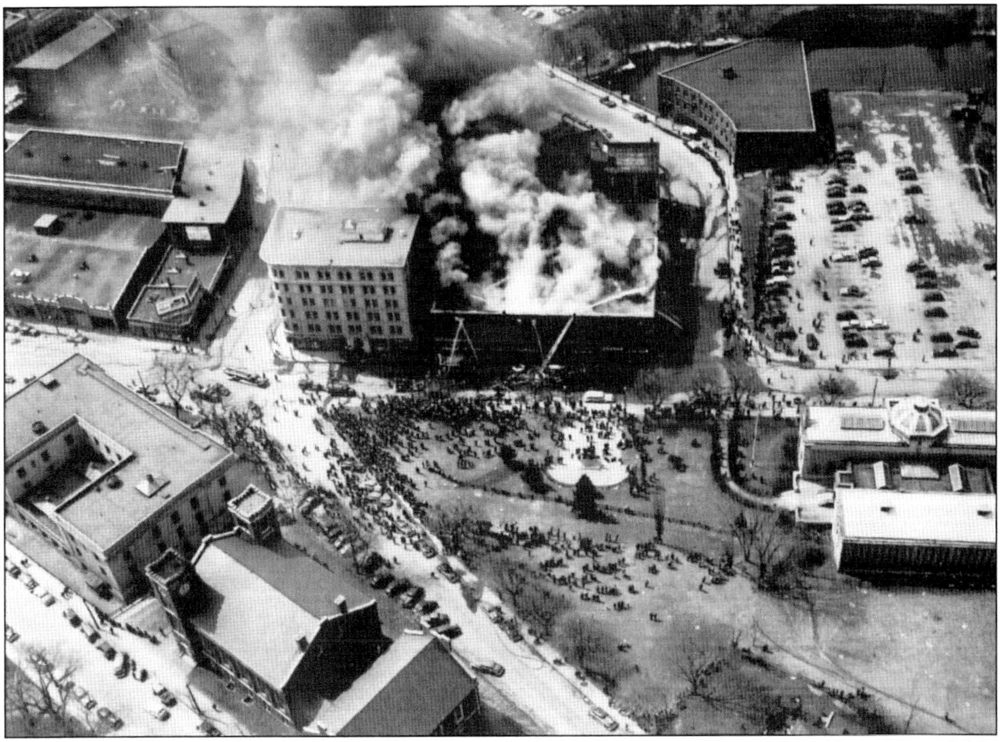

Few aerial photographs can match the drama of this one taken by Norm Houle and made available by publisher Pierre Dumont. Dated April 14, 1950, it shows the burning of the Windsor Hotel on Harlow Street, which resulted in an estimated $700,000 in damages. Quick work on the part of local firefighters contained the flames to the hotel block. As a result, the nearby Graham Building (immediately to the left of the burning block) was saved. Other landmarks identified are the Bangor Public Library and Peirce Memorial (lower right), the Murray Motor Mart (top right), the old post office building, now city hall (lower left), and the First Universalist Church which faces it.

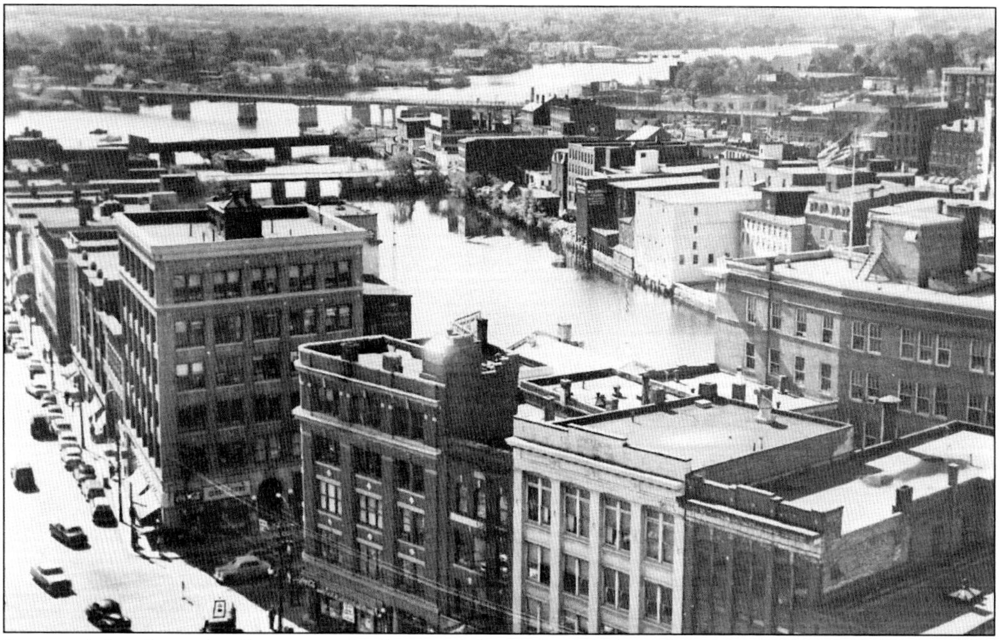

Some of the finest bird's-eye-view photographs weren't taken from airplanes but from church steeples and the upper floors of downtown buildings. This photograph, *c.* 1955, probably snapped from the top of the Telephone Exchange building on Park Street, shows Exchange Street and the confluence of the Kenduskeag Stream and Penobscot River. The stream area today is a parkway with concrete designed to increase parking and narrow the stream's width.

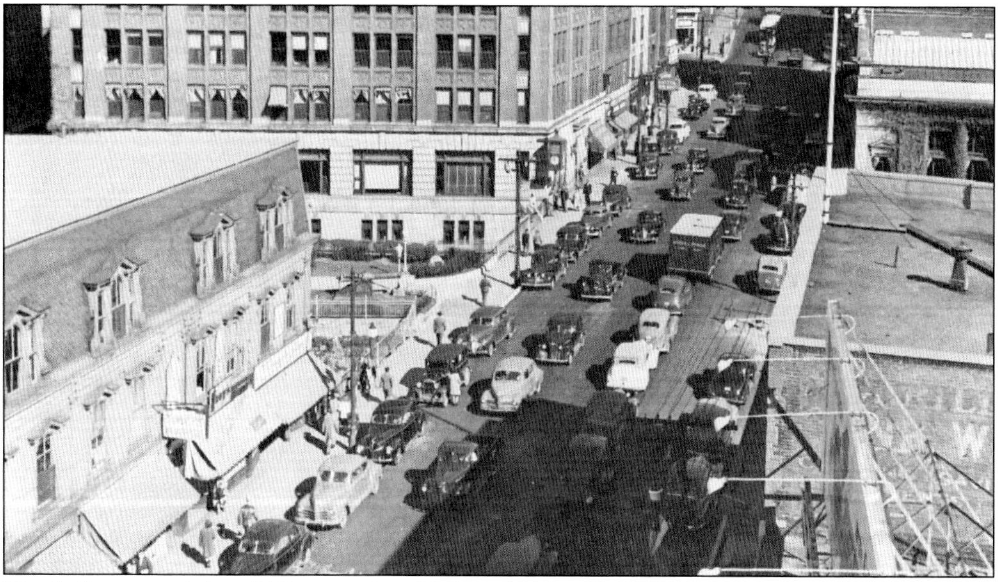

The bell tower of the old Bangor City Hall probably afforded this 1940s perspective of State Street in an era when downtown bustled with two-way traffic. The picture's focal point is the handsome Eastern Trust and Banking Company block (at left center). The entrance of the Park Theater is in the distance and the wooden block (in the lower left) is also visible. Both buildings have long since been demolished. The long billboard at the lower right (such signs are now banned in Bangor) also reminds us of long-ago times.

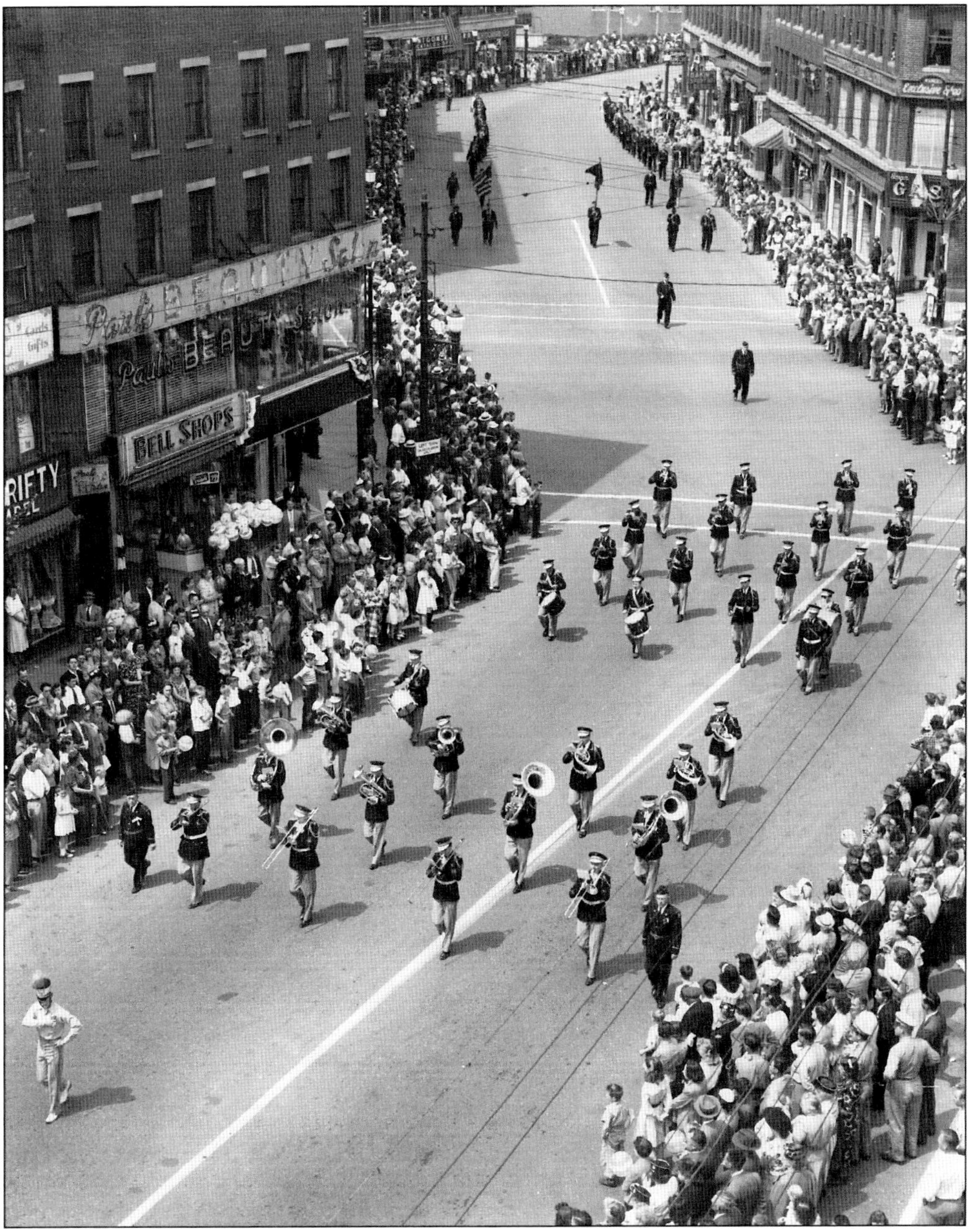

Bangor has always loved a parade, from early Independence Day processions that marched down a dirt Main Street, to later circus parades that started at the railroad yard and ended at the fairgrounds. This parade, apparently dating to World War II and probably photographed on Memorial Day or the Fourth of July, is viewed from an upstairs window as a marching band proceeds up Main Street off from Central Street. Sharp eyes will discern uniformed servicemen in the crowd at the lower right, and a man selling balloons in front of the Bell Shops at the left. Most of the old businesses are gone now: the Bangor Gas Company at Hammond and Central is no more, along with Dakin Sporting Goods on Central Street and Paul's Beauty Salon at Hammond and Main.

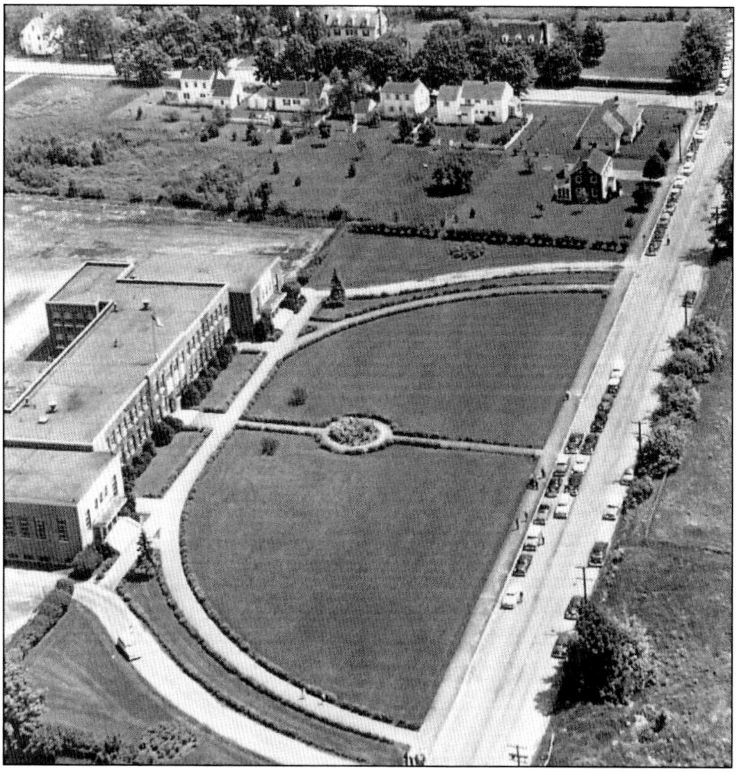

Evacuation Day in June 1955, as captured by an aerial photographer, saw parents hastily picking up their students from Garland Street Junior High School. The Cold War-era drill tested the city's civil defense preparedness in the event of a nuclear emergency. Minutes later this street, and Howard Street in the distance, were deserted.

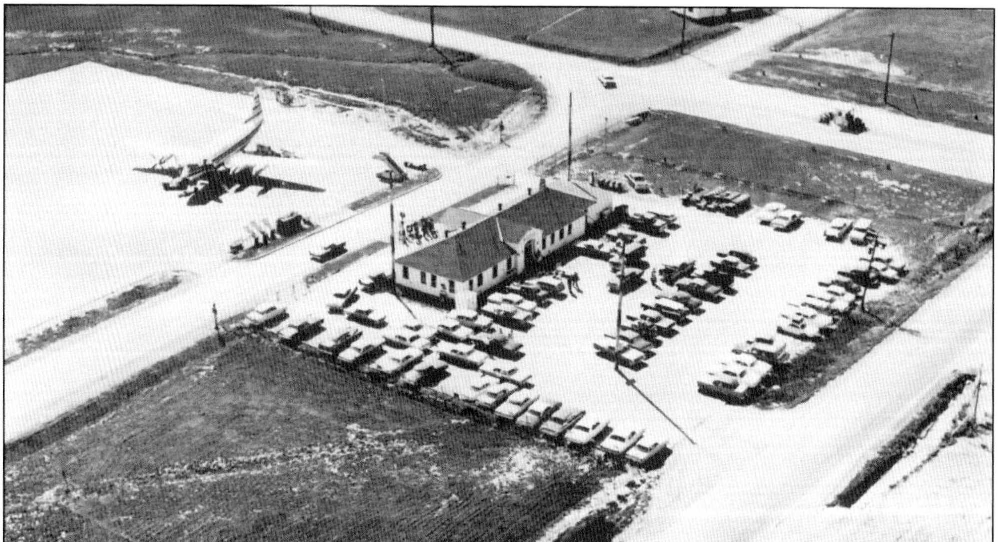

The old wooden terminal of Northeast Airlines, as it appeared in 1955. The building stood at the corner of Union Street and Griffin Road. Planes such as the airlines' Viscount aircraft shown here (the planes were later nicknamed Yellow Birds because of their canary-like paint jobs) taxied very close to Union Street and attracted many spectators on Sunday afternoons. Publisher Pierre Dumont, who received this photograph from the Maine Air National Guard, notes that the parking lot of the present Captain Nick's Restaurant is under construction at the bottom right.

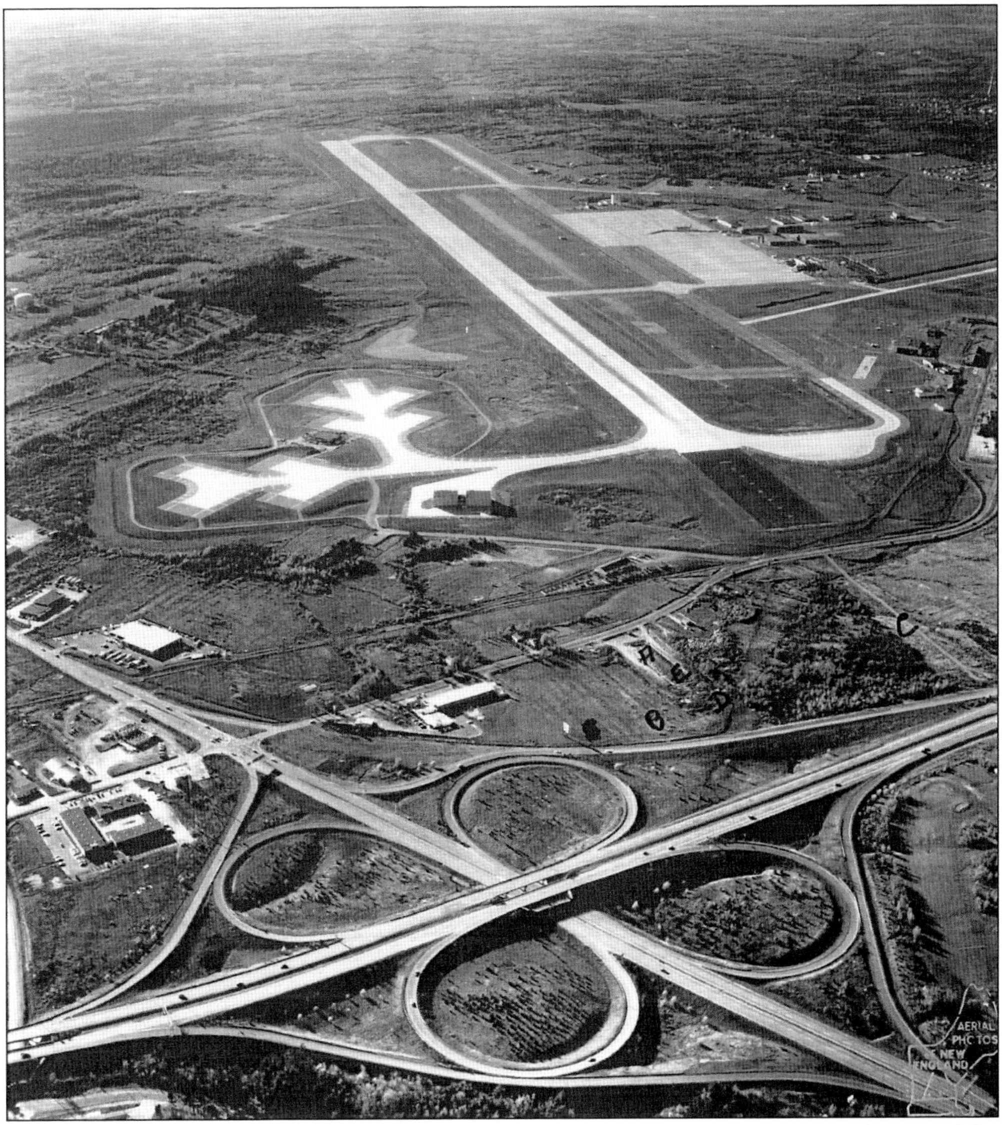

One of the more graphic aerials ever taken above Bangor pictures the geometric designs of the runway at Bangor International Airport and the clover leaf of Interstate 395 near Hammond Street and the Odlin Road. The curious part of the tarmac at the left center is a holding area for jets needing emergency clearance for takeoff. The photograph, dated May 25, 1972, illustrates the extremely long airport runway (dating to the airport's era as a Strategic Air Command base) which is so inviting to jumbo jets and military aircraft that make regular refueling stops here.

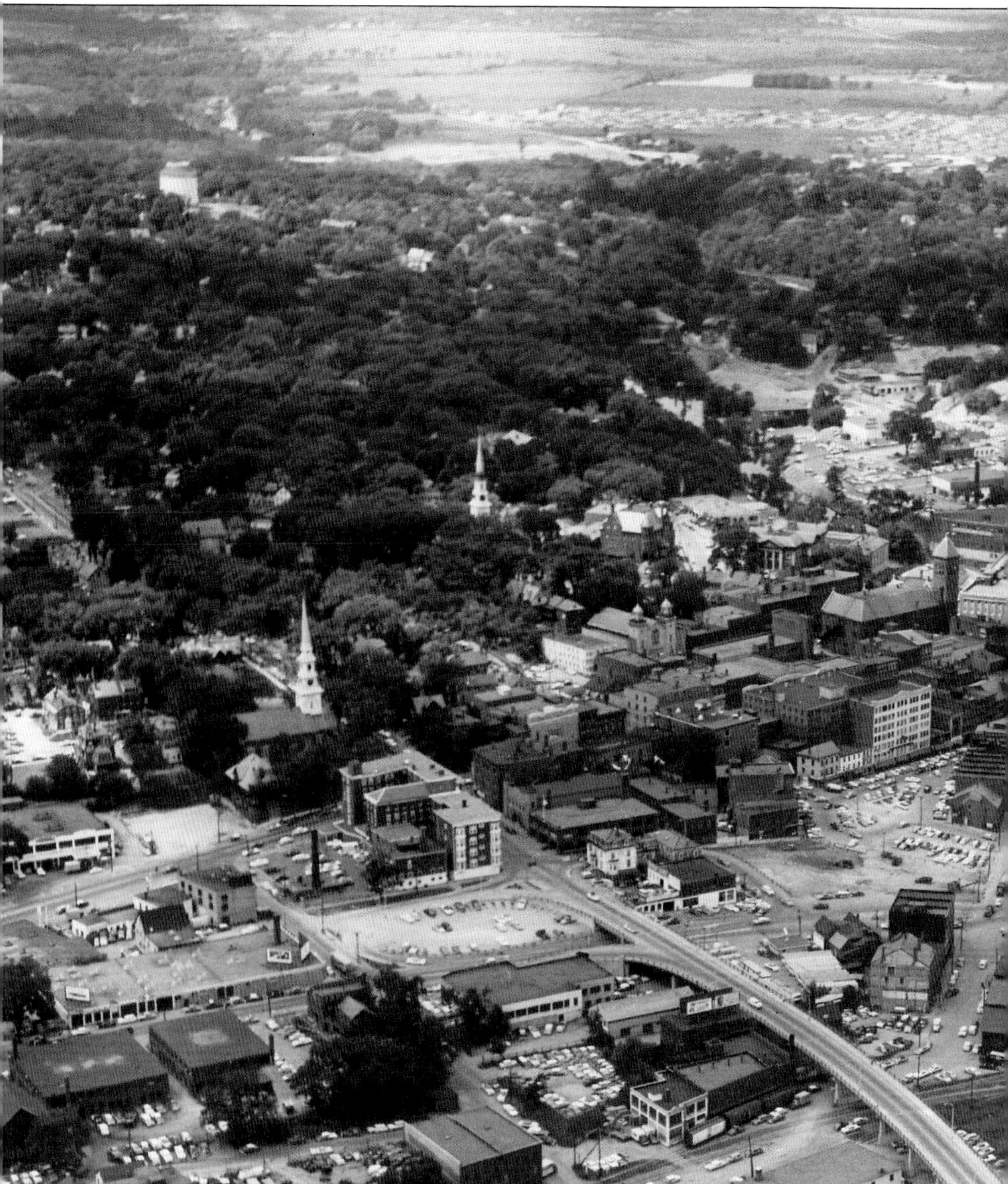

Bangor Daily News photographer Spike Webb, a master aerial photographer, snapped this panorama in June 1960 probably never knowing it would be the last time he would capture the city "intact." The beautiful Union Station (lower right, see pp. 126–7) would fall to the wrecking ball in 1961, and much of the downtown district would follow suit throughout the 1960s as a result of Urban Renewal. Light and shadow play onto the cream-colored Penobscot

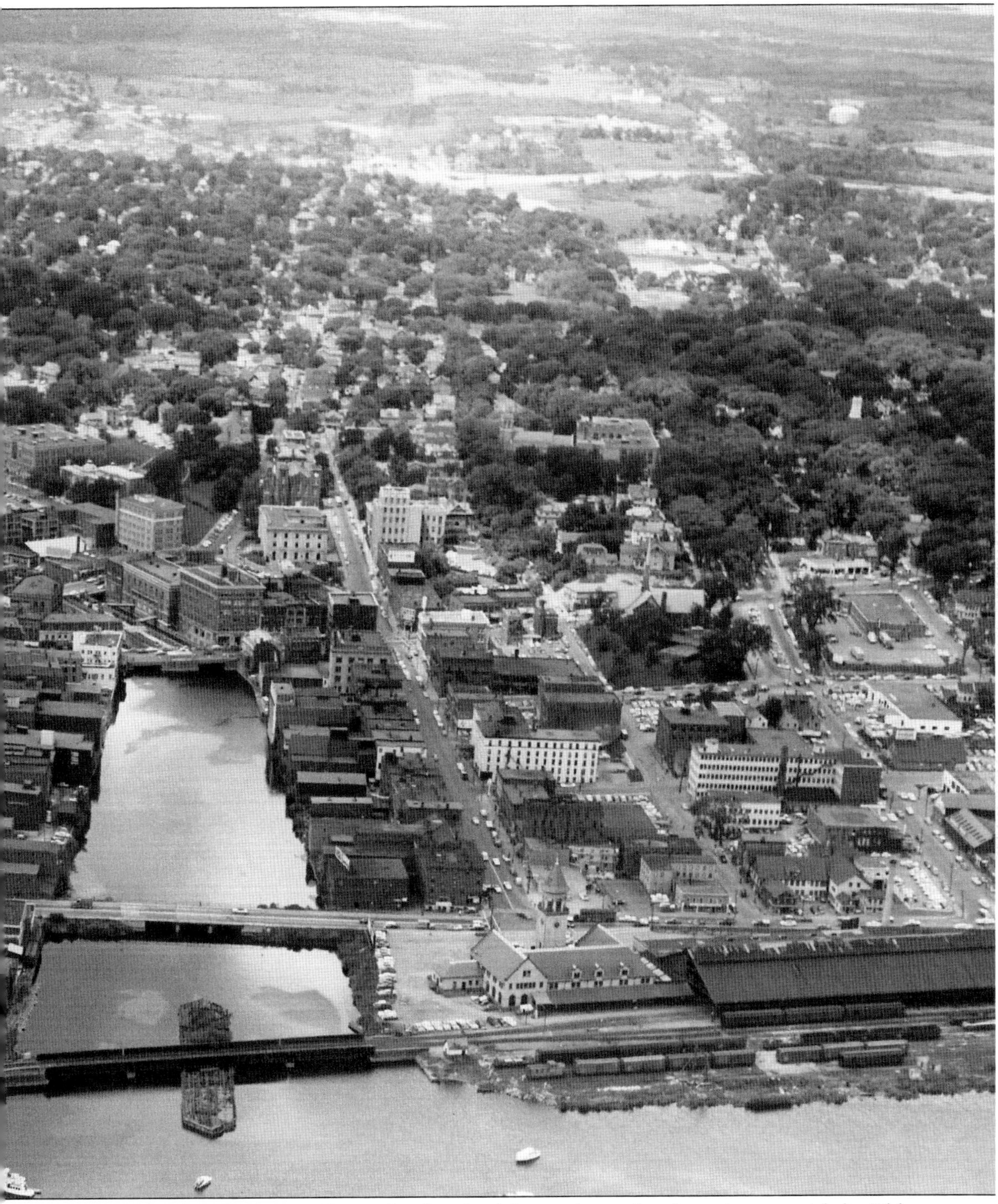

Hotel and other Exchange Street landmarks (above the railroad station, at right). Old warehouses line both the east and west sides of the Kenduskeag Stream (at center). Also visible are Freese's Department Store and the Flat Iron Block of Pickering Square (to the left of the stream), in addition to the twin steeples of the Unitarian (left foreground) and Hammond Street Congregational Churches.

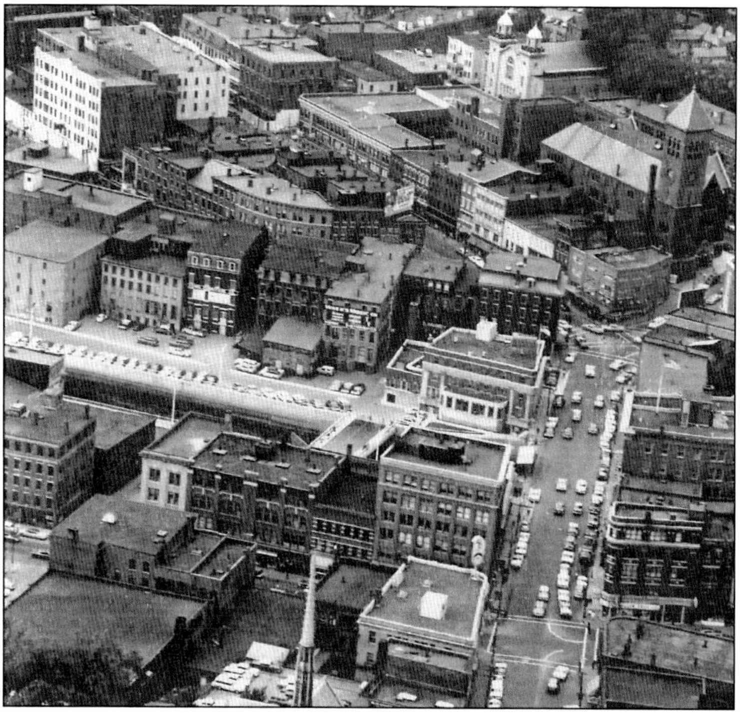

Bangor's downtown appears to be a succession of tightly grouped brick blocks in this 1963 view. The Urban Renewal project would soon claim the Bangor City Hall (top right) and other landmarks. The twin towers of the Columbia Street Baptist Church are visible at the top center, as well as the tower of All Souls Congregational Church (bottom center). Freese's Department Store is the large block at the top left of the picture.

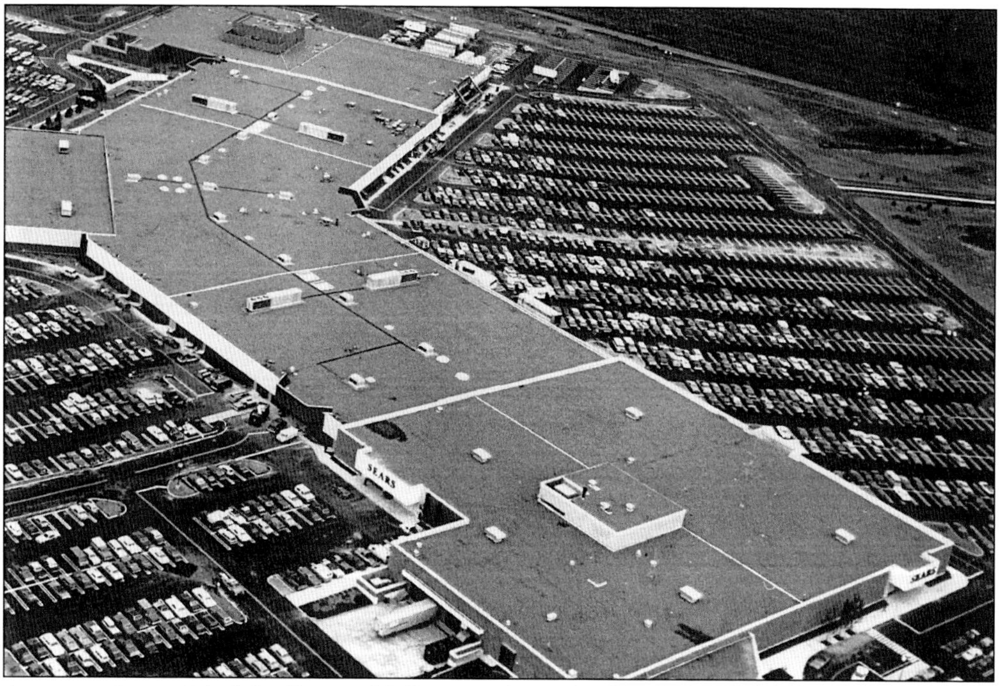

A contrasting aerial of the Bangor Mall is a study in the distribution of parking space and the square footage of retail area. Opened in 1978 in a former cow pasture on Stillwater Avenue, the mall's convenience and climate-controlled environment signaled the end of a vital downtown. Ironically, on a busy day many shoppers walk farther from their cars to the stores and back than they ever did downtown.

Three

People at Work and Play

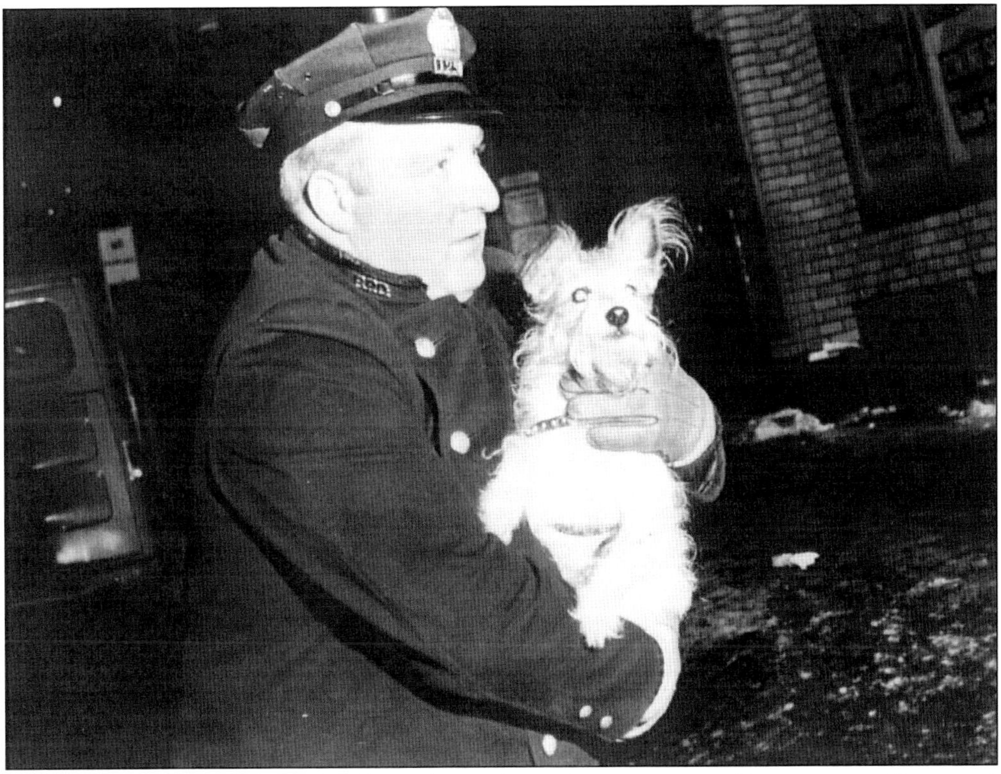

Bangor's firefighters and police officers have always been its true public servants. They work long hours without complaint, and in the course of a week go places and see things others will never see in a lifetime. Such was the life of John A. Elliott, for several years a city patrolman. There was no mistaking the rotund, gregarious man walking his beat. He even rescued pets from calamities, as seen in this 1950s-vintage photograph from the Fred Bryant police collection. Born in New Brunswick in 1926, Elliott lived on Sidney Street, marrying Jane Leard and fathering a son and a daughter.

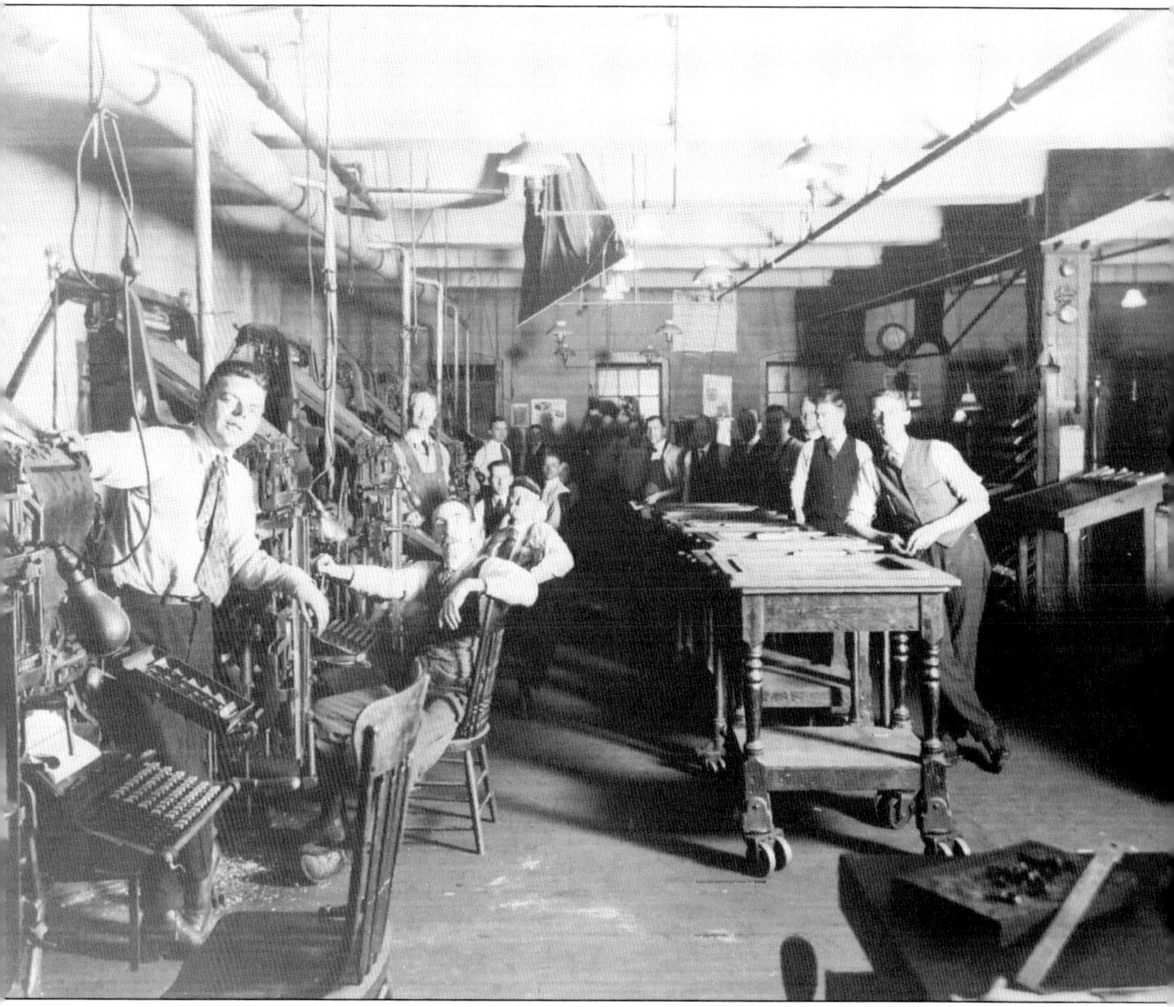

One of the earliest photographs of the old *Bangor Daily News* composing room and crew was taken around 1922. The newspaper was then located on Exchange Street in a block adjacent to the Bijou Theater. Founded in 1889, the *News* survived financial calamity, a fire, and numerous basement flooding (its back doors opened onto the Kenduskeag Stream) to become the state's largest daily newspaper. The composing room staff consisted of about twenty workers at this time. Among them are Henry Thibodeau (seventh from the right), head of the ad room, or "ad alley." Walter Washburn, a Linotype operator, is shown at the far left. The Linotypes on which all of the newspaper copy was set were gas-operated then. Some would even be collector's items in today's market as they were Model 1's. The oak pressed-back chairs and heavy wooden "turtles" (wagons on wheels) are a far cry from equipment in today's modern, computerized composing rooms. The *News* converted to "cold type" in 1974, meaning that most uses of hot lead type were discontinued.

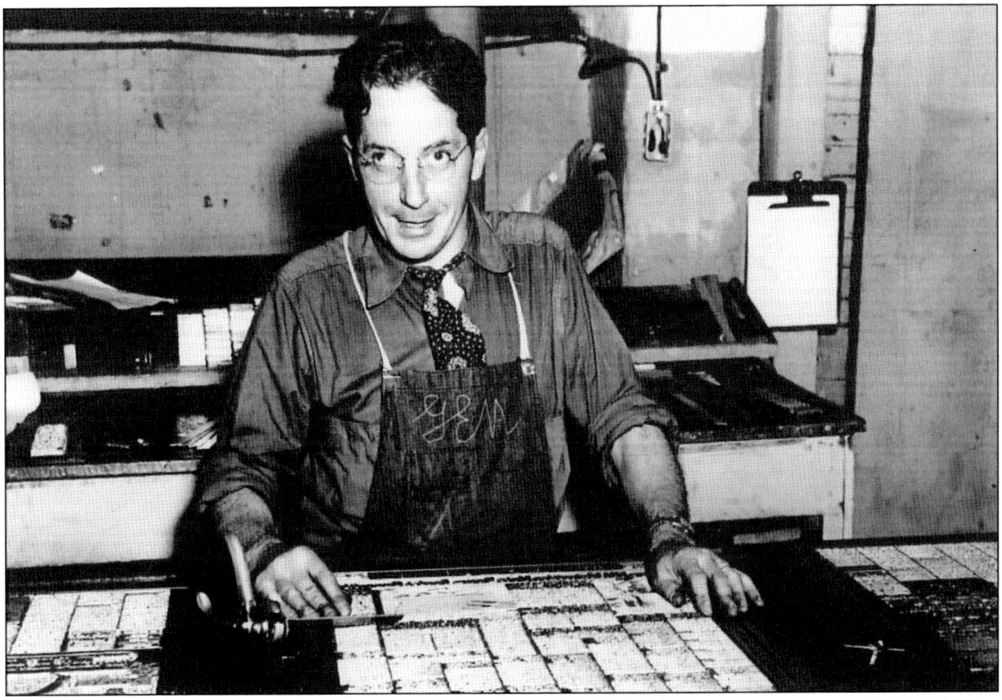

George Mugnai learned the printing trade in Machias, where he grew up. Around World War II, *Bangor Daily News* production manager Ray Cox invited Mugnai to work for his newspaper. For many years after that, the friendly man typically made up the *News*' front page. The type was all hot lead then, and the composing room was a lively, even hectic, place to work. Arthritis finally slowed Mugnai's work time in later years and he retired from the business.

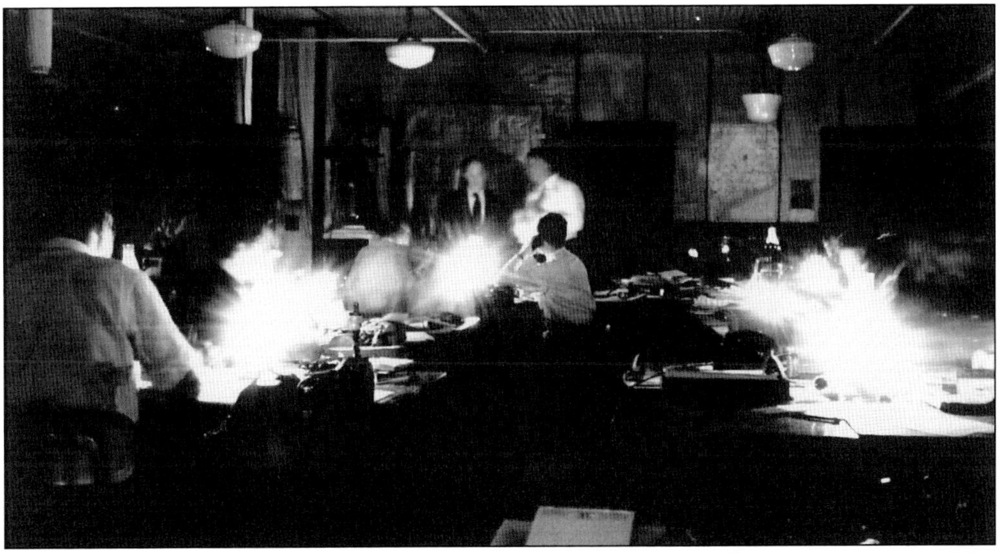

Putting together a newspaper by kerosene lantern was always a challenging experience. This scene in the old *Bangor Daily News* city room was taken sometime in the 1940s. The power went out, the lamps were lit, and city desk reporters like Anne Hannan (to the left of the center light, in a white blouse) made do under trying conditions. Power outages didn't affect the gas Linotype machines.

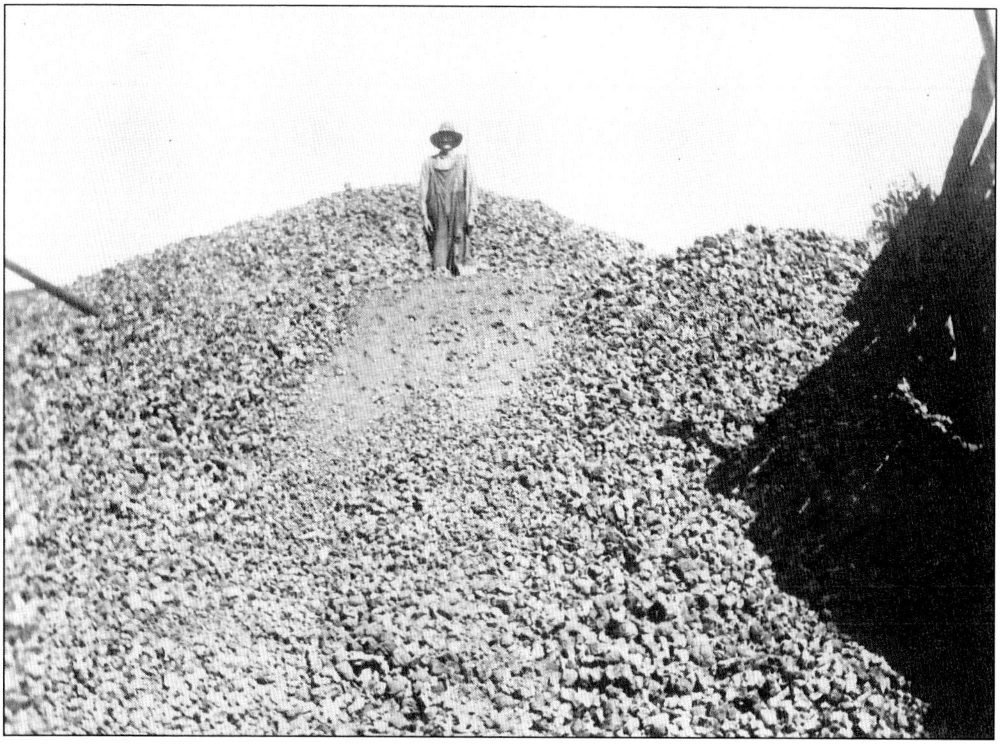

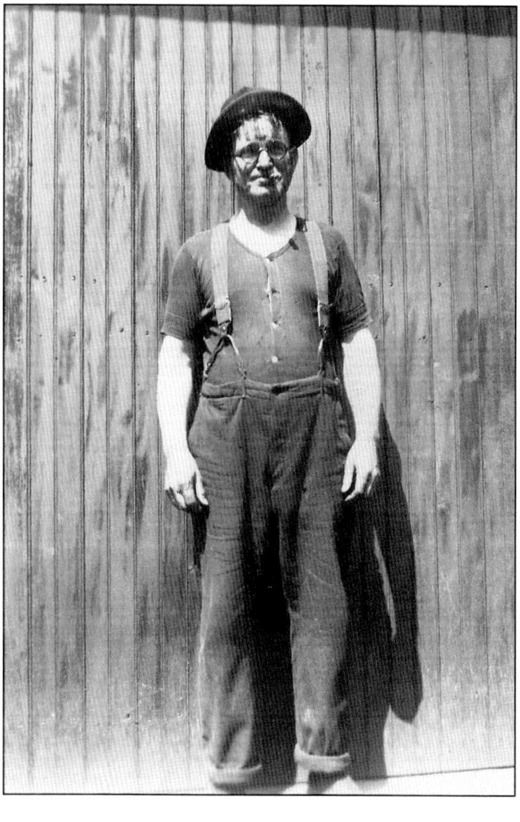

Scenes like this were common for many years at the Bangor Gas Light Company on Main Street. Tons of coal were delivered to the business by schooner, and later, by railroads located directly across the street. Workers would shovel the coal into large, circular furnaces to produce gas that was piped into Bangor area homes. The byproduct, known as coke, also had sales value. People would burn it in their coal stoves.

Every old business had its characters, and Tom Cuddy was definitely one around the Bangor Gas Light Company. The likable Irishman worked in his blacksmith shop, built on the property, to serve the needs of the laborers. Originally horses had to be shoed and iron work for tools and vehicles had to be attended to. Cuddy felt right at home in this part of town, an old working-class Irish neighborhood.

Long after the business ceased to exist, many people still heat their homes with Wood and Bishop Company wood stoves, a testament to their durability. Stoves, ranges, and furnaces were sold in this Broad Street showroom, but the company's foundry was, for many years, located at 329–339 Main Street. Formed in 1839, the business grew steadily until, by the early twentieth century, one hundred skilled men worked at the plant, which consisted of ten buildings on 2 to 3 acres of lands.

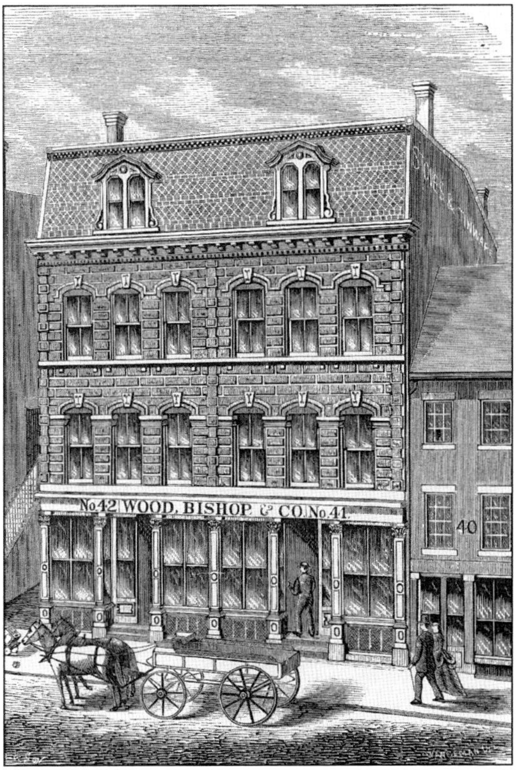

The Morse's Mill on Valley Avenue occupied more than a mile of space, a half mile on both sides of the Kenduskeag Stream. Founded by L.J. Morse and H.P. Oliver in 1850, the business was incorporated as Morse and Company in 1889. A crew of 210 men in 1906 worked around the clock to produce such items as doors, blinds, mouldings, and stairways from the finest hemlock, spruce, whitewood, and southern pine.

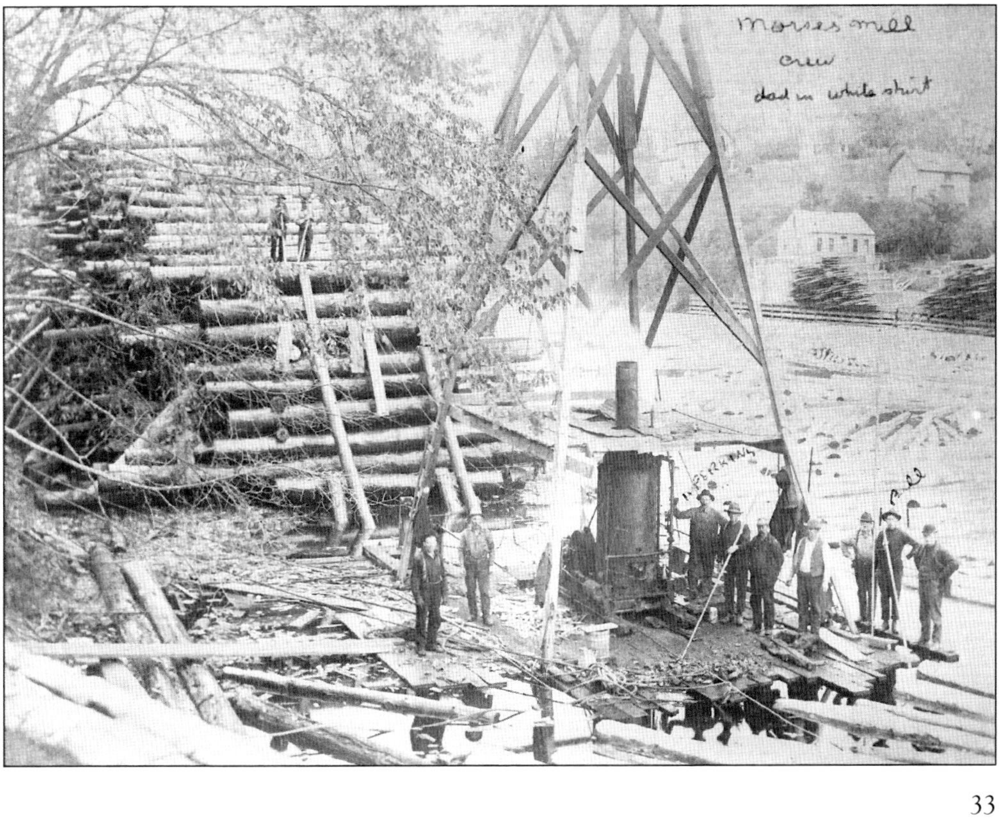

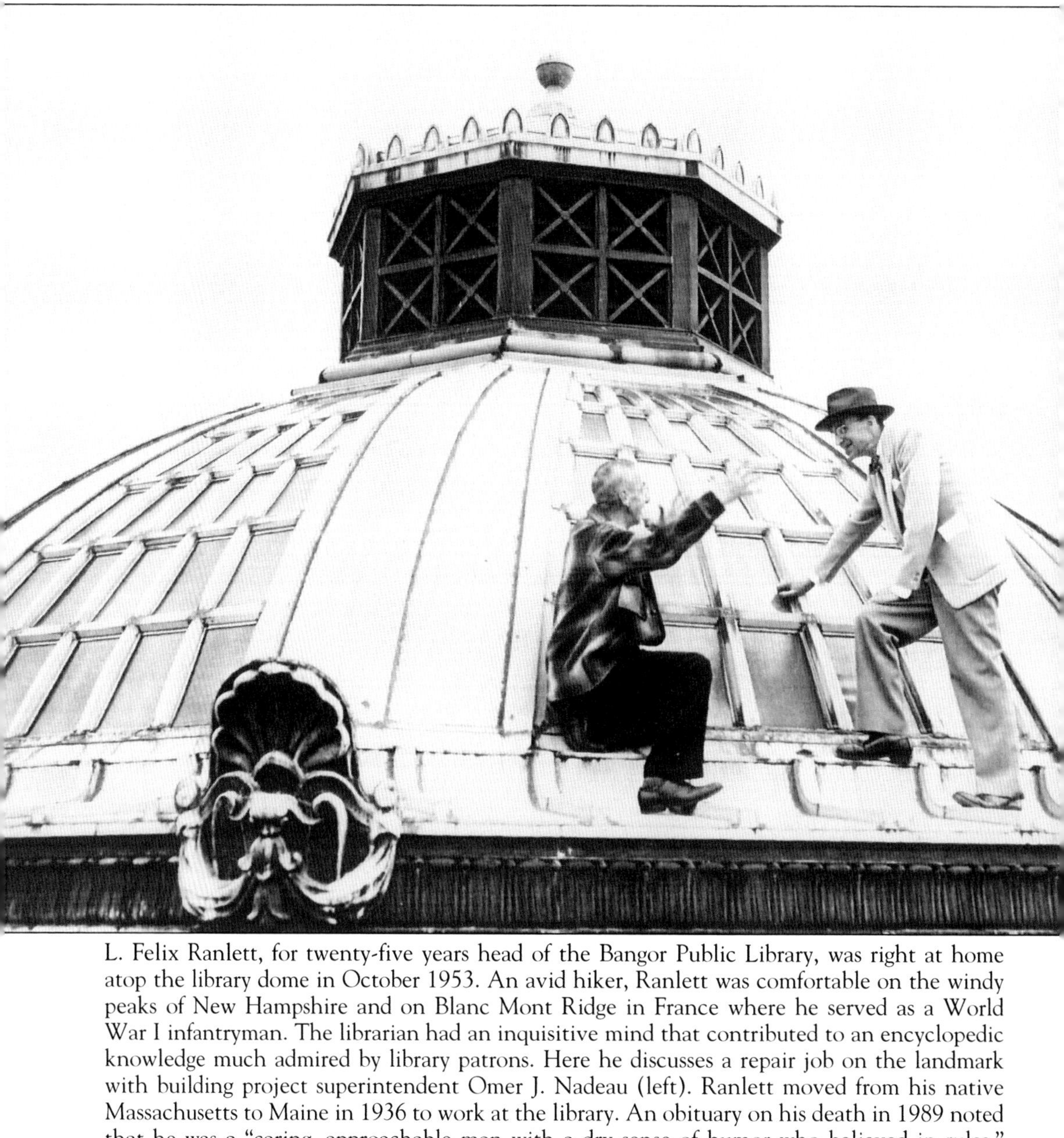

L. Felix Ranlett, for twenty-five years head of the Bangor Public Library, was right at home atop the library dome in October 1953. An avid hiker, Ranlett was comfortable on the windy peaks of New Hampshire and on Blanc Mont Ridge in France where he served as a World War I infantryman. The librarian had an inquisitive mind that contributed to an encyclopedic knowledge much admired by library patrons. Here he discusses a repair job on the landmark with building project superintendent Omer J. Nadeau (left). Ranlett moved from his native Massachusetts to Maine in 1936 to work at the library. An obituary on his death in 1989 noted that he was a "caring, approachable man with a dry sense of humor who believed in rules." It also mentioned one of his books, *Let's Go!*, the story of his wartime service. Ranlett was wounded in World War I, losing the sight in his left eye. He received the Purple Heart. He was also a noted civic leader and Rotarian. The trusted husband and father of three was known to neighborhood children, who were invited into his Montgomery Street residence for Halloween treats, and to sign his guest book.

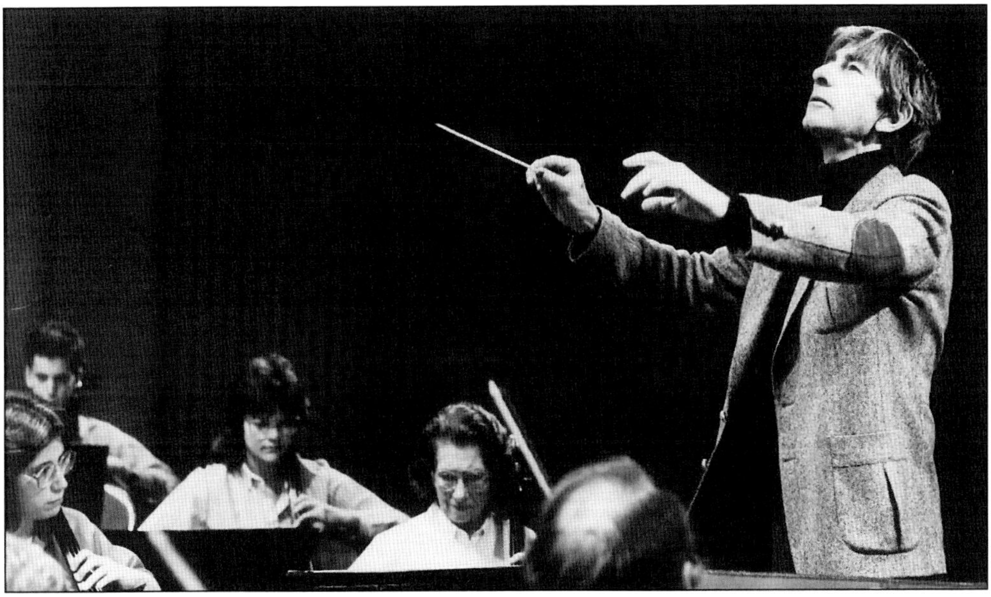

Werner Torkanowsky's musical brilliance and driving personality moved the Bangor Symphony Orchestra, founded in 1896, into a whole new realm of understanding. An accomplished violinist, the German native (he emigrated to Israel at age six, later moving to the United States) took the baton of America's oldest community orchestra in 1981, retiring in 1992 because of failing health. Wrote arts critic and friend Robert H. Newall, "He was internationally known, and we were fortunate that he happened to live in Maine."

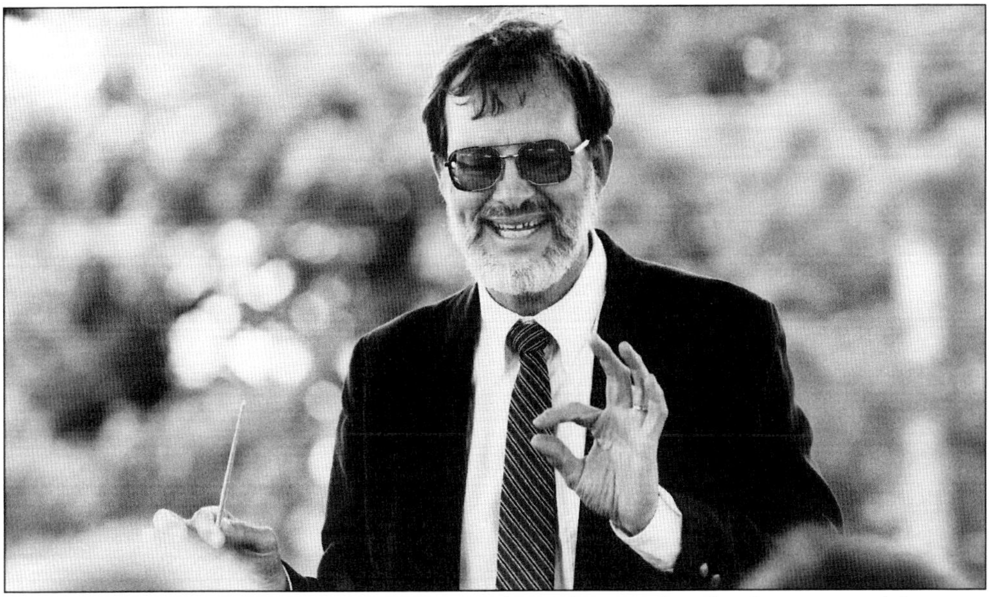

Gordon Bowie, seen here with the Bangor Band in July 1992, has the distinction of directing the nation's second oldest continuously performing town band. Since its inception in 1859, the band has never failed to perform indoor and outdoor concerts each year to please the public. It played for Maine Civil War regiments, for Spanish-American War troops, and for many visiting dignitaries, including presidents. Summer concerts are performed at the Bass Park bandstand, with occasional outings in the Chapin and Fairmount Parks on the city's east and west sides.

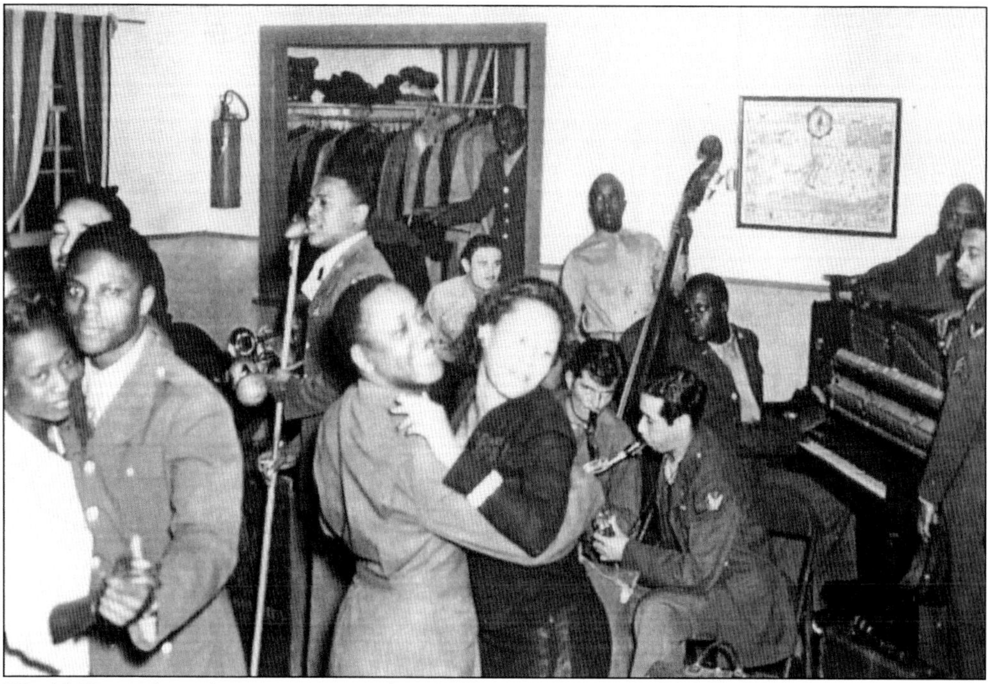

World War II brought an exciting cultural mix to Bangor with the opening of the military base in 1942. When they weren't on duty at Dow Field, couples congregated in base clubs, where jazz combos played while couples danced. Note the man singing at the microphone, and another checking coats and hats in a separate room at the rear.

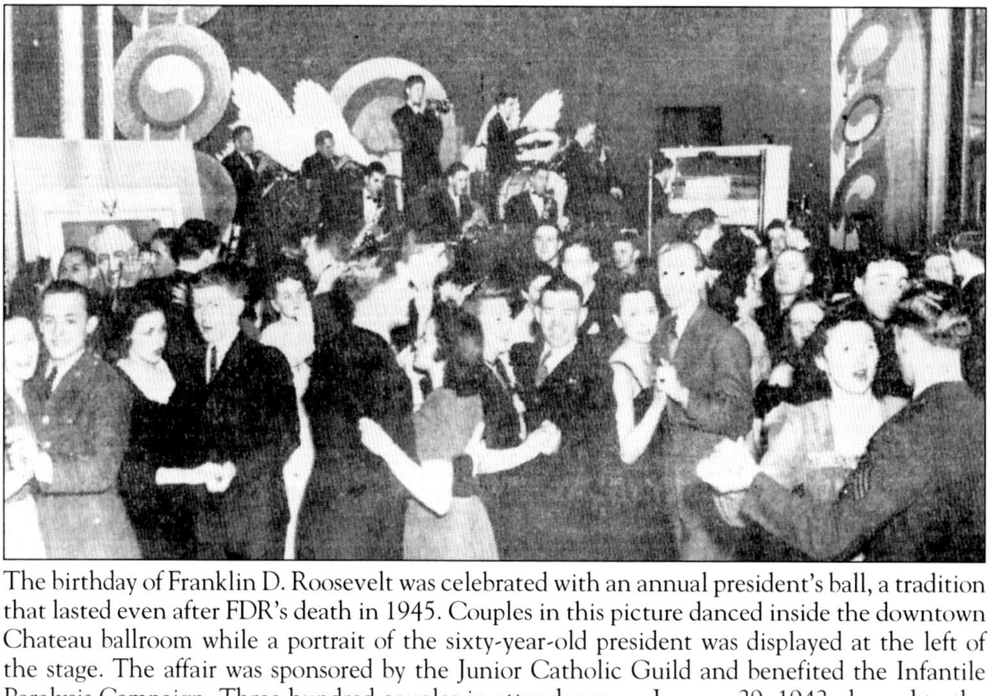

The birthday of Franklin D. Roosevelt was celebrated with an annual president's ball, a tradition that lasted even after FDR's death in 1945. Couples in this picture danced inside the downtown Chateau ballroom while a portrait of the sixty-year-old president was displayed at the left of the stage. The affair was sponsored by the Junior Catholic Guild and benefited the Infantile Paralysis Campaign. Three hundred couples in attendance on January 29, 1942, danced to the music of Sammy Saliba and his Southernaires.

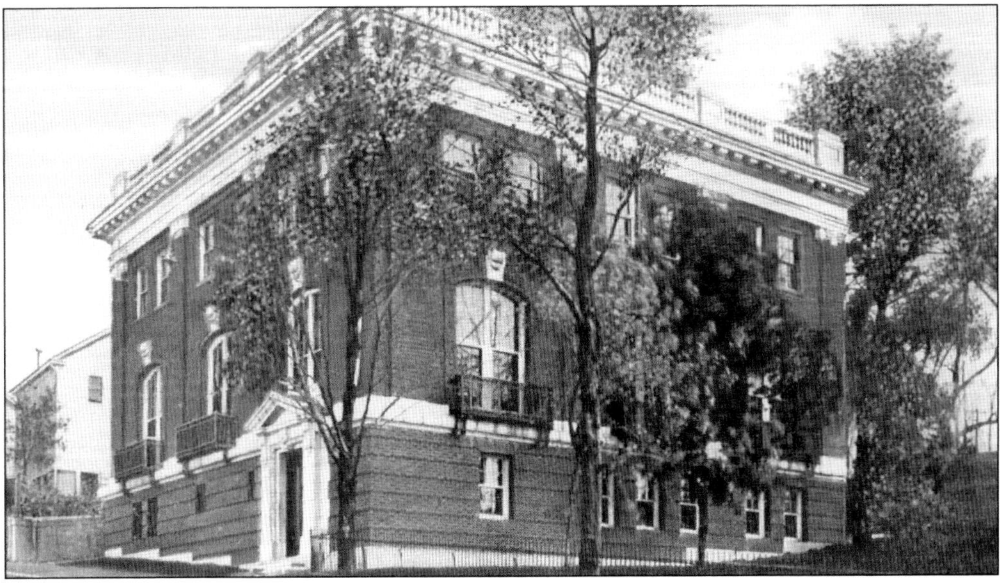

The Tarratine Club, the city's premier social club, financed the construction of this stately brick building in 1907, using it as its headquarters until 1991, when it was sold to Kork Systems Inc. The club was founded in 1884 by former Vice President Hannibal Hamlin and other prominent Bangor businessmen. In its heyday, club rooms were filled with gentlemen who played cards and drank cocktails. The building survived the Great Fire of 1911, which destroyed the surrounding buildings.

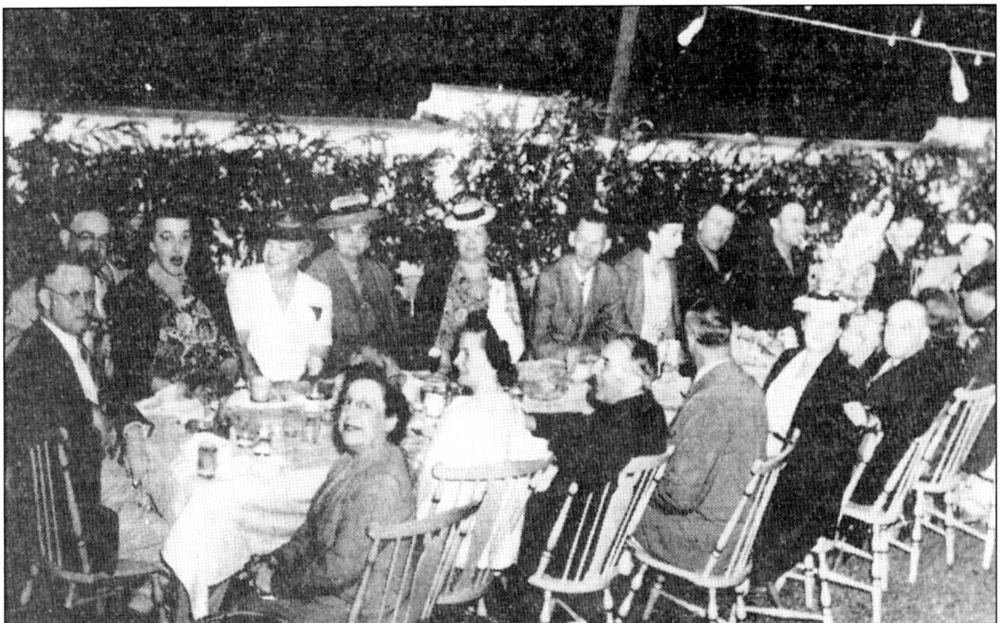

More than sixty people were present on July 8, 1942, for the opening of the Molly Molasses Roof Garden at the Tarratine Club. Dinner was served, followed by games and dancing. The roof garden was named for a Penobscot Indian woman whose portrait hung inside the club for many years. The 1940s were transitional years for the club as it opened its doors to servicemen stationed at Dow Field.

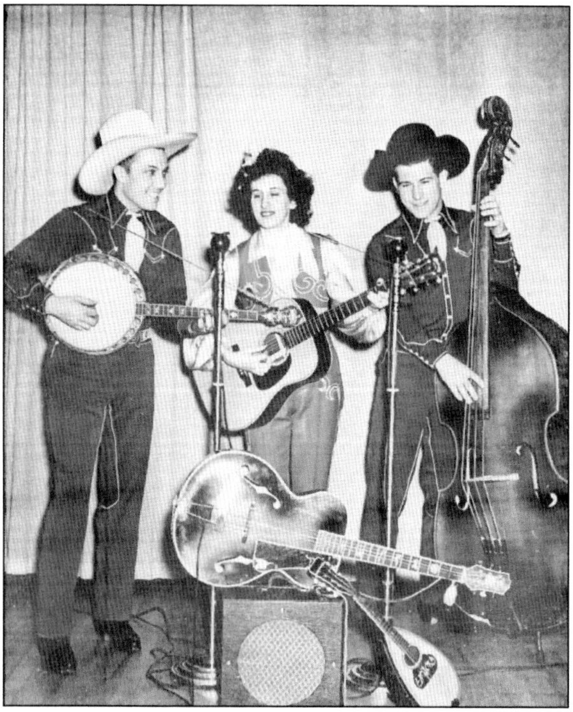

In the days when country acts were called hillbilly bands, WLBZ radio and other local stations featured live weekly programs such as Ray Little's Radio Cowboy Show. Bands typically consisted of three or four musicians, with a banjo, guitar, string bass, and sometimes other instruments included. Hal Lone Pine and Slim Clark were other local names who built a listening audience on local radio.

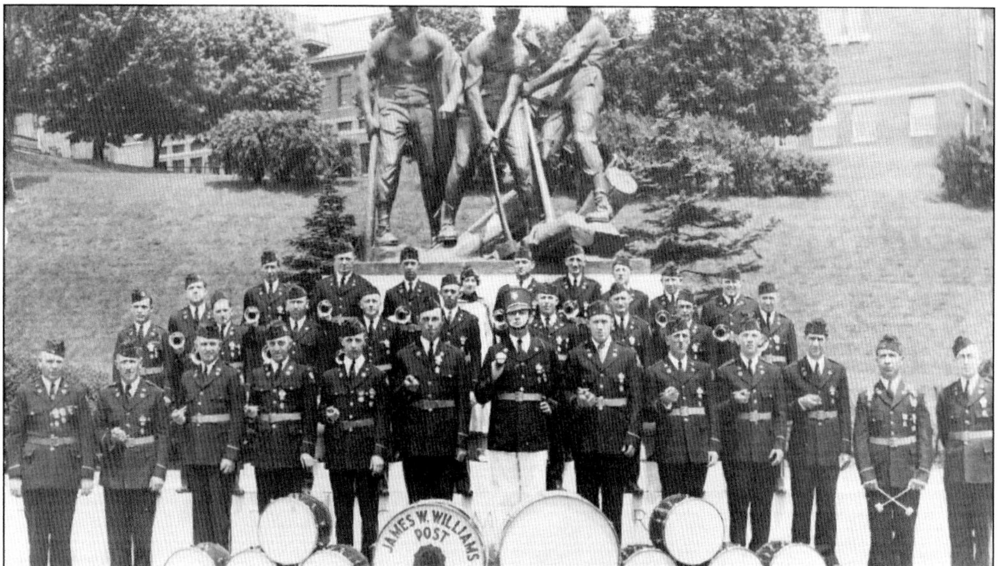

One of the city's finest marching bands was the drum and bugle corps of James W. Williams Post No. 12 of the American Legion, pictured here around 1934 in front of the Peirce Memorial. From left to right are as follows: (front row) Laurel Ross, Gerald Atwood, Philip Plummer, Gay White, Louis Cushing, Carl Dahlberg, Dutchy Carr, Al Greenlaw, Earl Bowen, Lewis Graffam, W.I. Brookings, Everett Allen, and Ernest Gibbons; (middle row) Jimmy Smith, Sam Cohen, Harold Casey, Carl Johnson, Herbert Hewes, Harold Noddin, Bill Skinner, Bob Finn, and L. Goodell; (back row) Punk Howard, Joe Cushing, F.E. McNamara, Bill Hastings, Pearl Bowen, Pete Marquis, Lawrence Libby, Caldwell Sweet Jr., Cobby O'Brien, and Irvin Kelley.

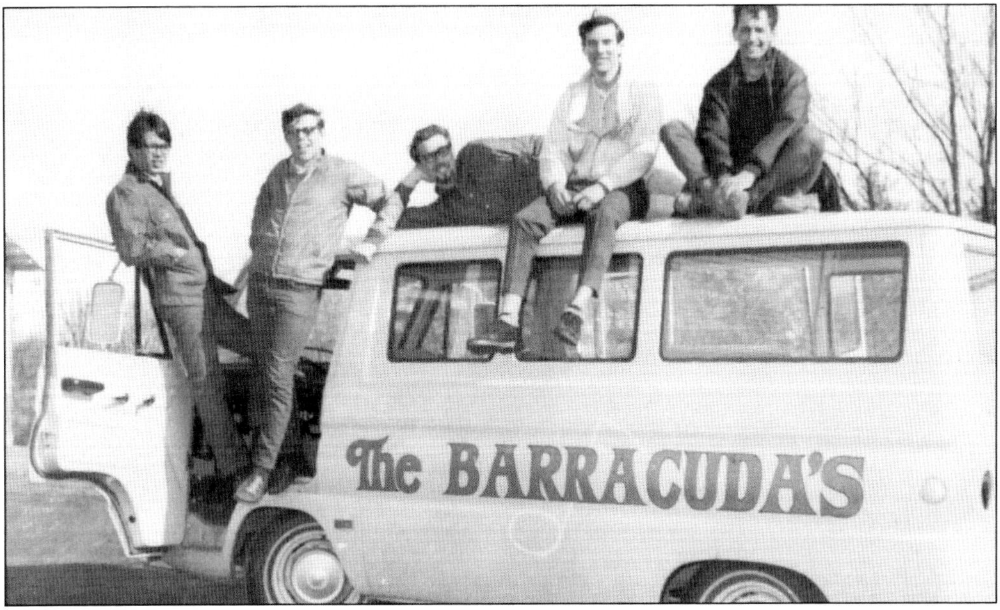

With lots of practice and the right promotion, local rock 'n roll bands could go places. Rick Bronson managed the Bangor-based Barracuda's in the 1960s. Steve Robbins, a musician in The Jesters, another local band of the period, had no trouble identifying all of The Barracuda's. From left to right are Mike Akins (keyboards), Tom Gass (lead singer and tambourine), Rob "Bear" Rolsky (drums), Pat Storey (guitar), and Roby Robichaud (bass).

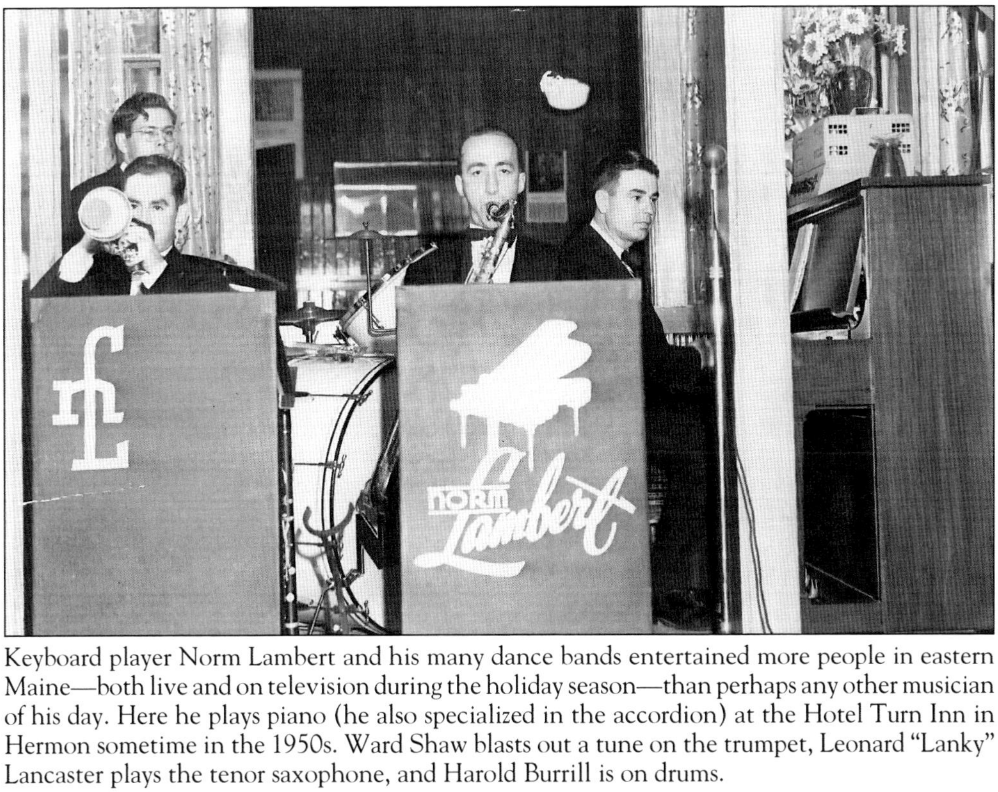

Keyboard player Norm Lambert and his many dance bands entertained more people in eastern Maine—both live and on television during the holiday season—than perhaps any other musician of his day. Here he plays piano (he also specialized in the accordion) at the Hotel Turn Inn in Hermon sometime in the 1950s. Ward Shaw blasts out a tune on the trumpet, Leonard "Lanky" Lancaster plays the tenor saxophone, and Harold Burrill is on drums.

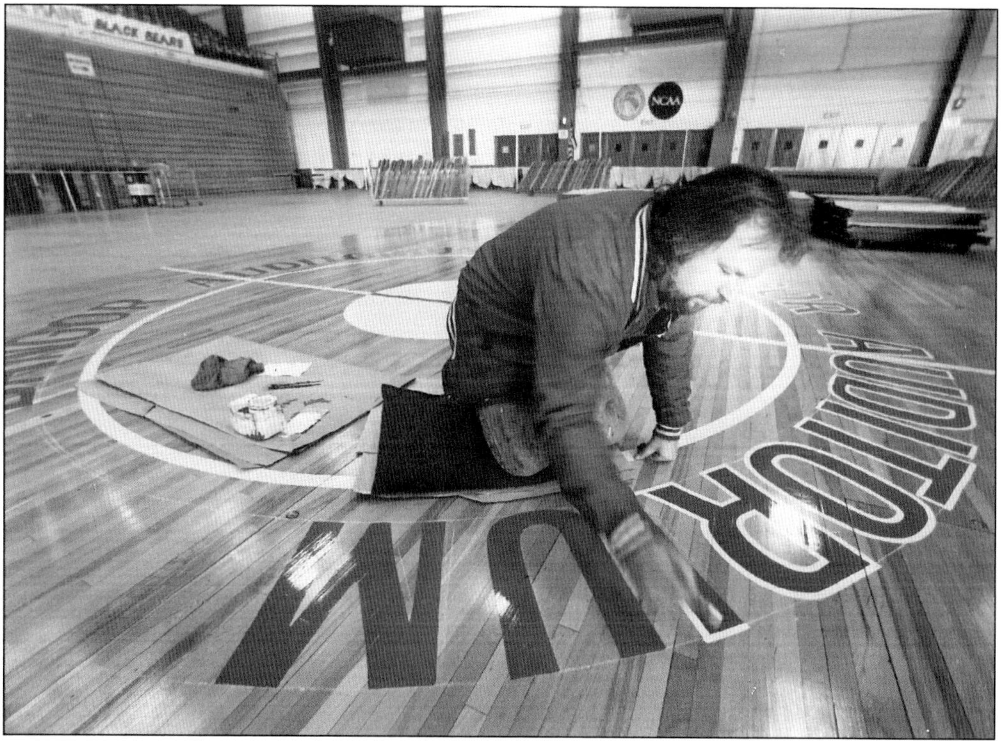

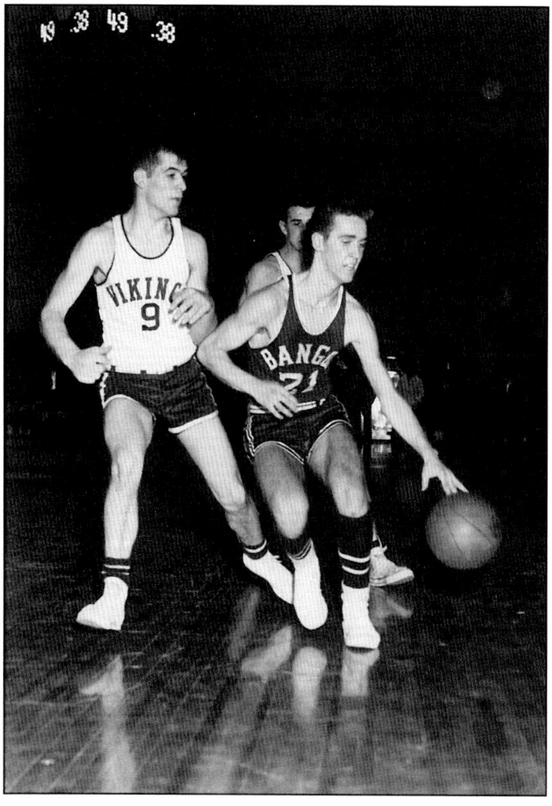

Brewer sign painter Harry Lord spent a good part of December 15, 1988, on his knees painting the words "BANGOR AUDITORIUM" on the jump circle at the center of the arena's basketball court. At the time, the refurbished facility served as the home court of the University of Maine men's and women's basketball teams as well as the John Bapst Crusaders. Funds were raised by City Councilor Marshall Frankel and the university to spruce up the auditorium and the floor was painted as a final attraction.

Basketball tournaments can still fill the Bangor Auditorium to the very top row of seats. The exciting 1958 game between Bangor and Caribou was no exception. One of the finest players in the school's history was Bill Cohen, wearing no. 21 in this photograph. Cohen (also pictured on pp. 86–7) went on to use his competitive skills in the Congress as both a representative and senator. Bangor's uniforms are still maroon and white.

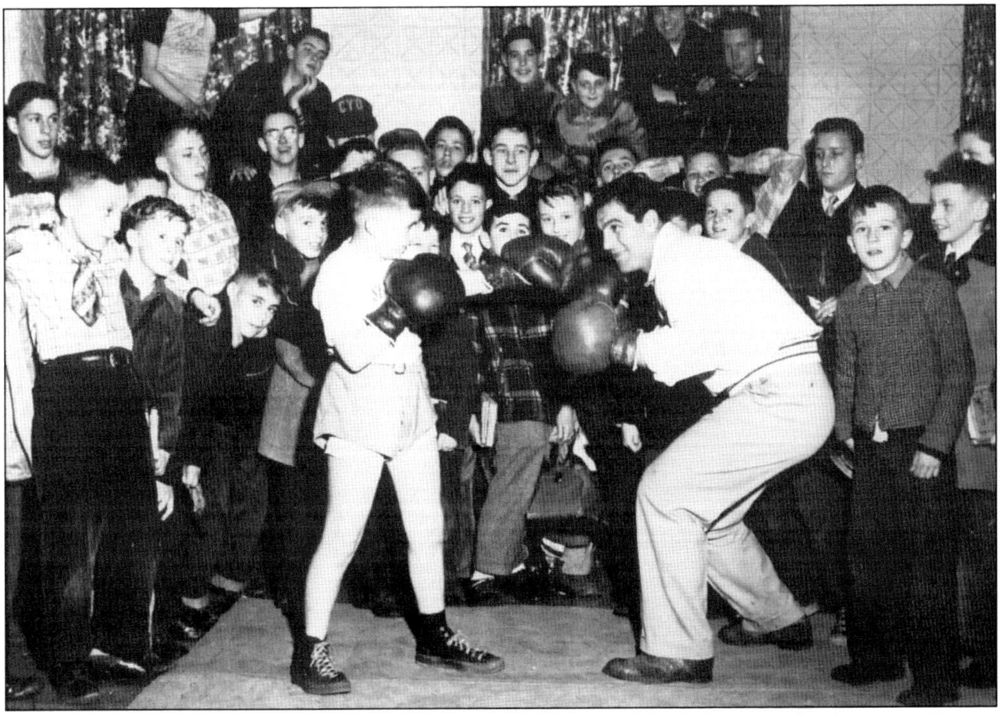

St. John's Grammar School was the setting of this 1952 boxing "match" between Rocky Marciano, who was visiting Bangor on a publicity tour, and future automobile executive Edward Darling. Among those attending the Catholic Youth Organization event were these boys; standing in the front, from left to right, are Thomas McDonald, James Whitty, Lester Verow, John Whitty, Albert King, Warren Wallace, John Largay, Michael Abbott, Patrick Welch, and Shaun Dowd. On September 23 of that year, Marciano knocked out a real boxer, Joe Walcott, in Philadelphia to capture the world heavyweight title.

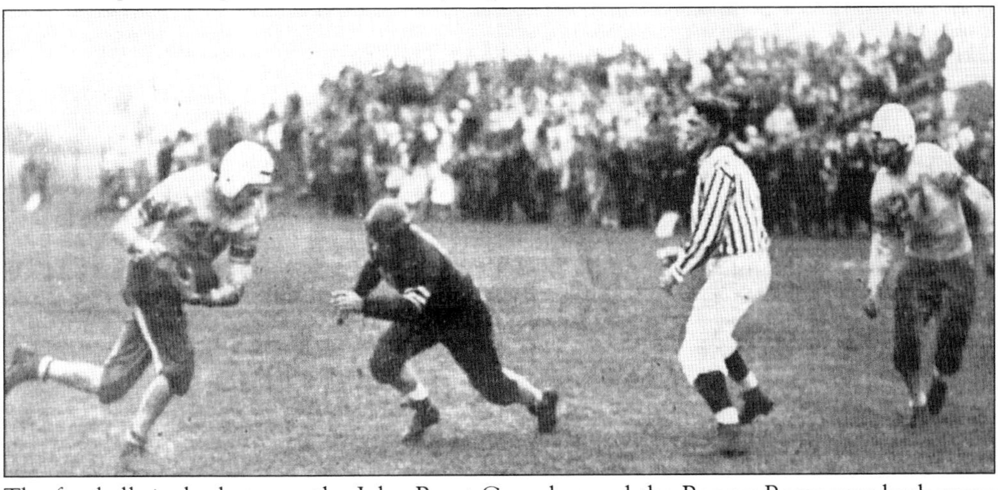

The football rivalry between the John Bapst Crusaders and the Bangor Rams goes back many years. In October 1944, the Crusaders upset the Rams for the first time in eleven years. The score was 13–12. Playing in a drenching rain, Bangor player Ronnie Smith tried to tackle a Bapst player named Booker, but he was too late. The Bapst player at the right was identified in newspapers only as Royal; the official was Mr. Hebert.

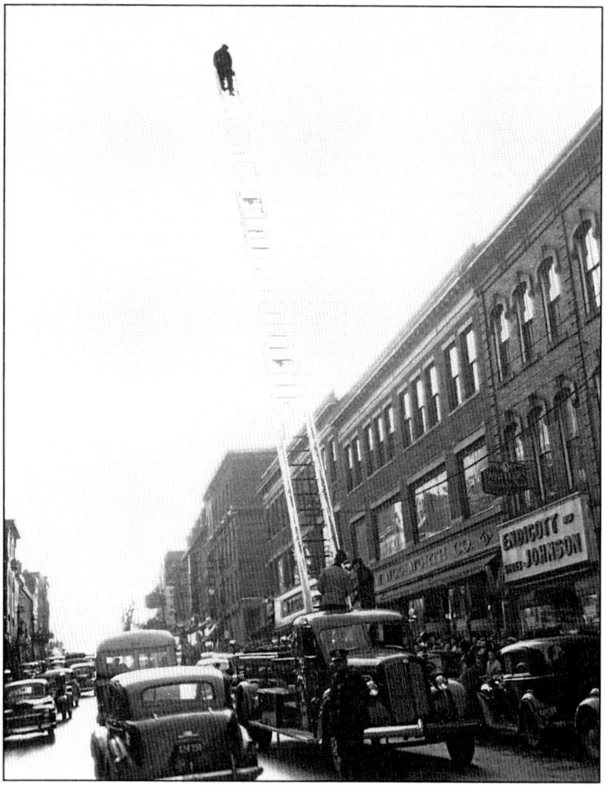

A Bangor firefighter who obviously doesn't fear heights demonstrates the department's new Segrave aerial ladder truck on Main Street in December 1946. The ladder extended to 65 feet, quite a length for its day. Later innovations such as the Snorkel truck made the fighting of fires in upper stories even more exacting. Firemen had their mettle tested many times fighting stubborn fires in Bangor's old buildings. Historian Paul E. Tower loaned this picture for publication.

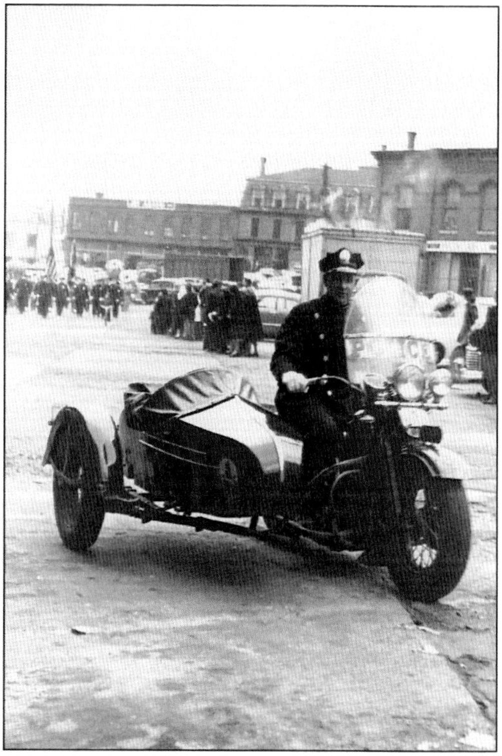

Perhaps every schoolchild in Bangor during the 1950s and '60s knew Warren "Bubba" Brown, the friendly police officer with the motorcycle side car. Also known as "Brownie," the patrolman often worked at crosswalks on the East Side, notably at the Mary Snow and Abraham Lincoln Schools. Here he is captured on film by Orlando Frati Sr. while leading a parade through downtown's Pickering Square, *c.* 1950.

Four

Planes, Trains, and Automobiles

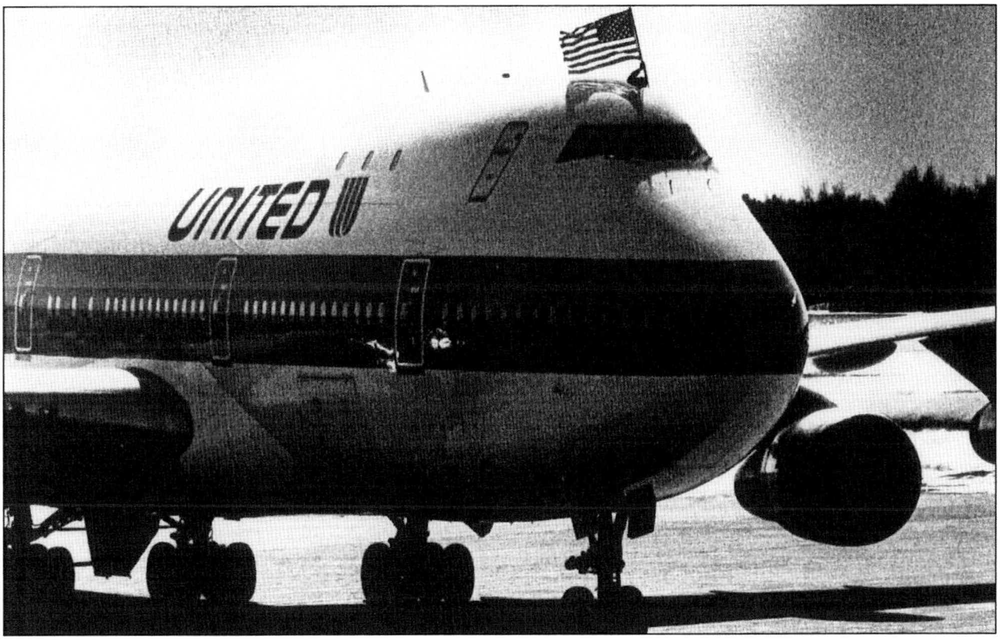

Scenes like this came to symbolize the patriotic fervor that surrounded the Persian Gulf War homecoming flights at Bangor International Airport in 1991. Lynne J. Cole and Brian Swartz, who both have written books chronicling emotional scenes inside the terminal, recall along with many others the sight of the first 747 jetliner landing in Bangor with an American flag flown from its hatch. This *Bangor Daily News* photograph of Captain David Young flying Old Glory was republished throughout the country. Federal Aviation Administration safety concerns nearly stopped the practice, but it eventually continued to the delight of many spectators.

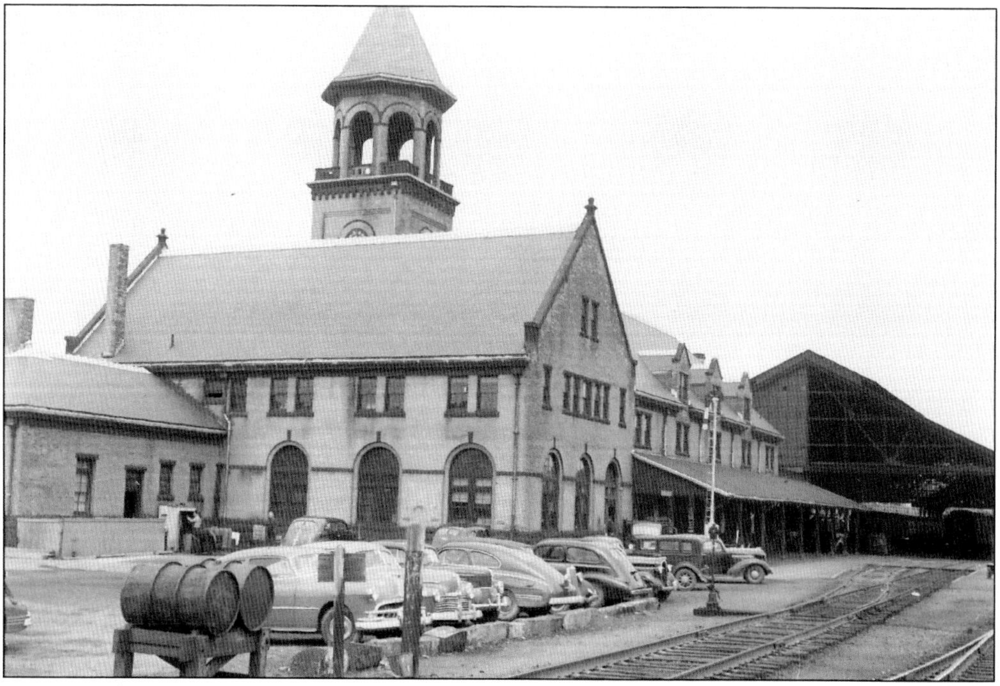

An unusual view of Bangor's Union Station, from the tracks, on April 11, 1949. After it began serving Maine Central and Bangor and Aroostook Railroad travelers in 1907, the station became one of the city's most beloved landmarks. No other building in town was so busy with people. Everyone, it seemed, had passed through the station at least once in his or her life.

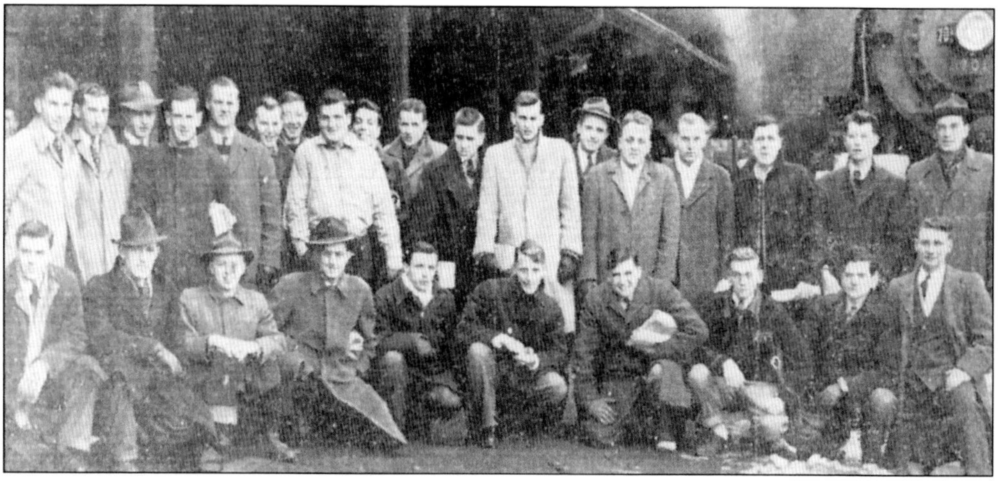

Thirty-two men from Bangor selective service board number 1 left Union Station for Fort Devens, Massachusetts, on December 22, 1942. Laurence Downes, the acting corporal of the group, is shown at the extreme right of the second row. Others in the group (not identified in order) are Guy Leonard, Byron Gardiner, Wilfred Richardson, Arnold Kelley, Clarence Melvin Jr., Carroll Polyot, Donald Ferguson, Joseph LaChance, Linwood Conners, Malcolm Carter, Augustus Parsons, Frank O'Connell, Charles Oakes, Robert Thibodeau, Fred Vardamis, Phillip Plummer Jr., Irving Robinson, Raymond Hansen, Francis Murray, Laurel Lawrence, Clarence Heath, Francis McDonald, George Brountas, Sandy DeRoche, Gilbert Gyr, Charles Carson, Paul Hamilton, John Hopkins, Orin Seeley, Clayton Redmond, and Paul McKenney.

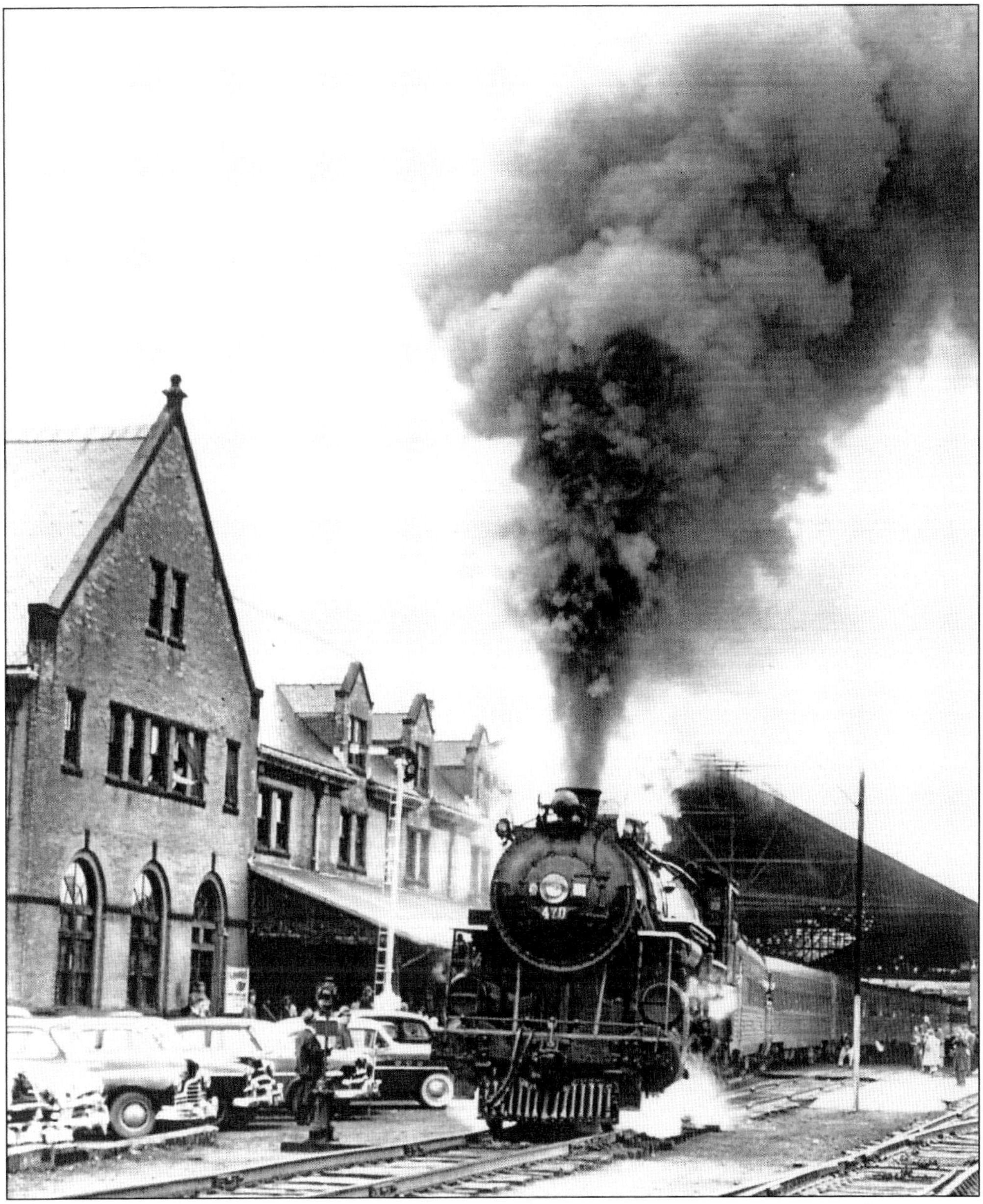

A colorful era of steam and romance drew to a close on June 13, 1954, as steam locomotive 470 left Union Station for the last time. On board the twelve cars coupled behind the old locomotive were Governor Burton M. Cross, Maine Central Railroad President Spencer Miller, and scores of railroad enthusiasts who tried to enjoy themselves on the Bangor-to-Portland round trip. But many were saddened knowing the days of steam travel in the city, which began in 1855 when the Penobscot-Kennebec Railroad started to serve Bangor, were soon to become only a memory.

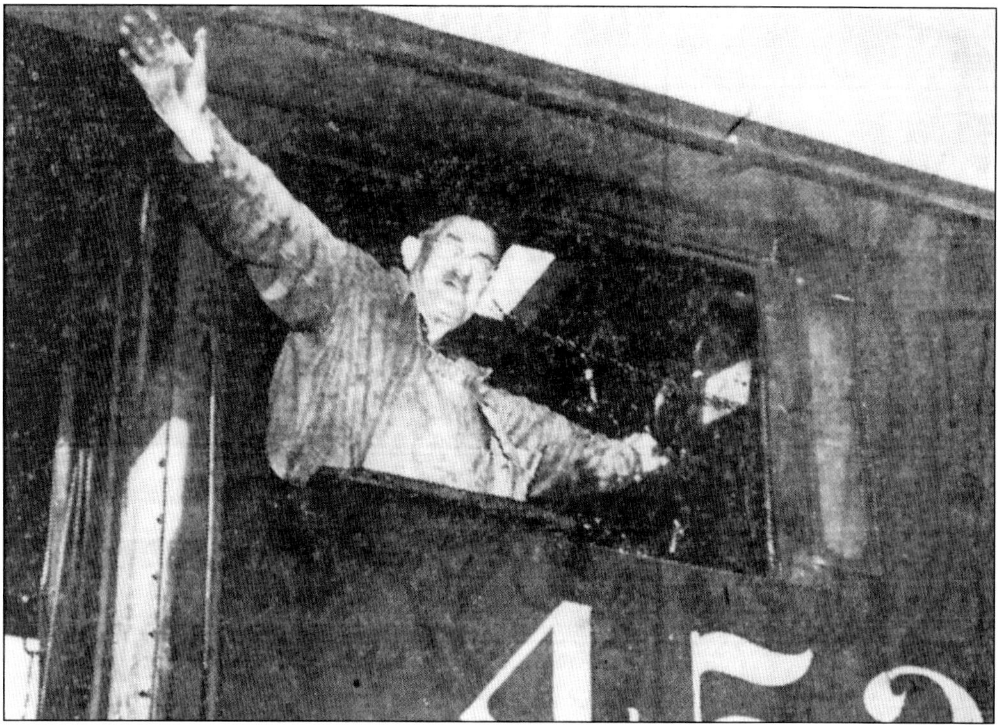

Engineer Harvey Colby saw fifty years of service with the Maine Central Railroad before retiring in 1944. Seen here leaving Union Station on his farewell run to Vanceboro, the Bangor man was an engineer on every part of the railroad's system except the Mountain Division. His most famous passenger was President William Howard Taft (see p. 11), who in 1910 rode the Bar Harbor Express from Bangor to Hancock Point and took a steamboat across to Mount Desert Island, where he vacationed with James G. Blaine.

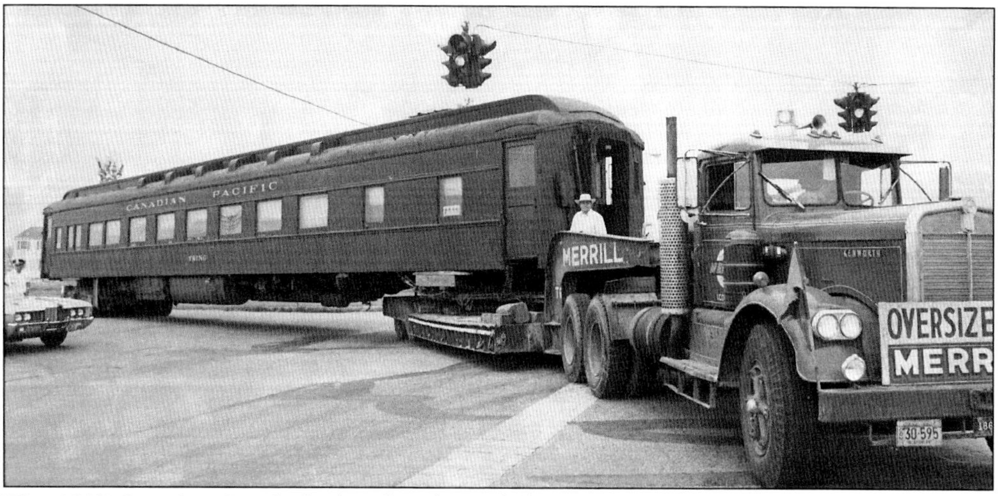

This 1895 Canadian Pacific Railroad parlor and sleeping car is shown being eased onto tracks next to the Chuck Wagon Restaurant (now Captain Nick's) on Union Street in July 1972. Restaurant owner Paul Nadeau reconditioned the car for elegant dining in the nineteenth-century mahogany motif of the Canadian west. The 60-ton car, which once traveled from Vancouver to Halifax, came to Portland by rail and then was trucked to Bangor.

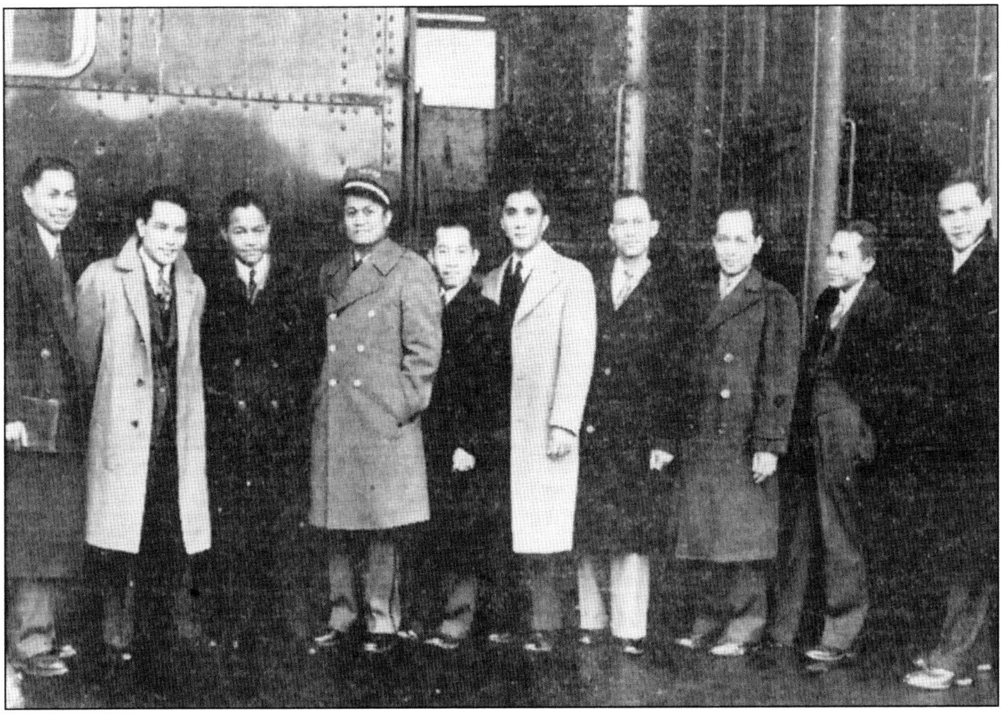

These ten Filipino nationals were chefs and waiters on the Bangor and Aroostook Railroad's passenger trains. They immigrated to America during World War II to get an education and to work, enduring the humiliation of being labeled Japanese because of their appearance. Pictured in 1942 are, from left to right, Jaime Bernal, Lucian Channay, Primo Dauz, F.G. Gonzales, D.G. Madarang, Val Mangawang, Greg Quijano, Jerry Umel, Calle Duque, and Carlos Quesada.

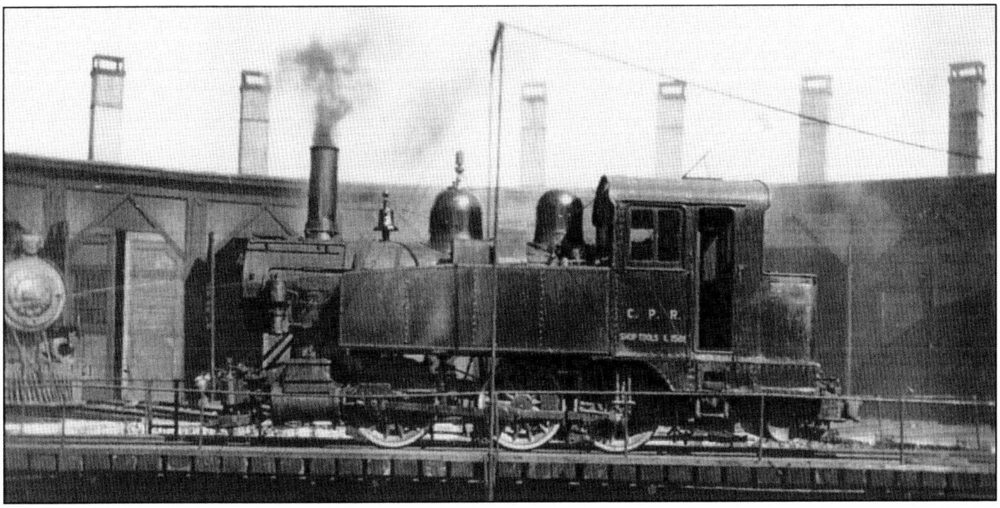

The Maine Central Railroad roundhouse at the foot of Dutton Street, beside the Penobscot River, was an engineering marvel when it was built in the summer of 1900. Architectural historian Deborah Thompson notes that the utilitarian building could accommodate thirty-five locomotives, each housed in one of five sections. A crew of forty men built what was said to be the finest roundhouse east of Boston. This picture from the Mildred N. Thayer collection shows a steam locomotive from the Canadian Pacific Railroad.

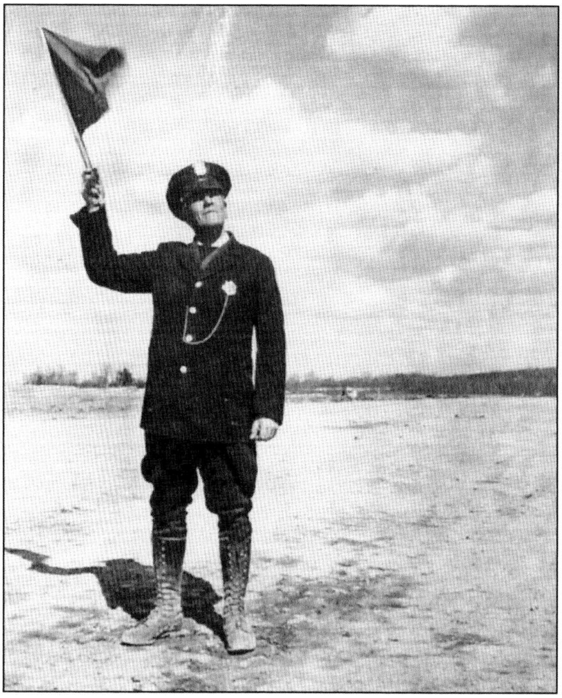

An unidentified Bangor police officer takes the wind direction sometime during World War II. Apparently photographed at Dow Field, the policeman stares intently at the clouds, perhaps waiting for an approaching aircraft. His long coat and high, laced boots would be oddities in today's police force.

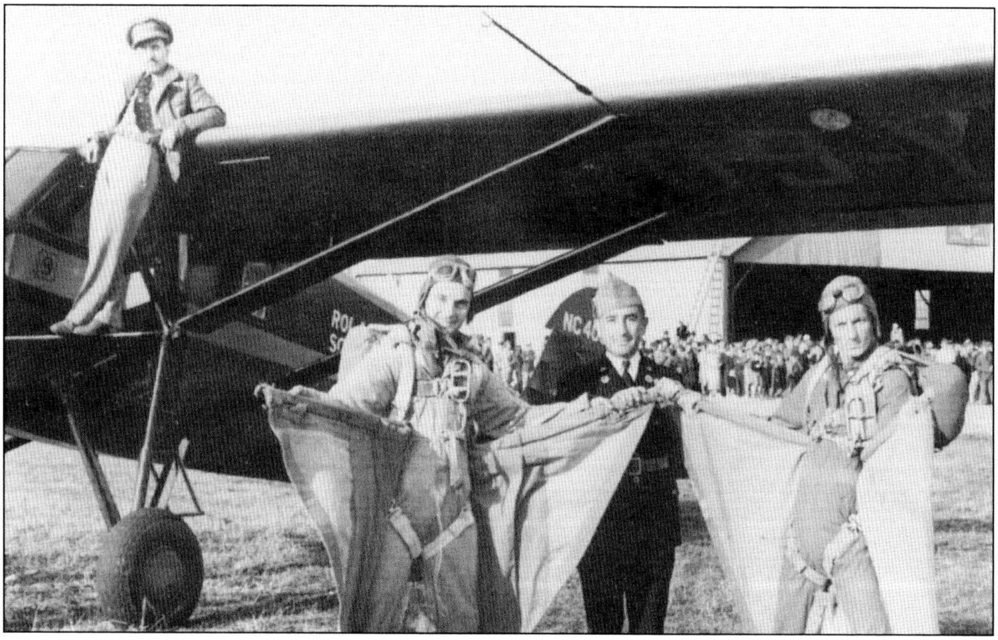

The 1940 Bangor air show featured two "bat wing" jumpers, Jimmy Goodwin (left) and Tommy Boyd (right). Leaning on the wing of his Stinson SM 8-A airplane is Roland Maheu, a popular Maine pilot of his day. Wilfred MacNeil of Bangor's American Legion post is standing between the bat wing jumpers. One of the big Bangor air field hangars is visible in the background. The government took over the property after the bombing of Pearl Harbor on December 7, 1941. Security was tightened around the base, although the public was invited to occasional air shows throughout the war.

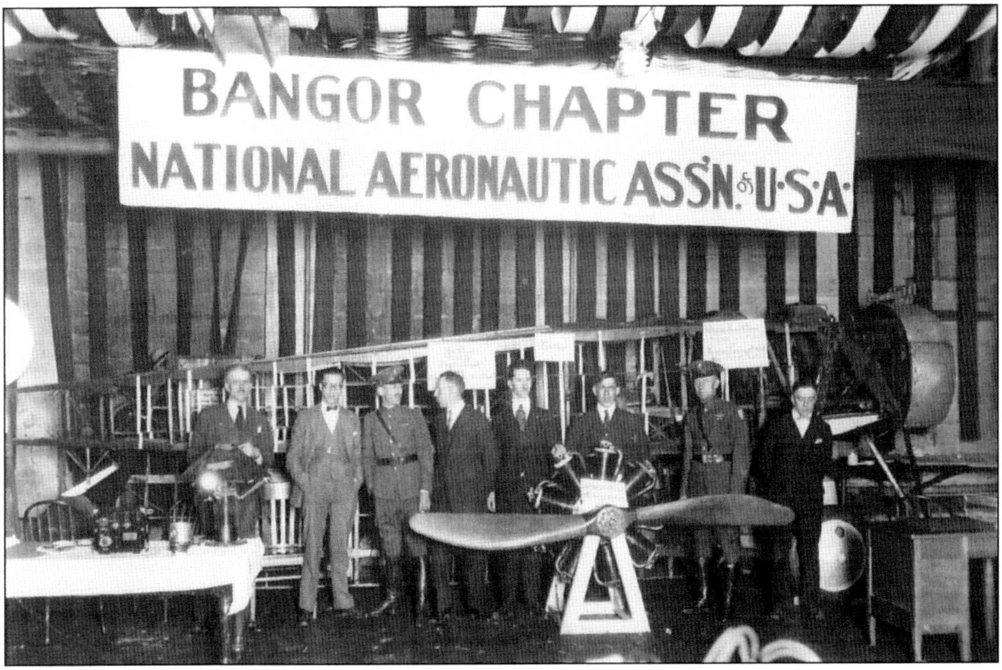

Bangor's old auditorium building was the setting of an aeronautical display, seen in a 1926 photograph from the Pat Denner collection. The wooden fuselage and engine shown in the picture were part of a British AVRO 404K wartime flying plane that was being restored by students of Bob Lowell, a World War I pilot. Lowell's school, the Maine Aerial Service, was located on Central Street but was short-lived. Maine aviation pioneer Edward R. Godfrey recalled seeing the plane parts being hauled through town, apparently a curious sight.

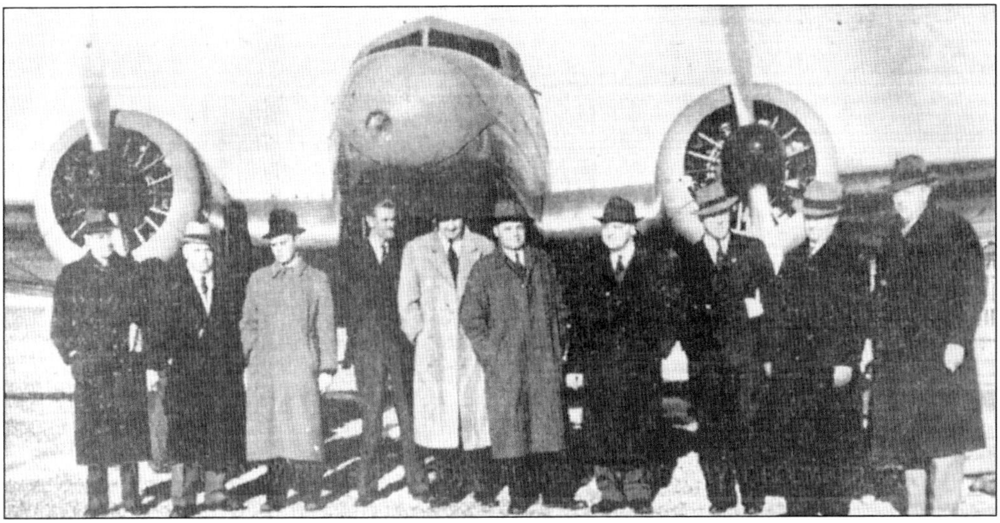

A Boston-Maine Airways Lockheed-Electra, like the plane Amelia Earhart was flying in 1937 when she was lost in the Pacific, provides a visually appealing backdrop for a scene from December 19, 1939. The picture was taken just before a survey flight departed from the Bangor Airport for Moncton, New Brunswick, for a proposed run between the two cities (flying time in those days was one hour, twenty-three minutes). *Bangor Daily News* reporter Wayne St. Germain (third from left) stands with other newspaper men, in addition to aviation officials.

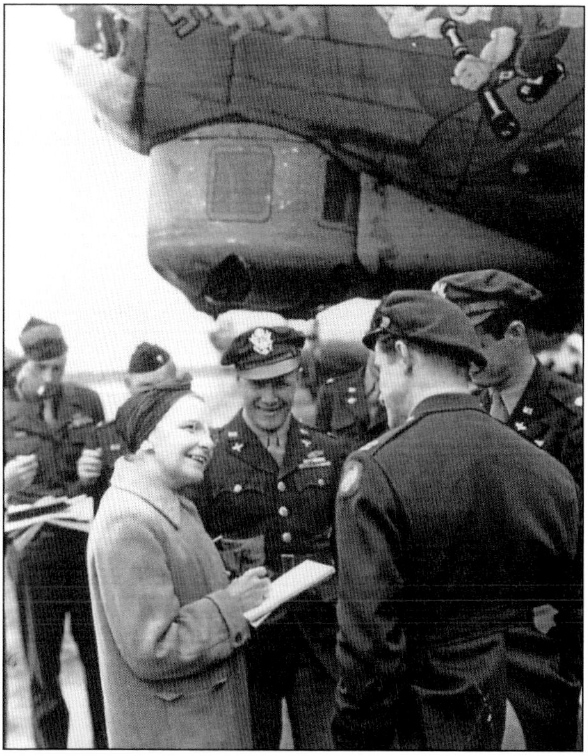

Nelle Penley, a *Bangor Daily News* reporter, liked to be where the action was, and on this day it was on the tarmac of Dow Field interviewing a trio of Army Air Corps officers. The top-security base was off-limits to most civilians during World War II, but on occasion Uncle Sam swung open the gates and allowed the press in to cover the arrival of visiting brass or an occasional aerial display. A row of swastikas and a cartoon character holding a telescope are painted on the bomber's fuselage.

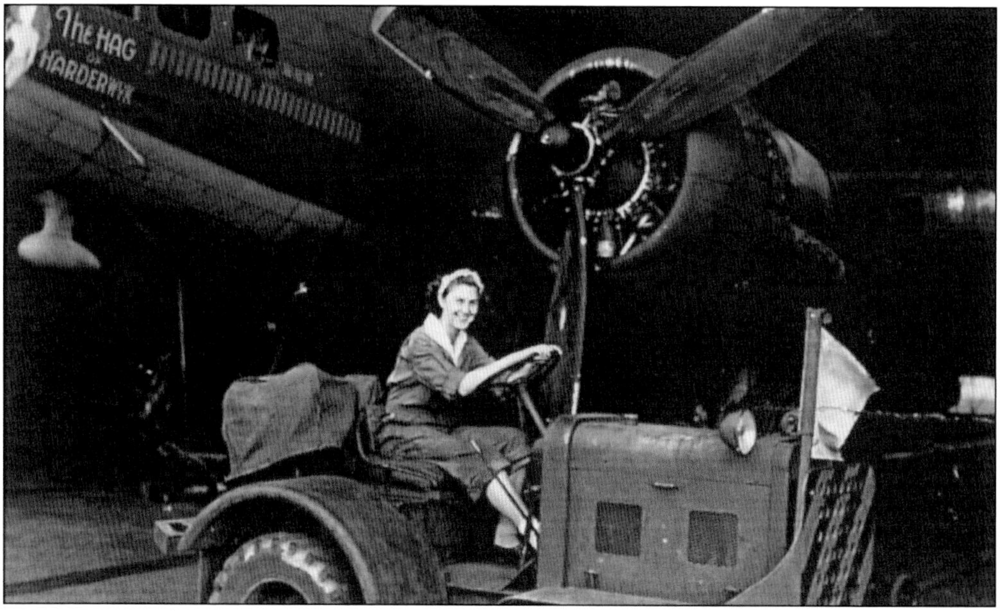

Women not only covered the airport for newspapers during World War II, they worked on base in important jobs. This woman is pictured driving a vehicle nicknamed a "tug" around the field with a bomber dubbed "The Hag of Harderwyk" in back of her (a racy painting of the hag is painted on the plane's fuselage). The Allies were winning the war by July 26, 1944, when this picture was taken, although thirteen more months of fighting remained before the aggression ended.

Careful inspection of the tail of Tony Guercia's fighter plane at Dow Field reveals scores of names painted on the side: Kearney and Berry and Madden and Tarr, to name a few. All apparently took credit for aerial combat in this aircraft. Women's names appear, too, for good luck: Jeanie Elam and Minnie May. Countless fighter planes passed through Bangor during World War II, each with its own signatures and gaudy artwork.

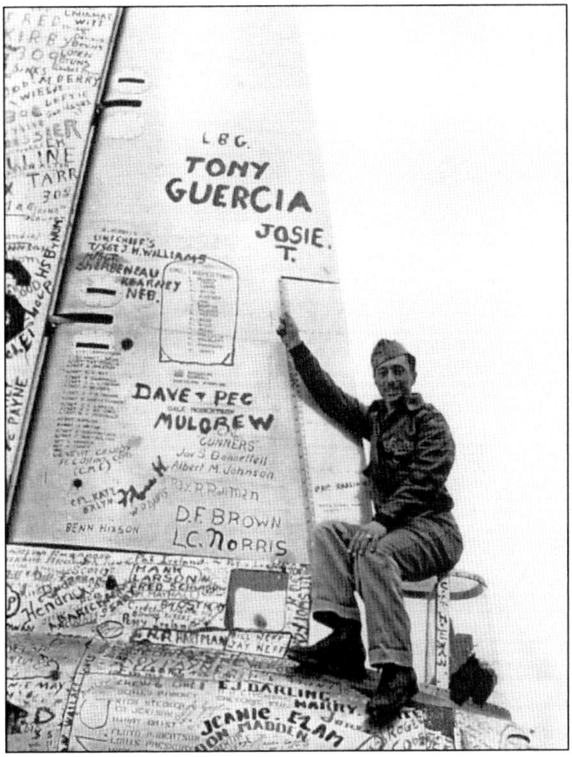

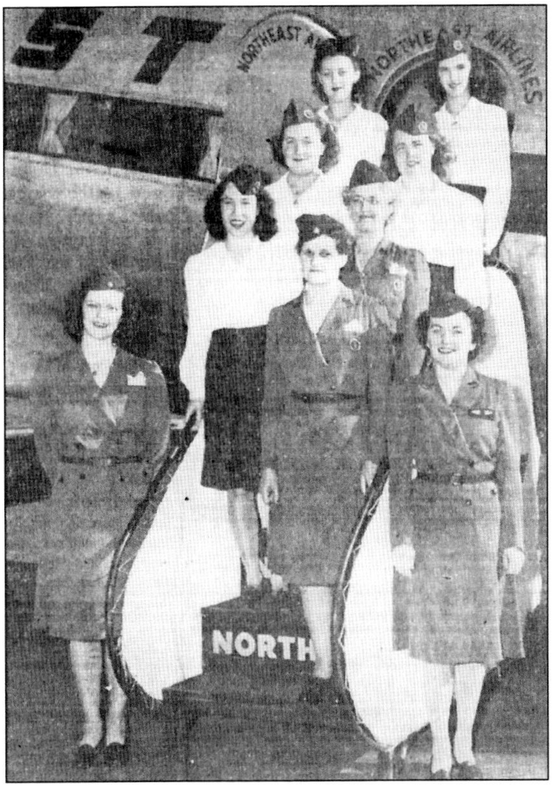

The Bangor unit of Wing Scouts leaves Bangor on Northeast Airlines' morning flight to Boston in June 1945, its members' first plane ride following a winter's study in aeronautics. The unit was named for Col. Frank Bostrom, a local hero whose wartime actions won nationwide commendation. Pictured are as follows: (bottom row, left to right) Hilda Courtney and Margaret Marley; (left row, bottom to top) Lorraine Ladner, Barbara Attner, and Helena Buskee; (right row, bottom to top) Mrs. Earl Perry, Mrs. Roy Ladner, Carolyn Gamble, and Carlene Paine.

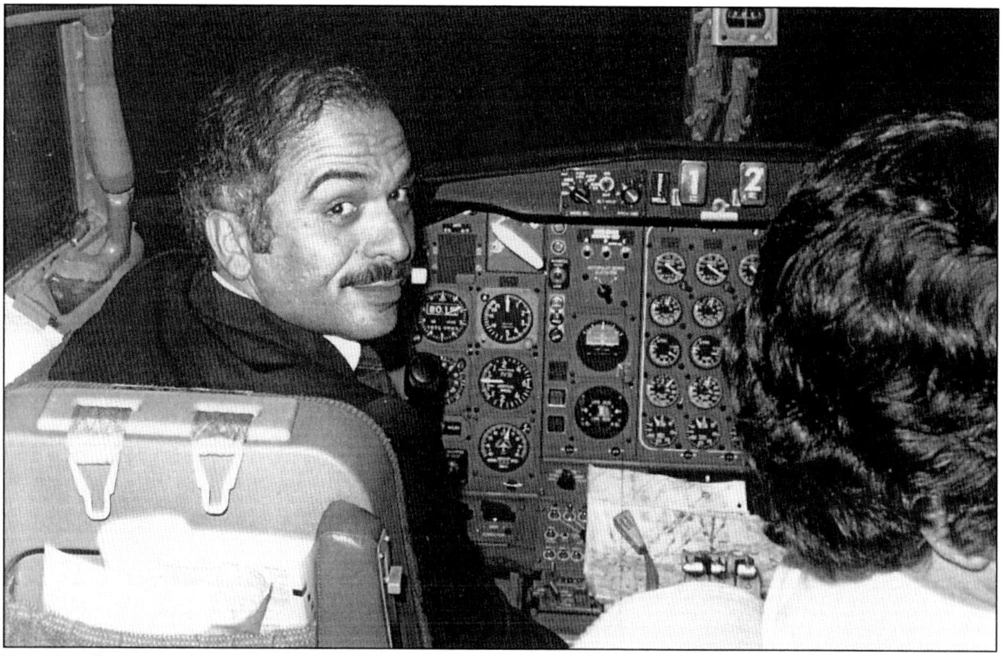

Royalty flew into Bangor International Airport on the night of August 18, 1974. King Hussein and his wife, Princess Alia Baha, made a brief refueling stop before returning to Jordan. Hussein was at the controls of his newly purchased Royal Jordanian 727 before he left the aircraft to stretch his legs in the domestic terminal. He even invited a local airline representative, Bruce Nett, onto the jet, where the king amiably posed for this picture.

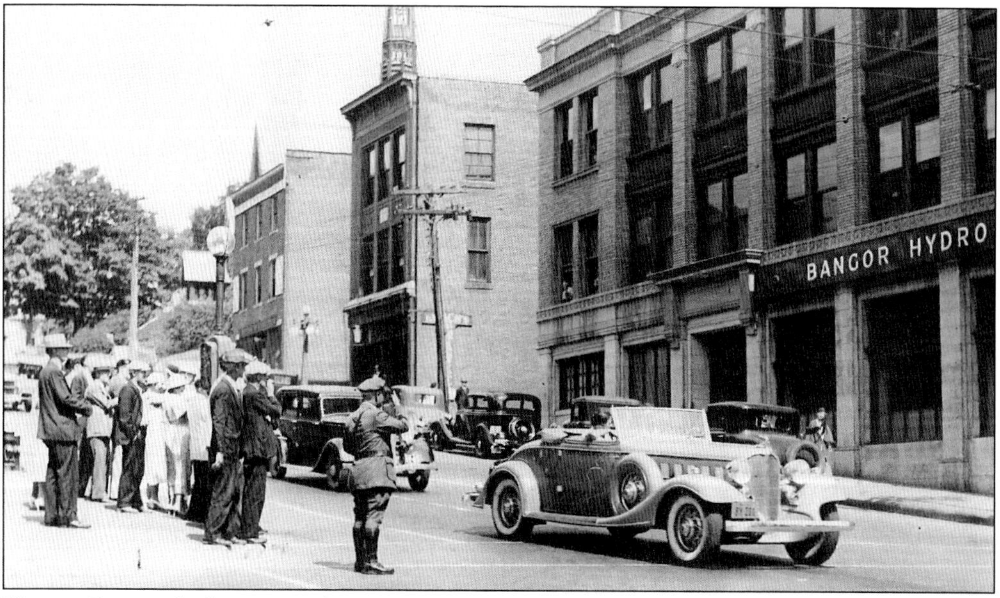

Eleanor Roosevelt, known as the nation's most famous auto tourist because of her love of the open road, drove down State Street hill in a blue Buick roadster in July 1933. Accompanied by her personal secretary, Lorena Hickock, the first lady was saluted by onlookers as she passed. Having refused a state police escort, Mrs. Roosevelt drove along Route 2 to the Lakewood Theater in Madison, where she watched a play.

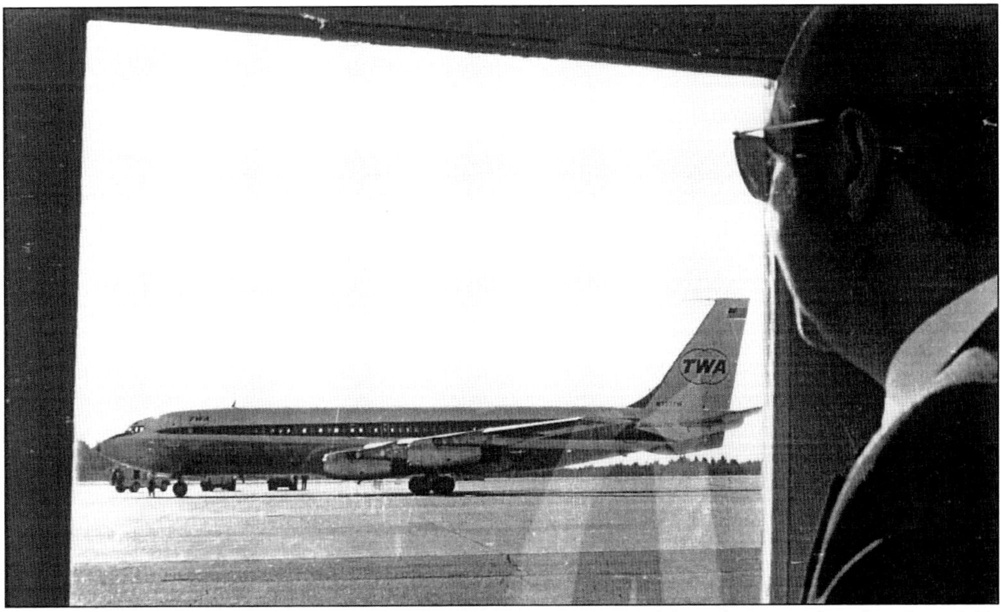

Bangor International Airport played a part in an international hijacking on October 31, 1969. A hijacked TWA jetliner, commandeered by an emotionally disturbed U.S. Marine armed with a carbine, landed at BIA for refueling. Flight 85 had been hijacked after it left Los Angeles for San Francisco; passengers were allowed to disembark in Denver. Pilot Billy N. Williams refueled in Bangor before flying on to Shannon, Ireland, and finally, Rome, where the 6,900-mile flight ended without injury.

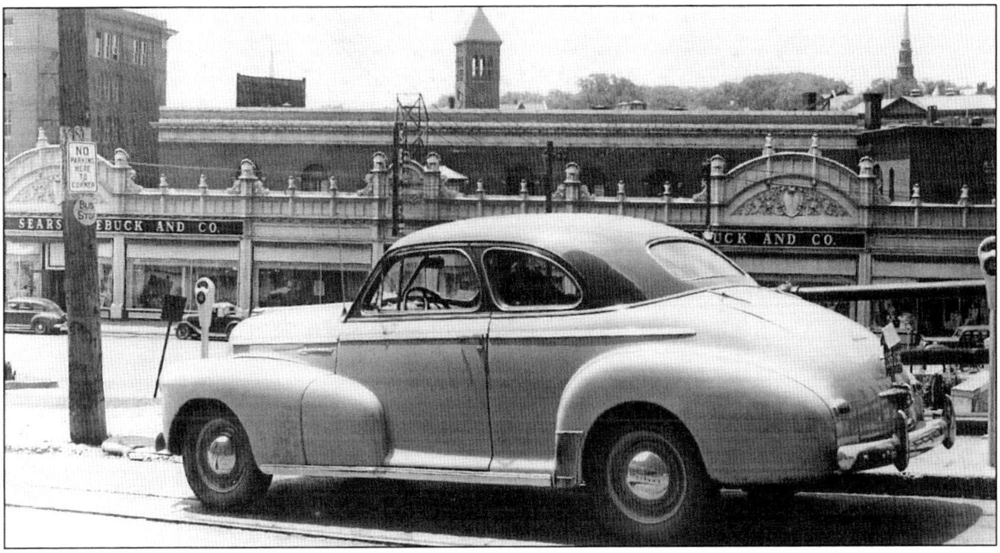

Before fuel injection and unabody vehicles, cars looked like this Chevy Fleetmaster—big and heavy with shiny silver hubcaps. Dan Maher snapped this photograph on Park Street hill in 1946 with a backdrop of parking meters and the old Sears Roebuck and Company store on Harlow Street. The store has now been demolished, and the old brick city hall in the distance was taken down in 1969. Most downtown streets are now free of parking meters, which were never much of a hit with motorists in the first place, but were a valuable source of municipal revenue.

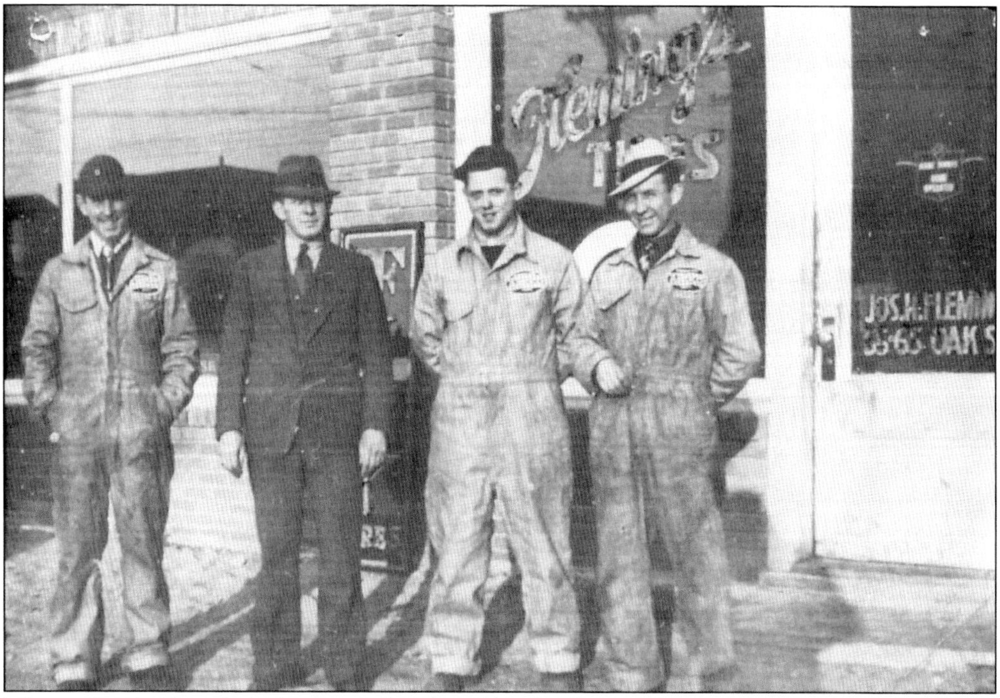

Johnny Quirk (far right), the future founder of his family's Subaru dealership, was a crackerjack mechanic when this photograph was taken around 1938. Joe Fleming's Amoco garage (Joe is second from the left) started as a tire and auto mechanic business at the corner of York and Oak streets, later relocating to Oak and Hancock by the late 1920s. The other mechanics are Leo Webb (far left) and Burnie Welch (second from right). The garage closed in the late 1960s.

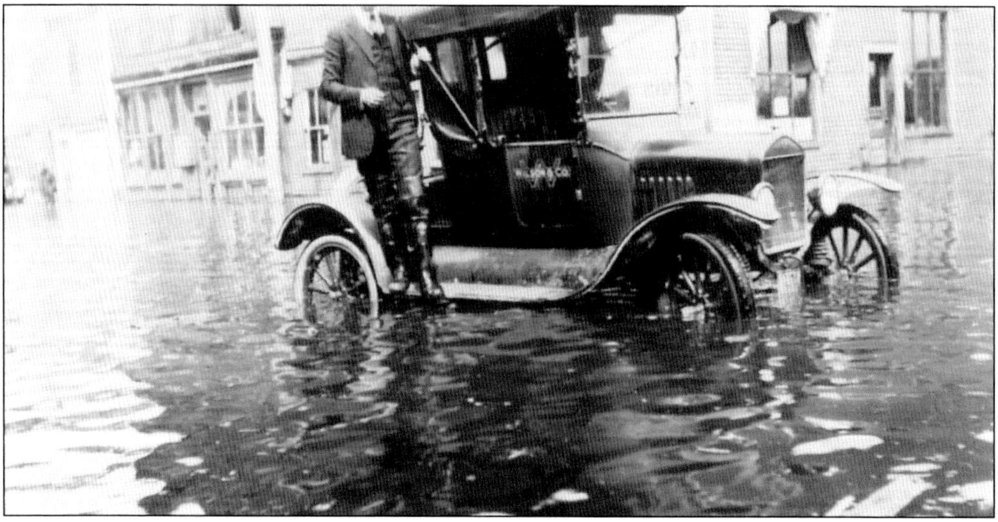

Try driving through flood waters this deep in today's automobiles with their low-built chassis. This early model apparently had no trouble making it around Bangor during the spring flood of 1923. The driver is attired in a three-piece suit, but wisely wears rubber boots for protection. Lettering on the door of his "horseless wagon" notes that it belongs to Wilson and Company, suppliers of "beef and provisions," located at 139 Broad Street, a section of town that was often flooded because of its closeness to the stream and the river.

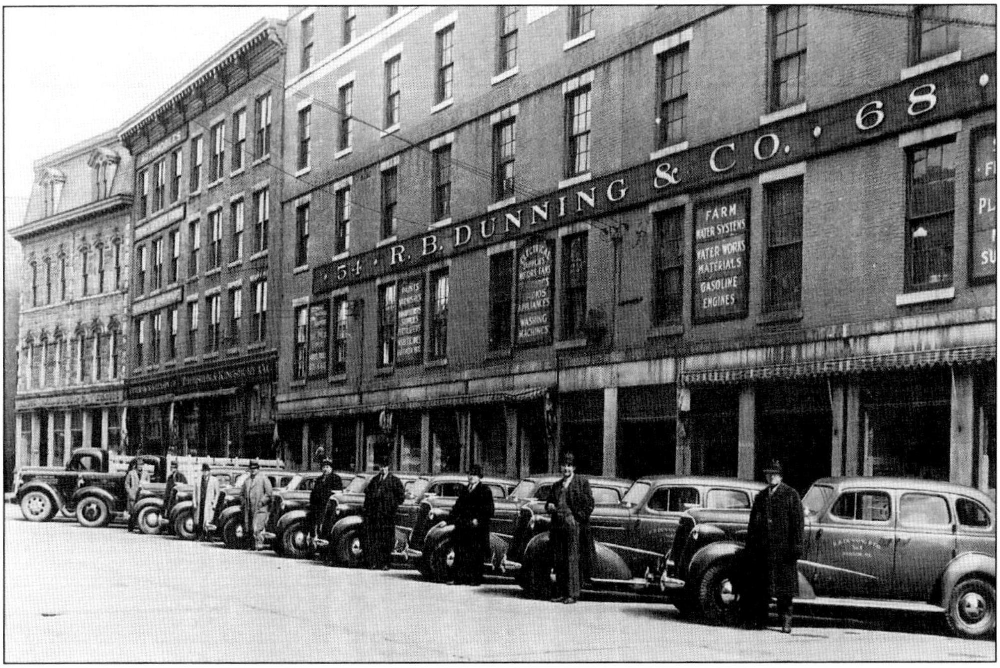

One of Bangor's best-known businesses, R.B. Dunning and Company, made deliveries with this fleet of automobiles while based at its store at 54 Broad Street. A newspaper caption of the time mentioned that this ". . . outside sales force (was) ready to scatter the products handled over the entire Great Northeastern State of Maine. These men—and the integrity of the company which they represent—are known from one corner of the state to the other." The company sold such items as washing machines, pipe fittings, and electrical supplies.

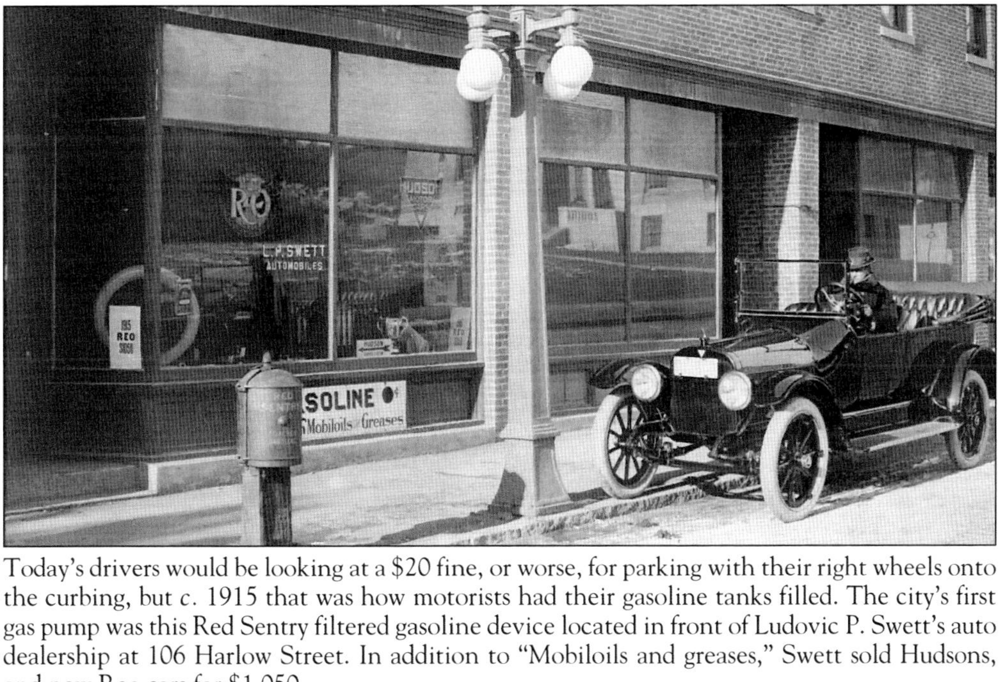

Today's drivers would be looking at a $20 fine, or worse, for parking with their right wheels onto the curbing, but *c.* 1915 that was how motorists had their gasoline tanks filled. The city's first gas pump was this Red Sentry filtered gasoline device located in front of Ludovic P. Swett's auto dealership at 106 Harlow Street. In addition to "Mobiloils and greases," Swett sold Hudsons, and new Reo cars for $1,050.

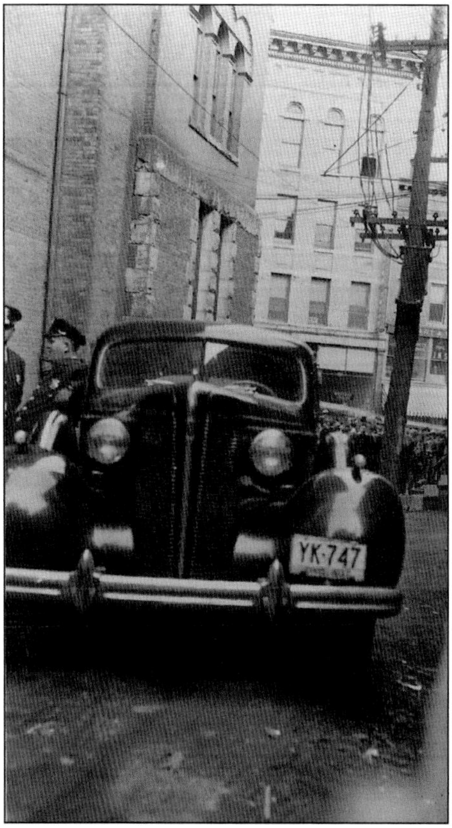

A trio of wanted criminals named the Brady Gang (see pp. 65–7) left behind this Buick Roadmaster when they drove it into a downtown trap laid by federal agents on October 12, 1937. While living in Baltimore in late 1936, the gang had carjacked the powerful new Buick, driving it thousands of miles for recreational, and criminal, endeavors. Downtown store manager Leo Mouradian took this photograph of the car with a crowd of curiosity seekers in the background. Bangor police officers F. Carr McInnis and William Bridges (barely visible at far left) guard the vehicle parked beside the police barracks, then located in the city hall building.

Brady gangster James Dalhover was flown out of Bangor to waiting federal agents in Indiana aboard this new Stinson Reliant "Gull Wing" (named for the curvature of its wing span). Dalhover was removed from his jail cell under tight security and driven to the municipal airport in the darkness. He became air sick en route during his first (and last) time in the air. That was nothing compared to his eventual destiny: found guilty of murdering a state trooper, he was executed at Michigan City, Indiana, in November 1938.

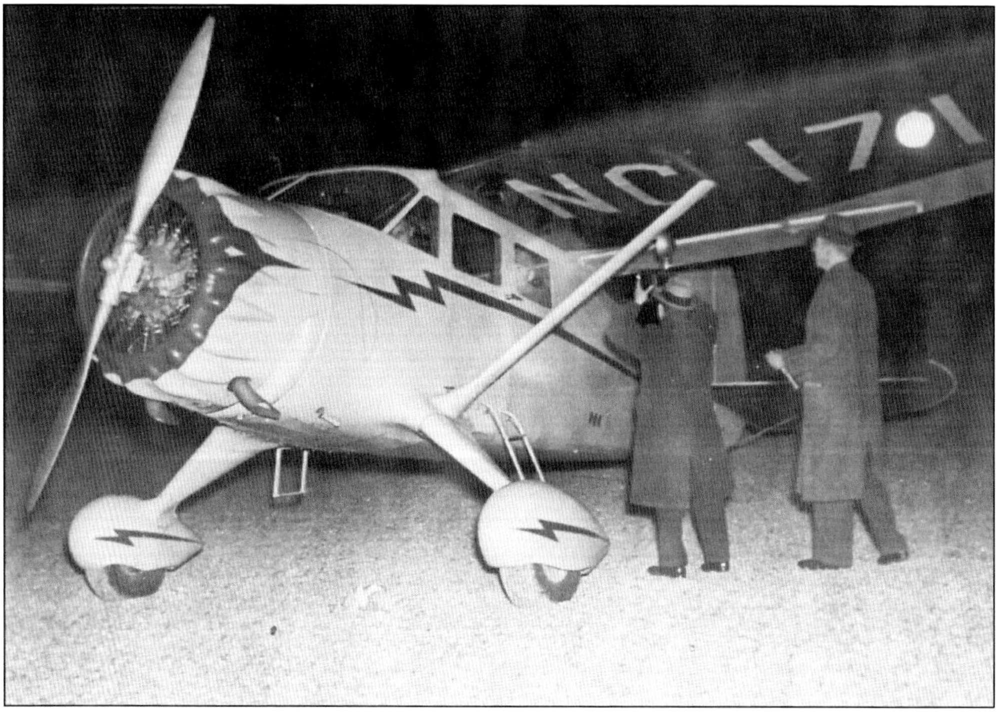

Five

On the Silver Screen

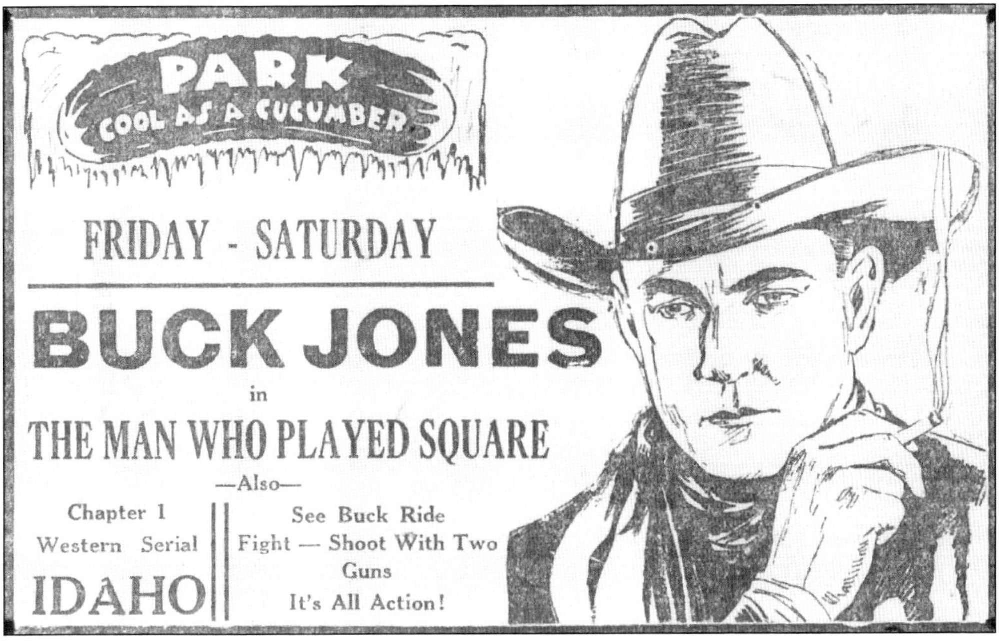

Patrons could stay "cool as a cucumber" at the Park Theater, situated at the corner of State and Park Streets. The Park never attained the status of the more opulent Bijou and Opera House theaters, both of which had balconies. Despite having no balconies, the Park was extremely popular with middle-class moviegoers, who liked the house's simplicity and cheap ticket prices. A silent movie starring cowboy hero Buck Jones was playing at the theater in 1925, when this newspaper advertisement appeared. A pit orchestra, or sometimes a single pianist, provided the accompaniment, often with sound effects of approaching trains and galloping horses.

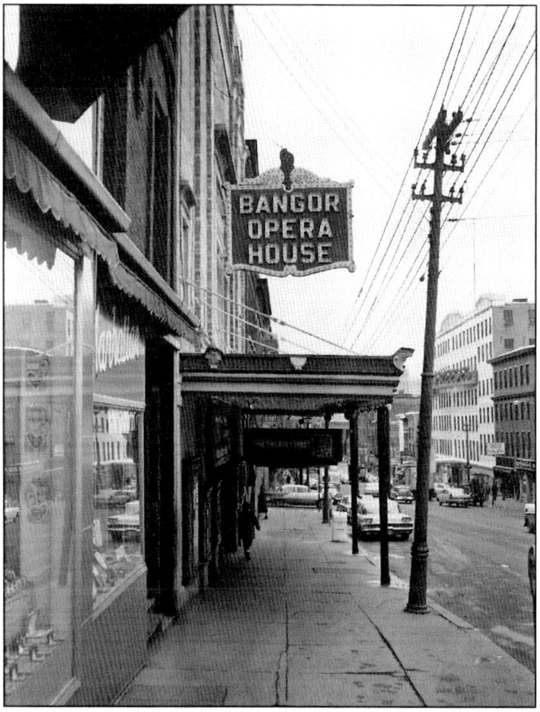

Main Street's appearance was soon to change when this bit of Americana was removed and the new sign of the Bangor Cinema put in its place. The Opera House was opened in 1920; organ music still accompanied silent movies and occasional live performances were still featured. The old Opera House, also located on this spot, dated back to 1882. Such diverse talents as Oscar Wilde and Ethel Barrymore performed there until January 1914, when a fire destroyed it. The present theater at 131 Main Street was converted to a performing arts center, and then a church, after modern theaters were built near the Bangor Mall.

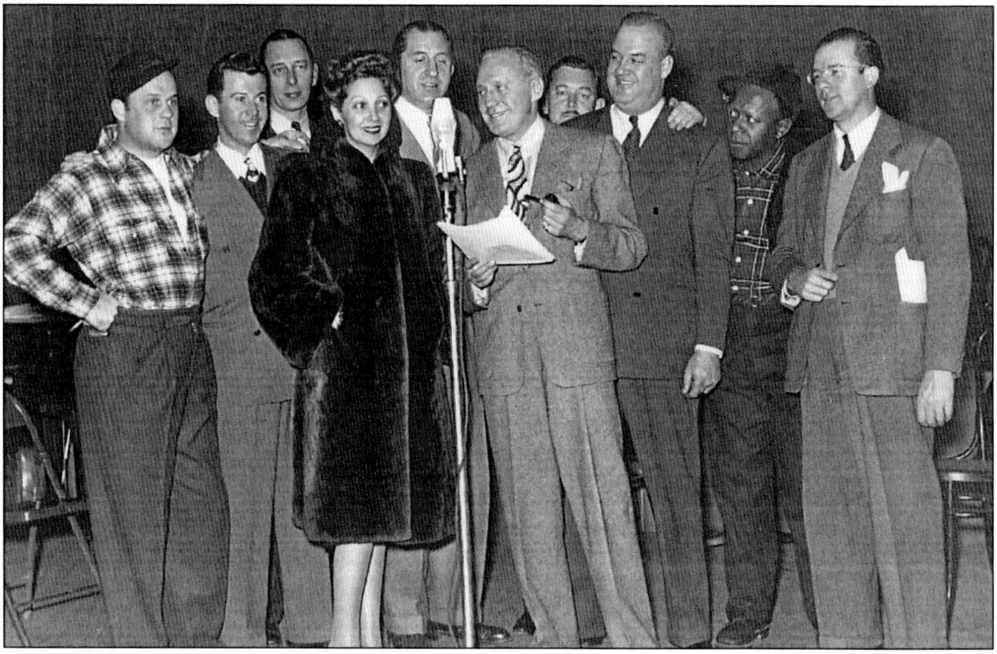

One of the biggest nights in the history of the Opera House wasn't the screening of a hot new movie, but a personal appearance by the nation's foremost radio star, Jack Benny, and his cast. In January 1943, Benny broadcast his weekly program from inside the theater, with Dow Field Army personnel as his guests. Cast members pictured are Dennis Day (second from left), Mary Livingstone (Benny's wife), Benny, master of ceremonies Don Wilson, and Eddie "Rochester" Anderson.

The strains of "Tara's Theme" and Rhett Butler growling, "Frankly my dear, I don't give a damn," echoed through the Opera House on February 8, 1940. The epic was scheduled to run for an entire week, an eternity in those days. Interest in the Academy Award-winning film was unprecedented in the city, with long lines of people extending down Main Street.

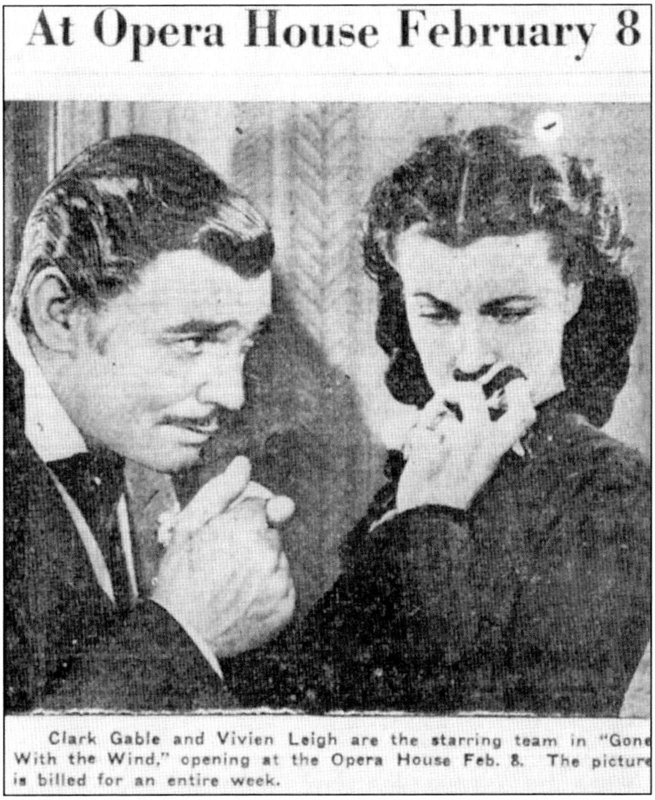

At Opera House February 8

Clark Gable and Vivien Leigh are the starring team in "Gone With the Wind," opening at the Opera House Feb. 8. The picture is billed for an entire week.

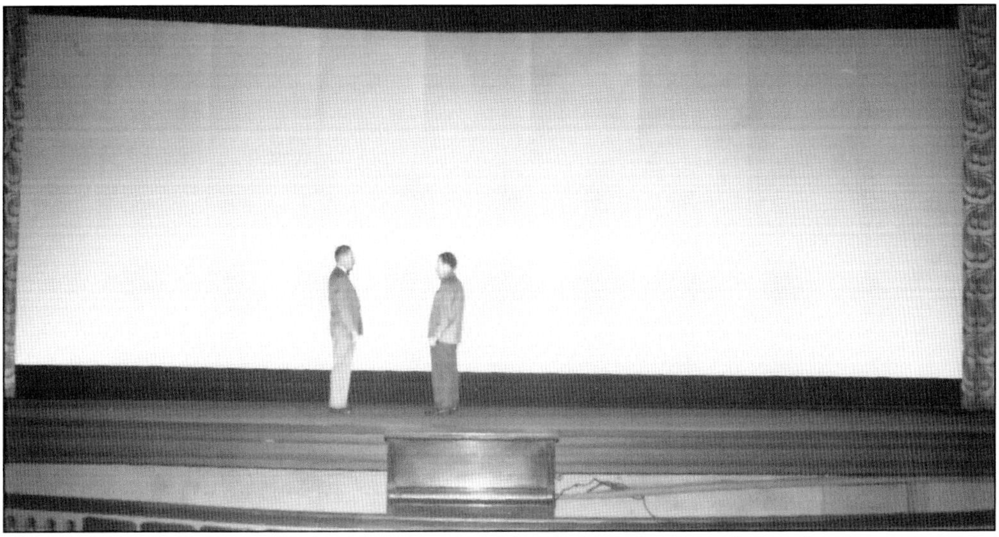

A huge new CinemaScope screen, measuring 36-by-14 feet, was installed at the Opera House in early 1954. Theater manager Arthur S. Allaire (left) and John J. O'Brien of the New England Theater Service for CinemaScope, who supervised the installation, are silhouetted against the screen. The Marilyn Monroe feature, *How to Marry a Millionaire*, a color short of Elizabeth II's coronation, and the first cartoon filmed in the new wide-screen process were the first films to be projected onto the screen. CinemaScope made its debut in Bangor at the Bijou on December 25, 1953.

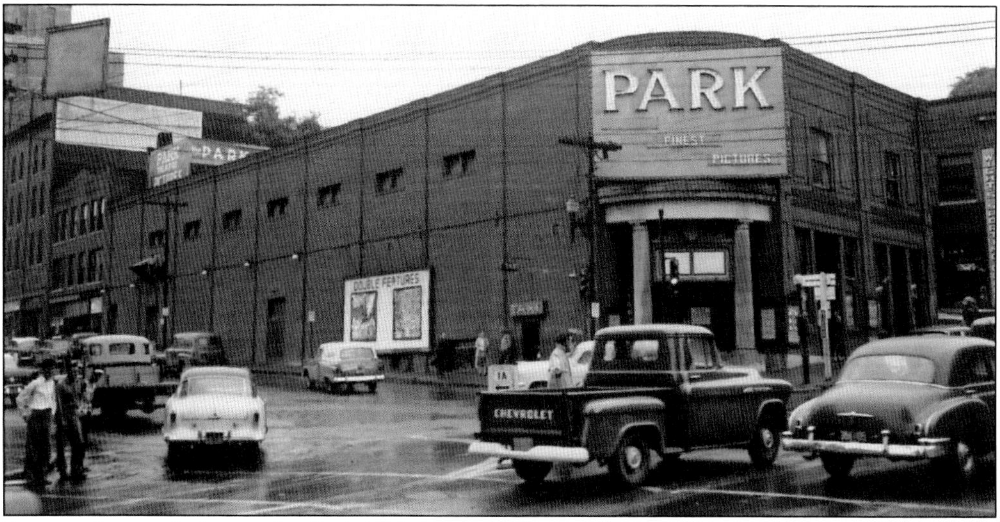

Even without a balcony, the Park had a ground-floor seating capacity of 1,200. It was opened in 1913 as the Palace Theater, but was soon renamed the Park Theater because of its location at Park and State Streets. Original manager Stephen Bogrett (who also managed the Bijou, which was owned by the same corporation) liked to boast of the ivory and salmon color of the movie screen's arch, the snow white and cream color scheme of the lobby, and the mahogany woodwork throughout. Eventually the property was purchased by New England Telephone and demolished in 1973.

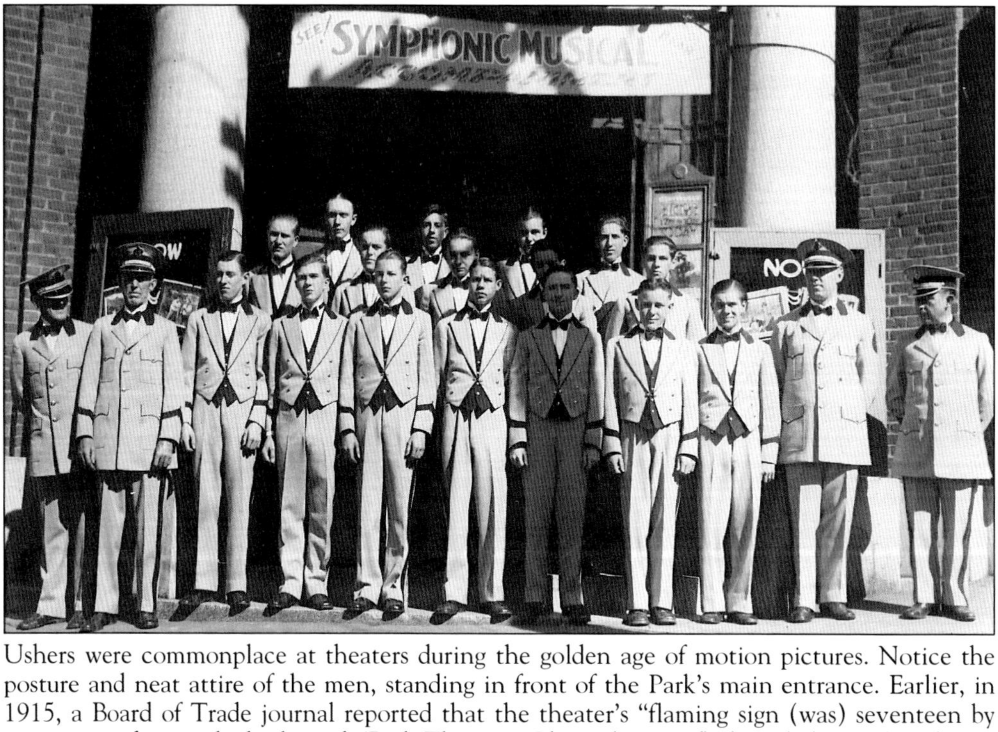

Ushers were commonplace at theaters during the golden age of motion pictures. Notice the posture and neat attire of the men, standing in front of the Park's main entrance. Earlier, in 1915, a Board of Trade journal reported that the theater's "flaming sign (was) seventeen by twenty-one feet, with the legend: 'Park Theatre—Photoplays' in flashing lights and a 'chaser' around the border—one of those snake-like electrical devices that are familiar sights along Broadway at night."

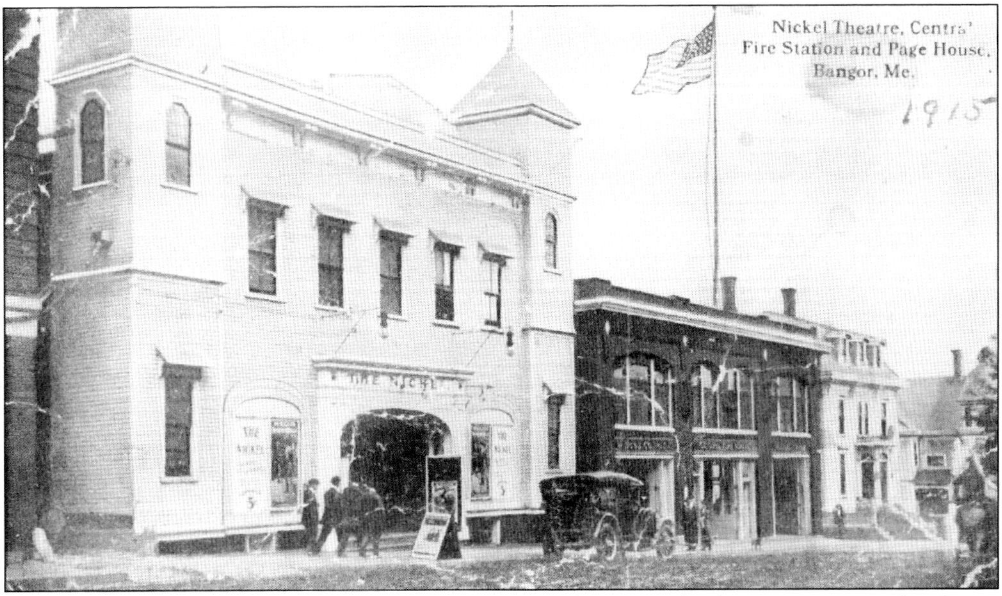

This old theater went by many names in the years after it was built in 1888, near the Opera House and across Union Street from the Bangor House. It was called the Nickel, the Olympia, even the Rathole (because of its dingy interior). The twin towers lured hordes of children on Saturday afternoons who paid their quarter and got their 12¢ admission ticket, lots of popcorn, and more than enough penny candy to keep them happy all afternoon. Cowboy movies starring Ken Maynard, Hoot Gibson, Tom Mix, Gene Autry, and Roy Rogers kept the place in business. Vaudeville also filled the theater in the early years.

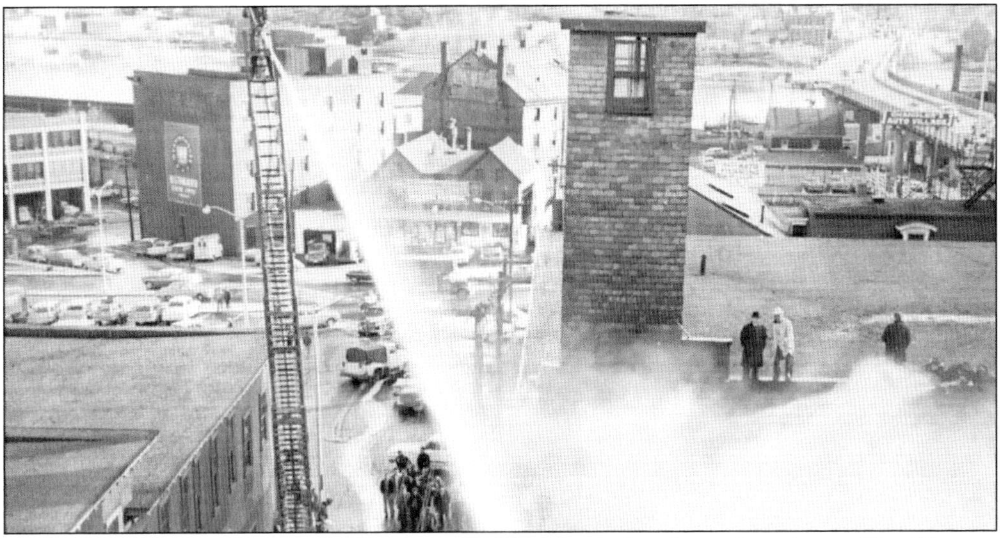

The majority of Bangor's old-time theaters succumbed to either fire or demolition. The Olympia fell into the former category in November 1963, the week John F. Kennedy was assassinated. It had long before closed its doors to theater patrons and was known as the Manhattan Bargain Center when it burned in a spectacular blaze. Being next door to the Central Fire Station didn't save the old wooden structure, but firemen merited praise for containing the inferno. Paul E. Tower, from whose collection this picture was selected, said the tall building at center was used for the drying of fire hoses.

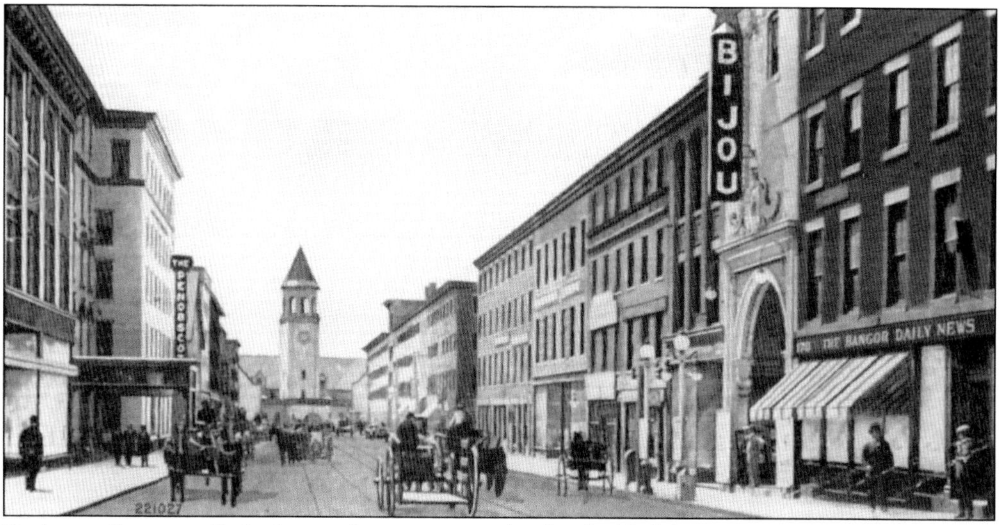

Exchange Street really had something going in the first half of this century. Visitors could step off a train at Union Station (center, in the distance), and walk up to the Penobscot Hotel (on the left) to have a sumptuous meal, then walk across to the Bijou Theater and be entertained all afternoon by vaudeville and motion pictures. The Bijou was opened in April 1912, having taken over the former Gem Theater. It was an instant hit because of its large seating capacity, balcony, and exquisite design.

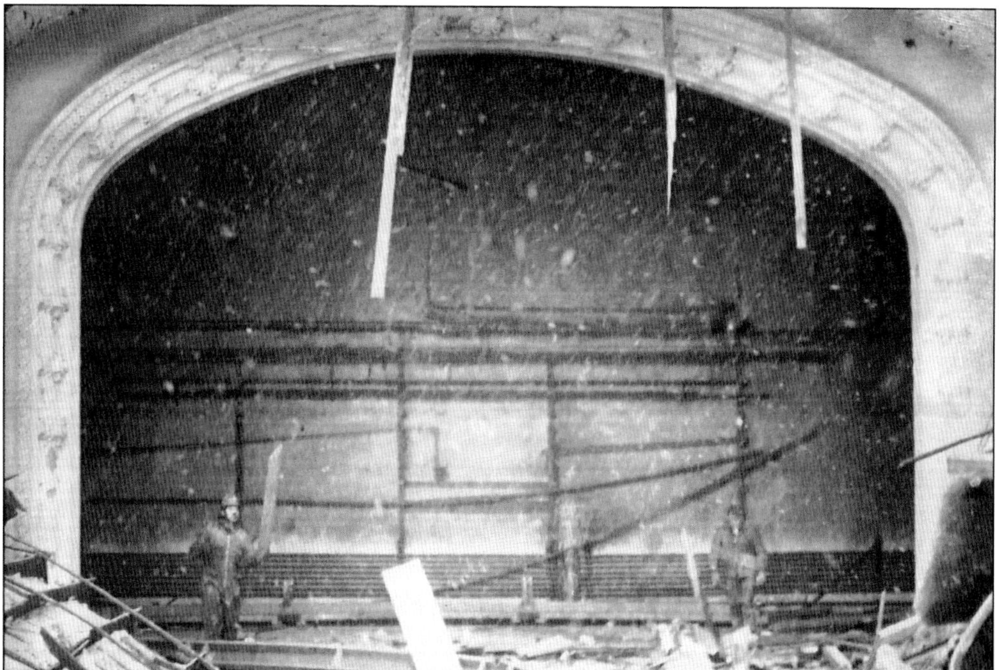

This was a sad day in Bangor, during January 1974. Only the proscenium arch of the old Bijou remained as demolition crews knocked down the theater to make way for a bank building. With the building went a thousand memories and the tears and laughter of audiences who recalled watching *The Wizard of Oz*, *The Sound of Music*, and *My Fair Lady* inside its walls. The theater's last picture show, on August 31, 1973, was a Walt Disney movie, *Lady and the Tramp*.

Cornelius J. Russell Jr. stood beneath the Bijou's marquee for the last time in 1973 before the theater closed its doors. His father, Cornelius Sr., came to Bangor in 1923 as a partner and general manager of the Park Amusement Company, which embraced the Bijou and Park Theaters in Bangor and the Strand in Orono. His son stepped into his shoes after his death. "Returns are good, if you've got a good picture," he said in 1973. "And with Disney pictures, I've made more with Disney pictures than with any other."

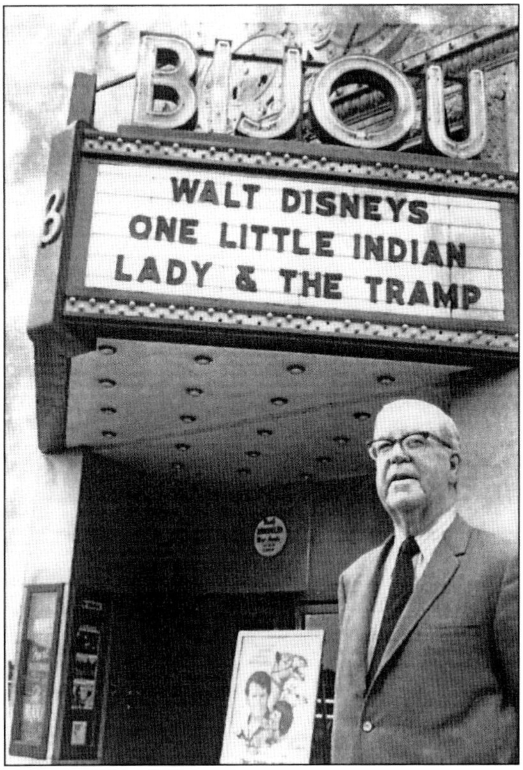

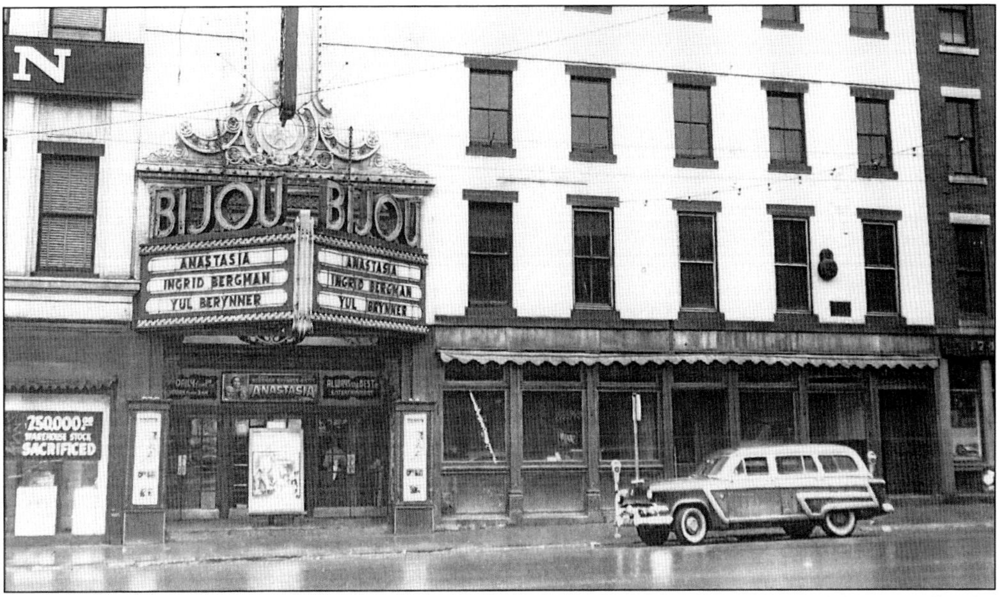

Once stars like Mae West and Hardeen Houdini, Harry's brother, appeared live inside the Bijou, and the F. James Carroll Players brought Broadway calibre entertainment to the theater. Many times the stars stayed in the Penobscot Hotel across the street. The theater's list of firsts is endless, but two worth mentioning are the area debut of the silent classic, *Birth of a Nation*, in October 1915, and, much later, the first showing, in 1945, in the northeastern United States of early newsreel scenes of a recently liberated German concentration camp.

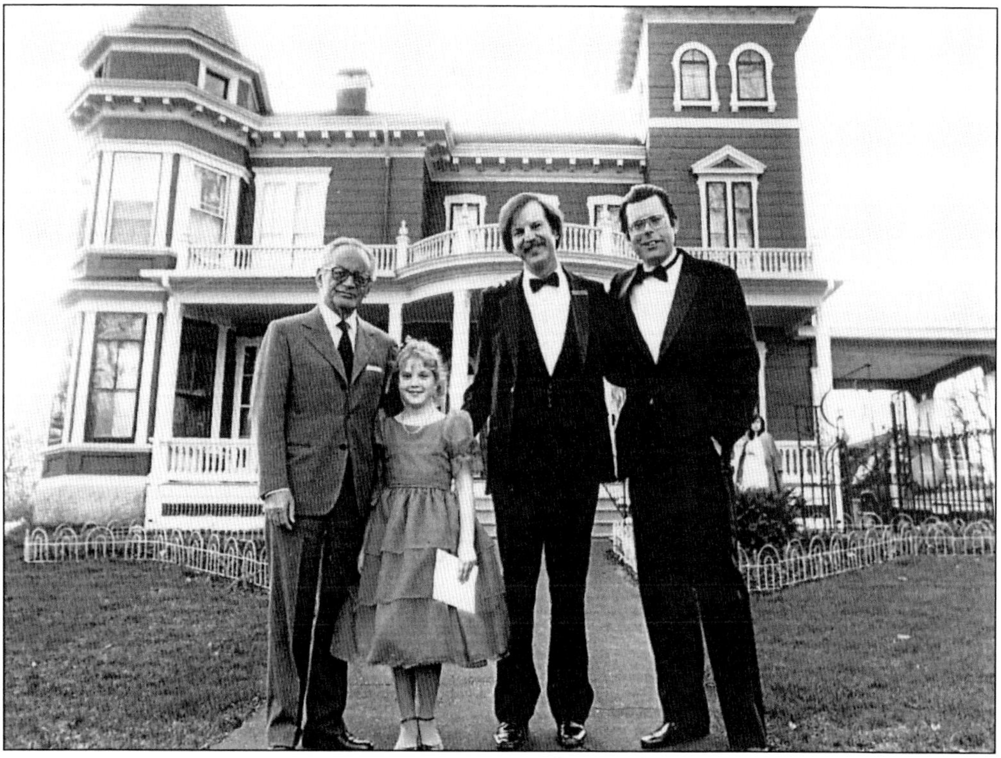

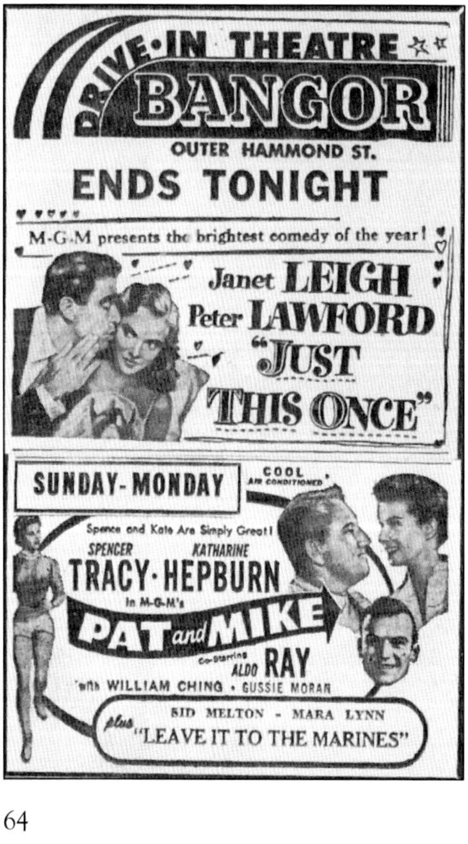

Novelist Stephen King (right) is also famous to movie audiences because of film versions of such works as *Firestarter*, brought to the big screen in 1984. A world premiere event to benefit Northeast COMBAT, Bangor's non-profit consumer help organization, brought together young star Drew Barrymore (second from left), producer Dino DeLaurentiis (left), and COMBAT executive director John Supranovich at King's Bangor mansion. The Opera House screening was sold out.

The summer of 1952 was golden at the Bangor Drive-in movie theater, located on outer Hammond Street. Audiences actually sat through double-features during those years, content to cuddle up in their cars eating popcorn. Like so many failing outdoor theaters, this one converted to adult movies in the 1960s and '70s before eventually going out of business. The Bangor-Brewer Drive-In in nearby Brewer was the other popular outdoor theater of its time.

Six

Days We May Never Forget

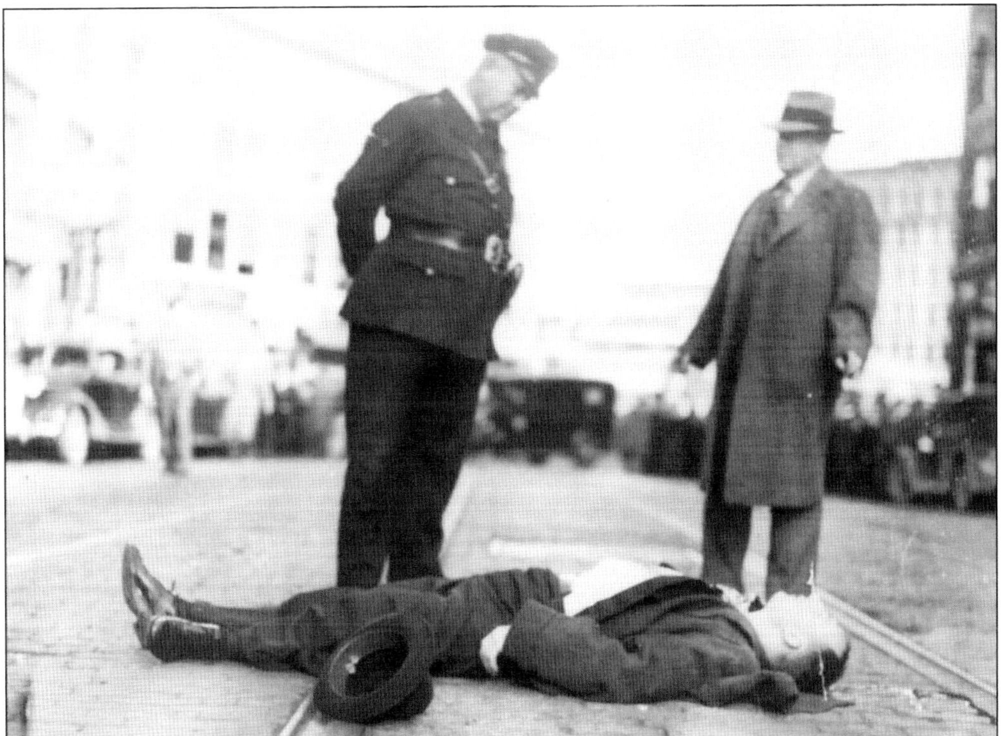

Bangor police officer Eddie Connelly and city physician Harry McNeil stand over the still-warm body of Alfred James Brady, America's most wanted criminal, minutes after he was gunned down by FBI agents on Central Street. Brady and his two pals had returned to Bangor to buy a machine gun, but instead drove into a trap set by J. Edgar Hoover's G-men. Connelly and McNeil had no actual role in the shooting; both were nearby at the time and acted as convenient props for a local newspaper photographer.

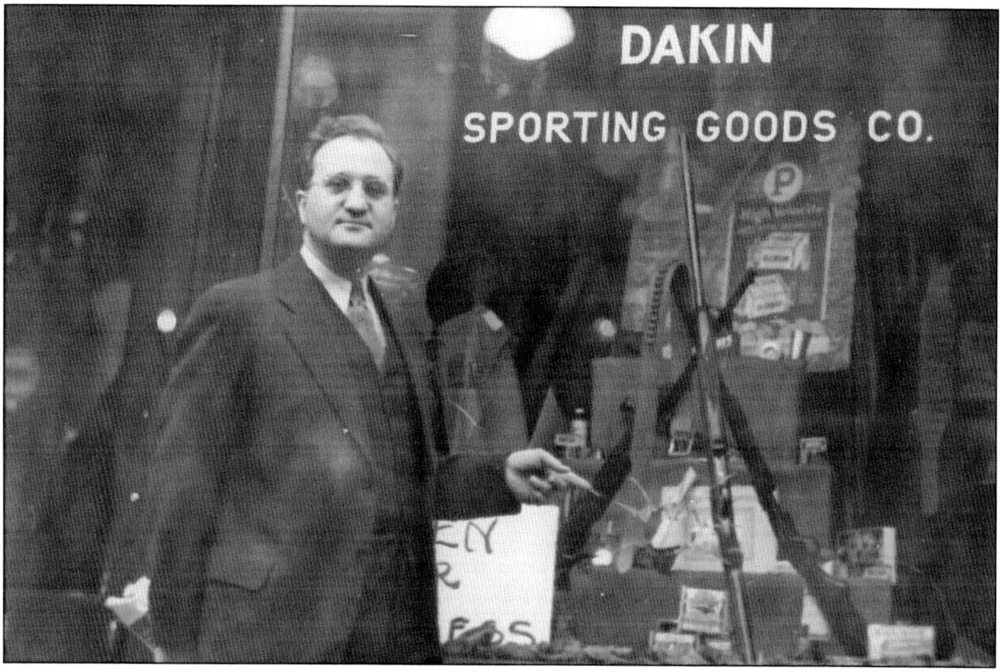

Store owner Everett S. "Shep" Hurd alerted the Maine State Police that a suspicious looking customer had returned to his sporting goods store on October 5, 1937, to buy more weapons and, in particular, to inquire about the purchase of a machine gun. When the Brady Gang returned on October 12, Public Enemy Number One Alfred Brady and an associate, Clarence Shaffer, were shot dead by federal agents, and a third criminal, James Dalhover, was captured inside the Dakin Sporting Goods Co. Hurd was awarded the entire $1,500 reward for the gang's capture, later sold snapshots of the shooting scene, and painted fake bullet holes on his store window after this bullet-shattered glass was replaced.

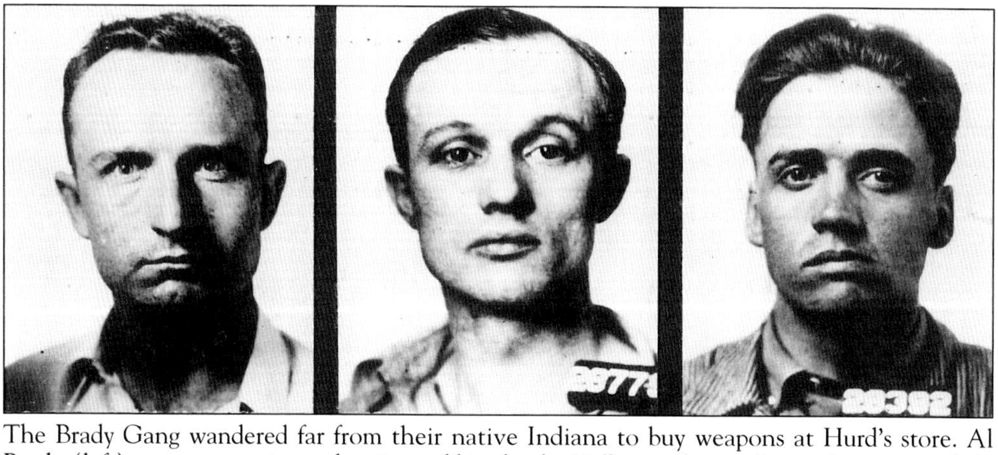

The Brady Gang wandered far from their native Indiana to buy weapons at Hurd's store. Al Brady (left) was twenty-six at the time of his death, Dalhover (center) was thirty-one when handcuffed inside Hurd's store, and Clarence Shaffer (right) was only twenty-one when he died after firing into the store window as he witnessed his pal's arrest. Nicknamed "the half-pint killers," all stood 5 feet, 5 inches or less and weighed no more than 150 pounds.

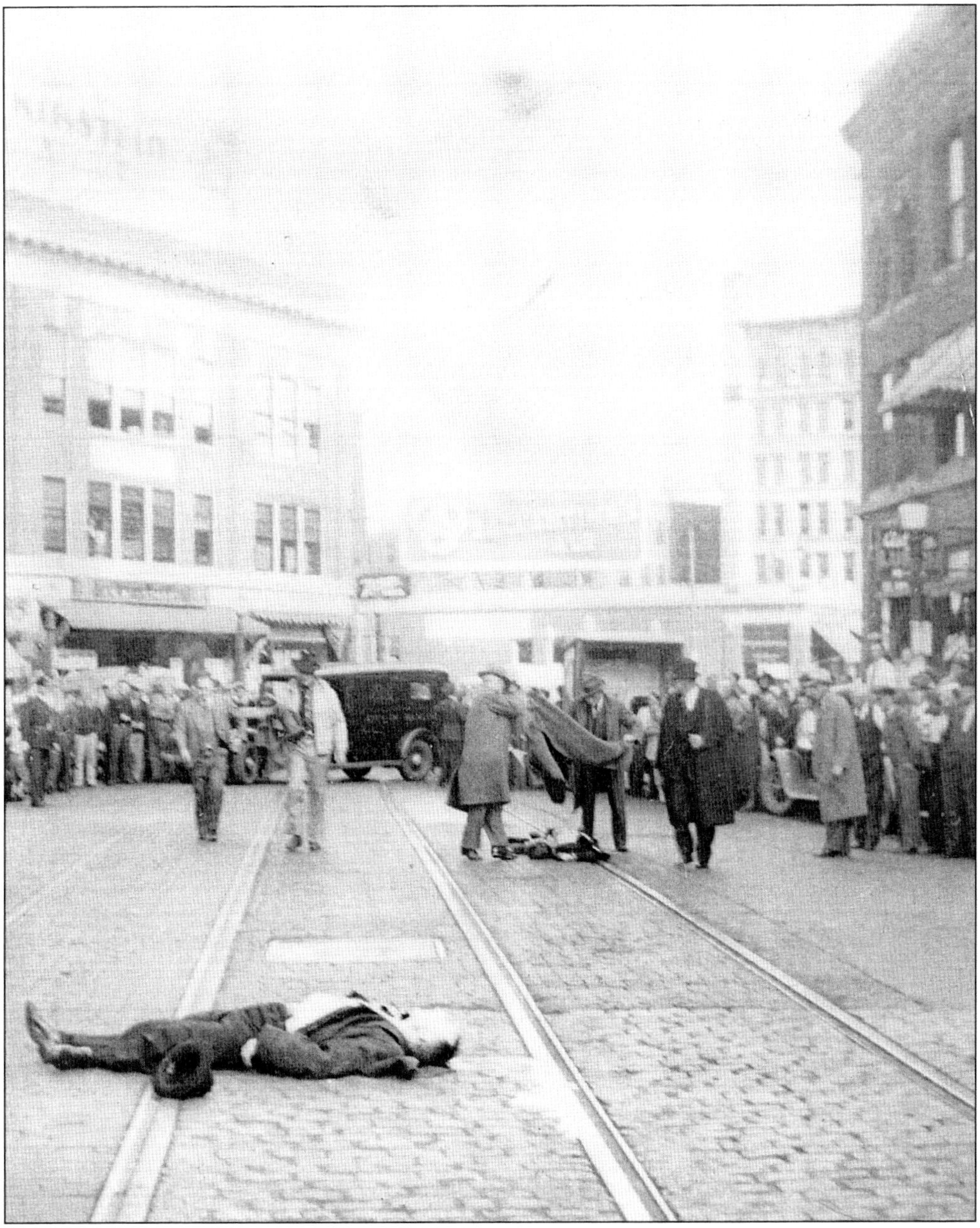

"The Battle of Bangor" erupted on Columbus Day 1937 and was witnessed by many pedestrians and motorists in rush hour morning traffic. Many others watched gruesome scenes like this, as funeral director Malcolm Hayes and others threw a blanket over the lifeless form of Clarence Shaffer and prepared to do the same for Al Brady (foreground). Both died of multiple gunshot wounds inflicted by federal agents who had trapped the murderers and bank robbers. All three had resisted arrest.

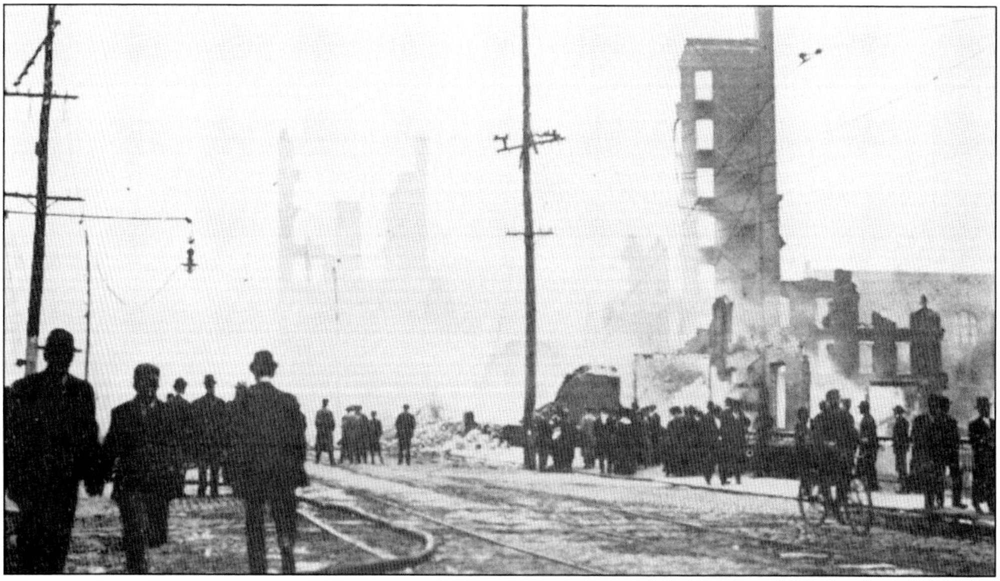

This study in devastation could be a scene from Dante's *Inferno*, but it actually shows the ruins of the Great Bangor Fire. Starting to burn on Broad Street around 4 pm on Sunday, April 30, 1911, stiff winds soon carried embers onto the East Side. Especially hard hit was this corner at State and Exchange Streets. A seventy-year-old Brewer shoemaker, John Scribner, one of two men to die in the fire (the other was firefighter George Abbott), was burned when the walls of the Morse-Oliver Building in this district collapsed.

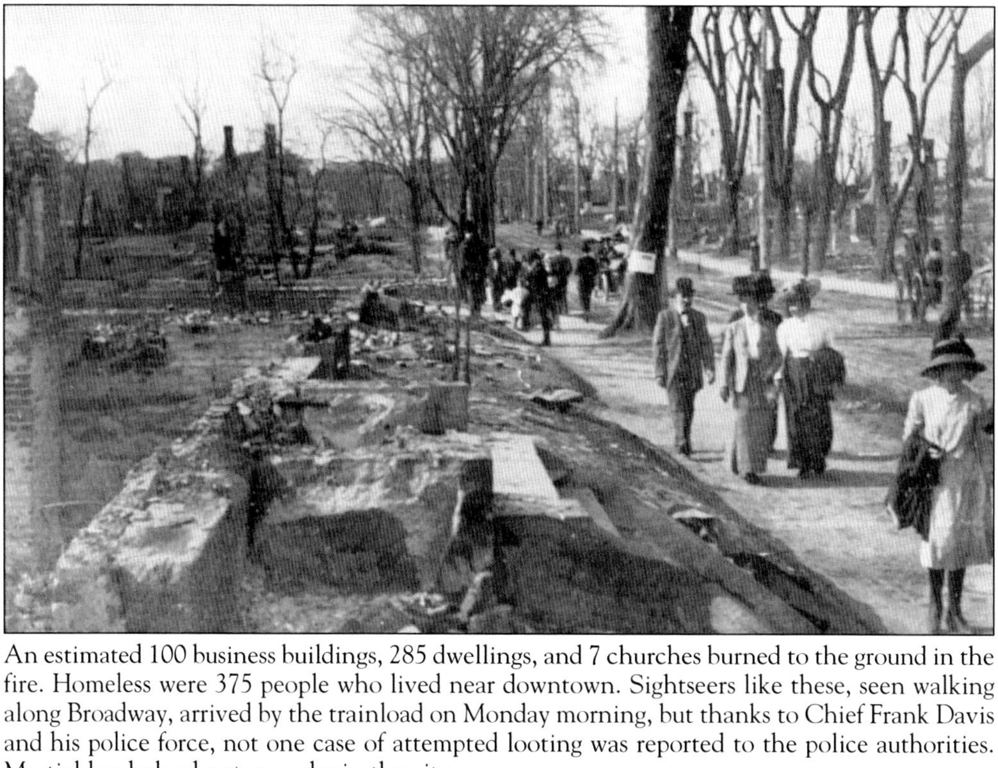

An estimated 100 business buildings, 285 dwellings, and 7 churches burned to the ground in the fire. Homeless were 375 people who lived near downtown. Sightseers like these, seen walking along Broadway, arrived by the trainload on Monday morning, but thanks to Chief Frank Davis and his police force, not one case of attempted looting was reported to the police authorities. Martial law helped restore order in the city.

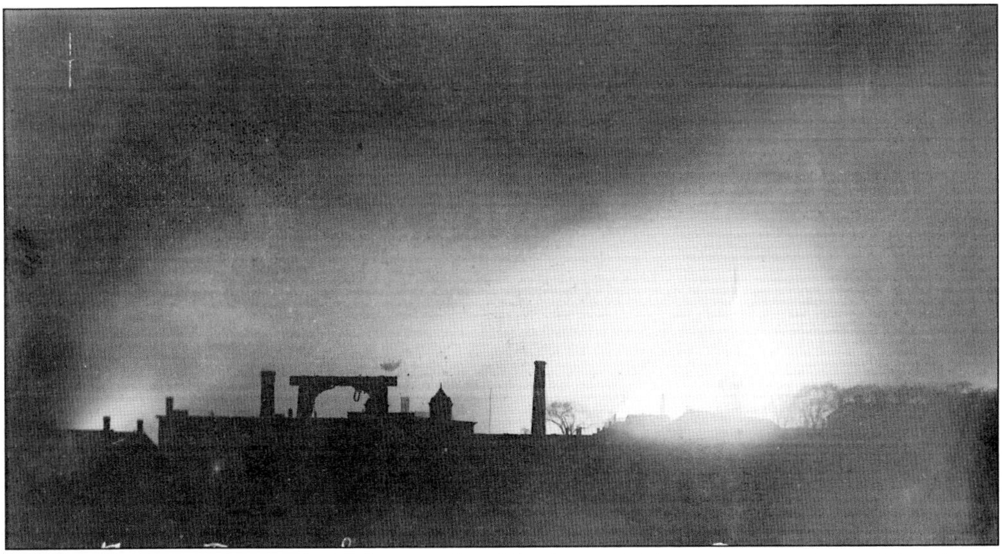

On Sunday evening at 8 o'clock, the steeple of the beautiful First Congregational Church was aglow. Wrote eyewitness M.J. Callinan, "A crew of firemen had worked for hours on the burning . . . church on Broadway and they did succeed in holding it there, much to the pleasure of all. Had the fire gone across the street it is doubtful if much of the east side could have been saved." All Souls Church stands on this site today.

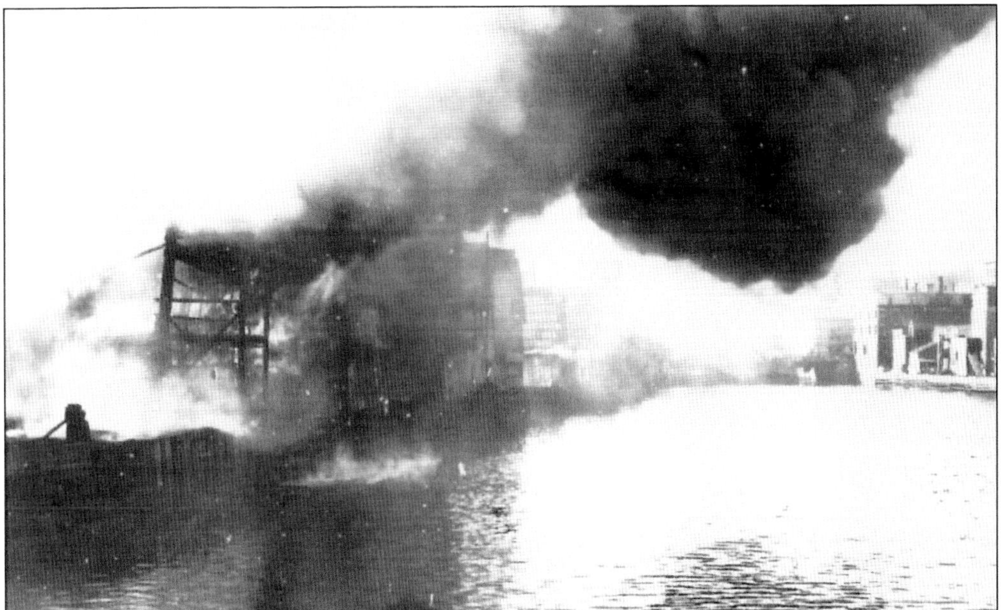

One of the earliest views of the fire was captured on this picture postcard, selected from the files of the Maine Historic Preservation Commission. J. Frank Green's hay shed at 176 Broad Street, the approximate site of the present-day Pickering Plaza parking garage, was the site of the fire's start, perhaps the result of a carelessly tossed cigar butt. Firefighters would have contained the fire if not for a high wind that carried the flames across the stream. On the back of this postcard, dated May 3, 1911, someone wrote the message, "Here is a picture of one of the scenes of the fire. You won't know Bangor when you see it again."

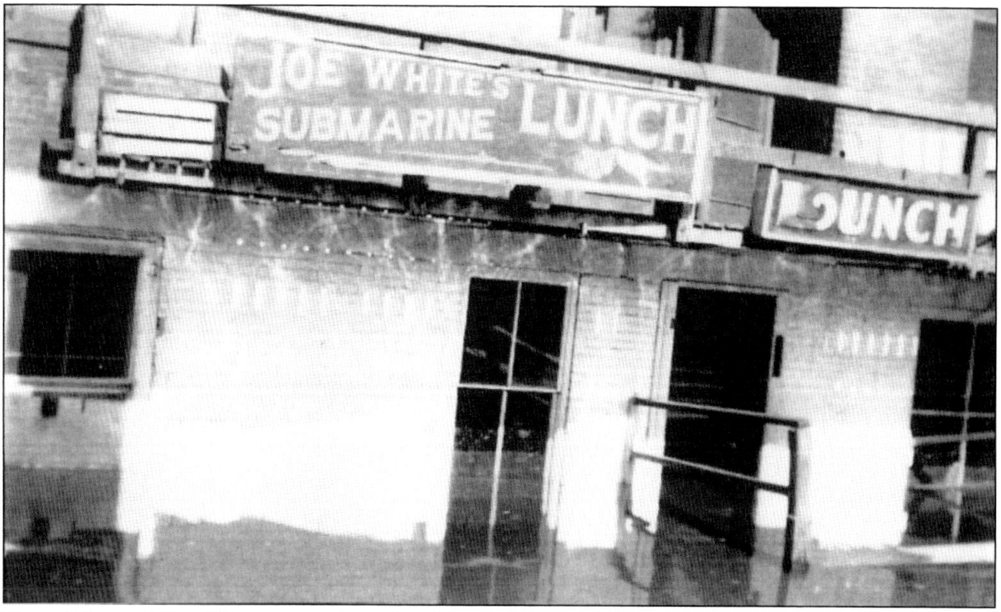

Enough! cried Joe White one day after his popular Submarine Lunch near the Kenduskeag Stream on Exchange Street was flooded yet again. He finally closed his business when he tired of bailing out from spring floods such as this one in 1936. White's aptly named business was a hit with businessmen and railroad workers, who gladly waited in line to feast on one of his sub sandwiches, Bangor's introduction to this new way of eating.

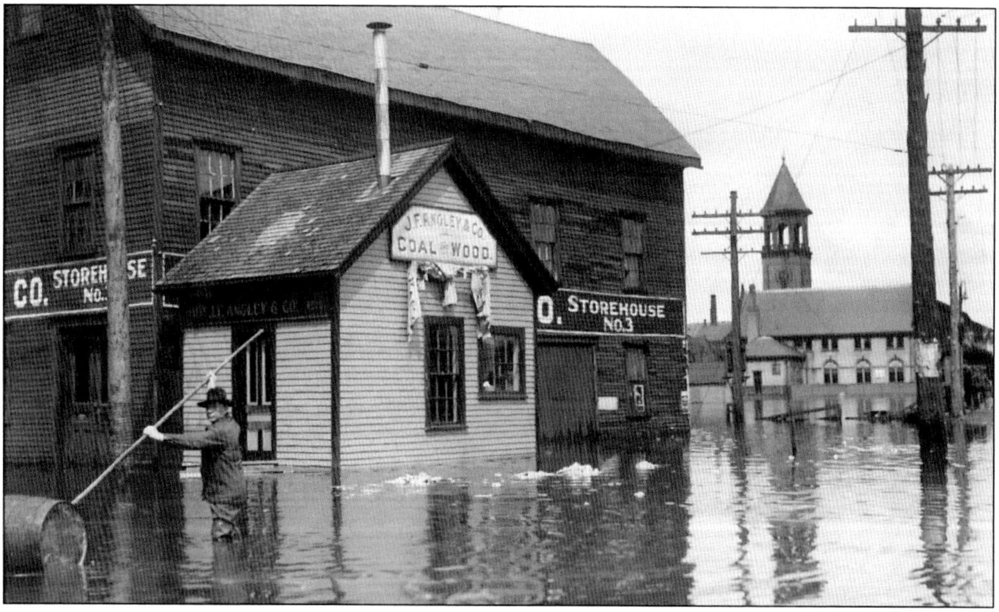

The spring flood of May 1923 was just as troublesome to businesses along Broad Street. This man is up to his knees in water while he tries to push a barrel along with a pole. It wasn't the first time J.F. Angley and Company, dealers in coal and wood, got a taste of Nature's fury. The railroad tracks of Union Station, visible in the background, were also flooded on several occasions. Floods are less common in the area today, the last notable one occurring in February 1976 at the Kenduskeag Plaza parking area.

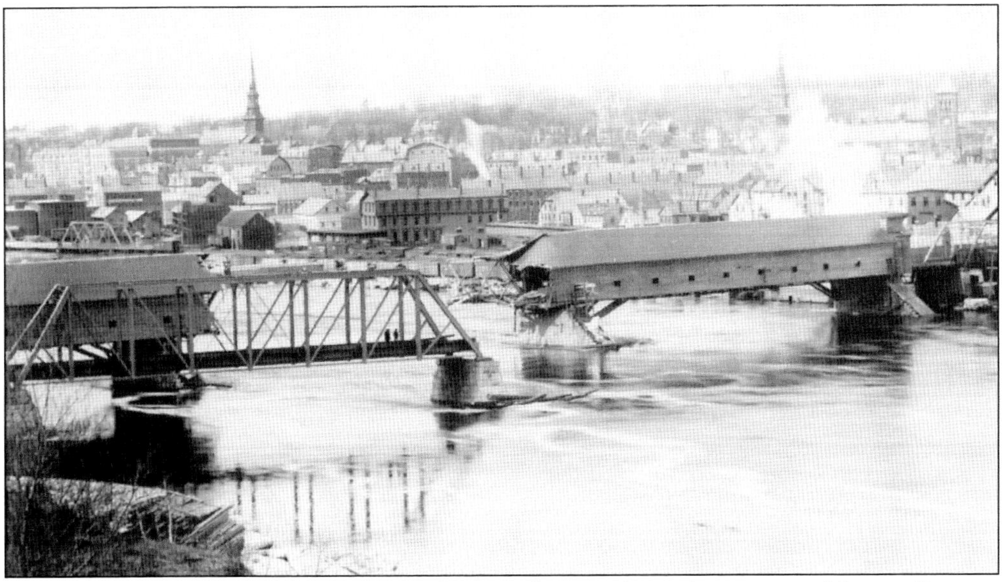

This dramatic view from the Mildred N. Thayer collection shows the remains of the two Bangor-Brewer bridges—one for vehicles and pedestrians, the other for trains—after the disastrous flood of 1902 wreaked its havoc. Much of nearby Broad Street was underwater. A famous picture shows people paddling canoes around downtown streets as if it were Venice. Renovations saved part of this, the state's longest covered bridge, and in 1912 the iron bridge that later generations remember was built in its place, along with a similar looking railway bridge.

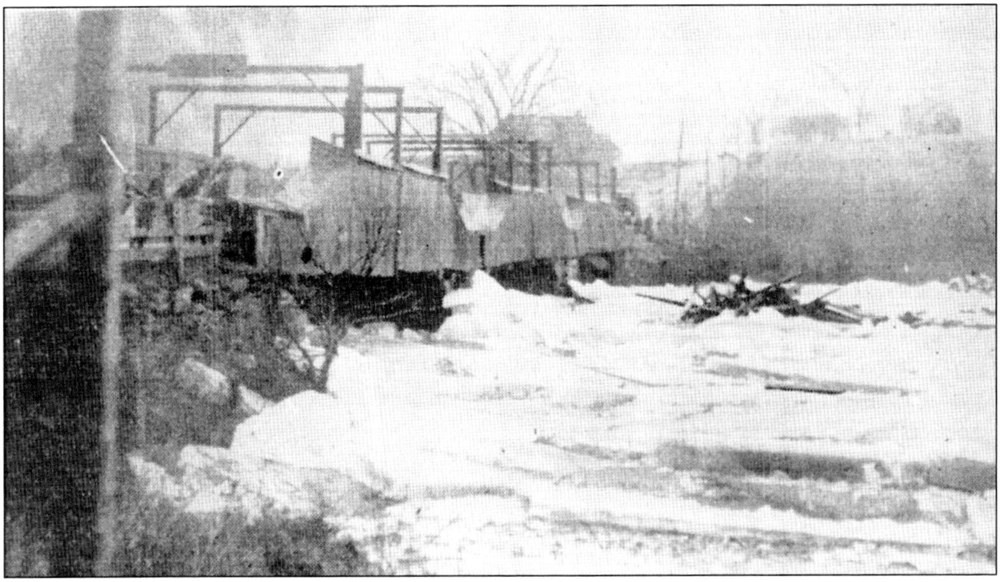

Hundreds of spectators rushed out Valley Avenue to watch the Bull's Eye Bridge be swept away in the spring freshet of 1936, but the old landmark never moved. This photograph from the March 28 edition of the *Bangor Daily News* shows the wreckage of the Dudley Bridge (at right) which collapsed farther upstream, along with ice, logs, and debris that slammed into the old landmark. Holes resembling bull's eyes once pierced the bridge's sides, hence the nickname which survives to the present day.

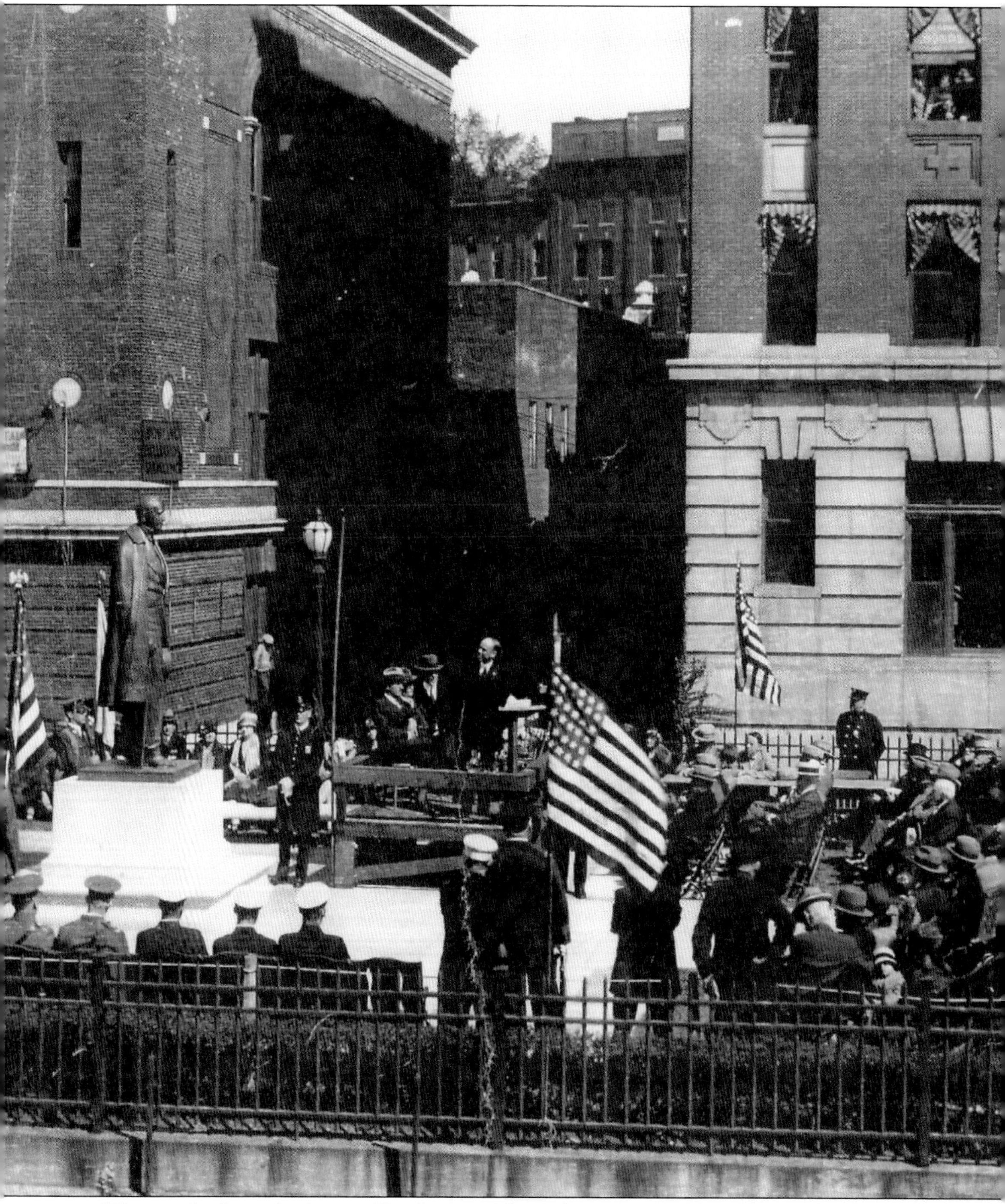

"Thousands cheer the bronze Hamlin," proclaimed a newspaper headline on September 16, 1927, the day after Charles E. Tefft's sculpture of statesman Hannibal Hamlin was unveiled at Kenduskeag Parkway. A flag veiling the statue was pulled aside, and once more Hamlin ". . . stood in his beloved Bangor, an heroic figure of the stirring past come back to us." Hamlin (1809–1891) was Abraham Lincoln's first vice president and a longtime Bangor resident.

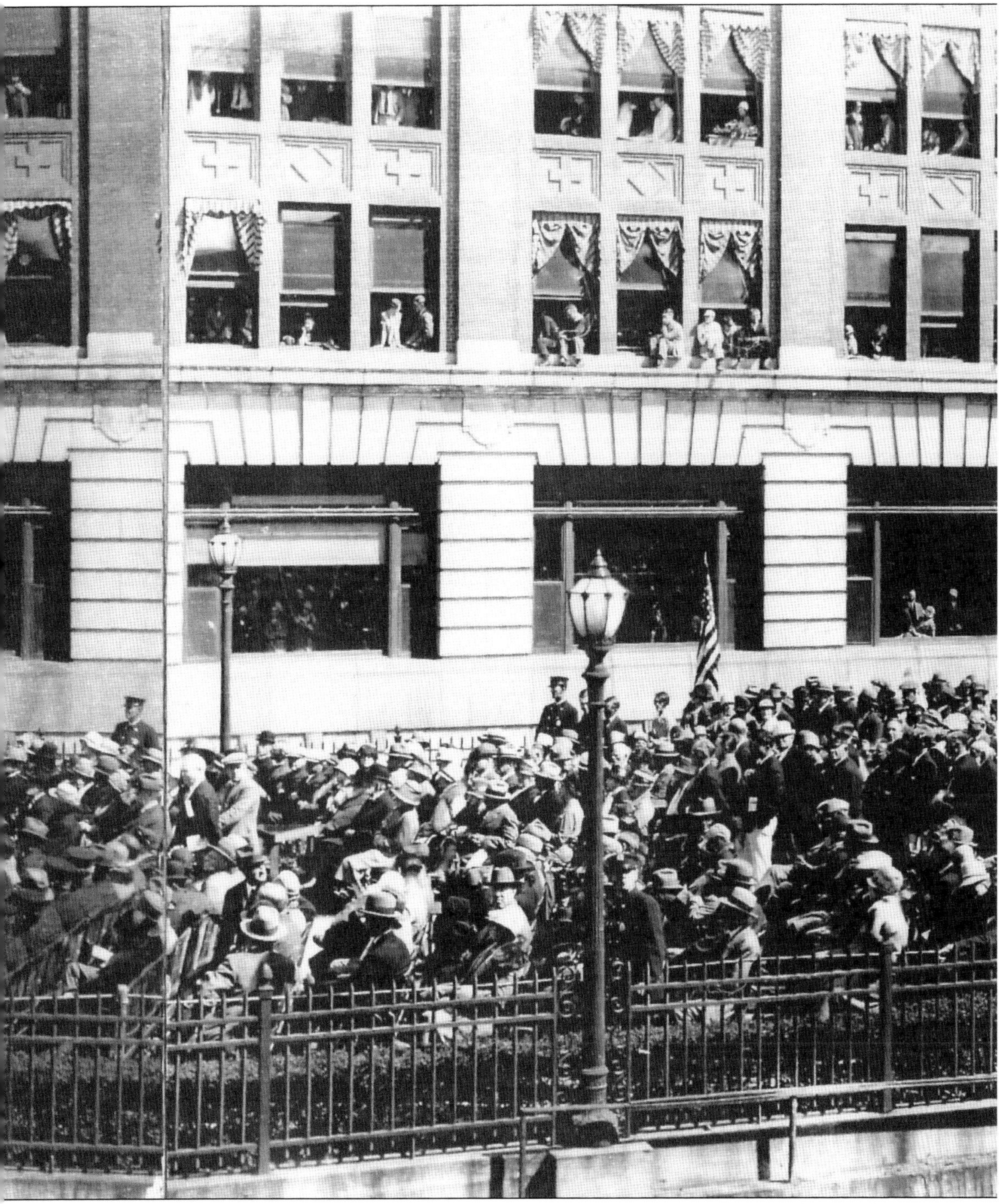

Governor Ralph Owen Brewster (seen on the platform looking up at the statue) delivered an address and the Bangor Band played "America." Tefft, though, occupied an inconspicuous place in the throng. Other guests of honor were former Governor Percival Baxter (wearing a hat, to the left of Brewster), and Civil War veteran William Z. Clayton, age ninety-two. The cane in Hamlin's right hand was stolen by pranksters in later years, but is now welded into place.

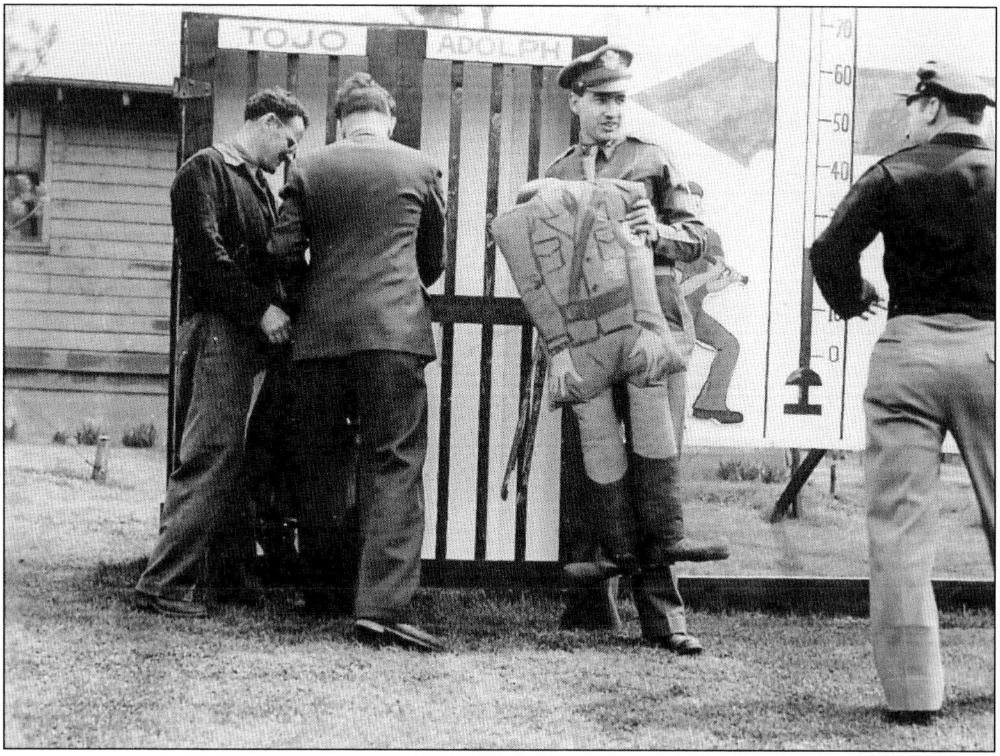

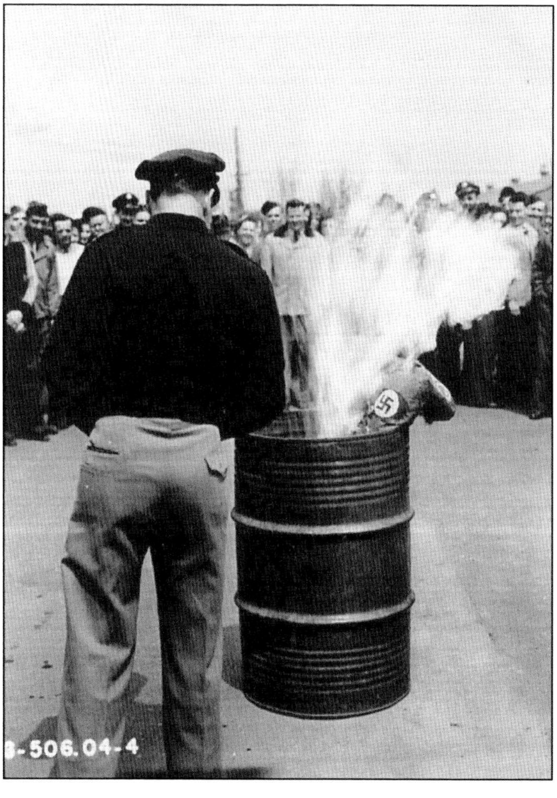

Just as Bangor crowds burned Germany's Kaiser Wilhelm in effigy on November 11, 1918, the end of World War I, officers and civilians at Dow Field hung, then torched, dummies representing Tojo of Japan and Nazi dictator Hitler on Victory in Europe Day, May 8, 1945. The men pictured had each bought a $1,000 war bond that day, allowing them the privilege of walking the two dictators to the gallows.

The burning of Adolf Hitler in a Dow Field trash barrel on VE Day signaled the end of the war in Europe, but there was not yet jubilation in the streets. Many Bangor families had sons and daughters still fighting the Axis powers in the Pacific and celebrating was out of the question until the Japanese surrender was announced in August. Students in local schools sat at their desks and heard President Harry S. Truman announcing the German surrender on the morning of May 8.

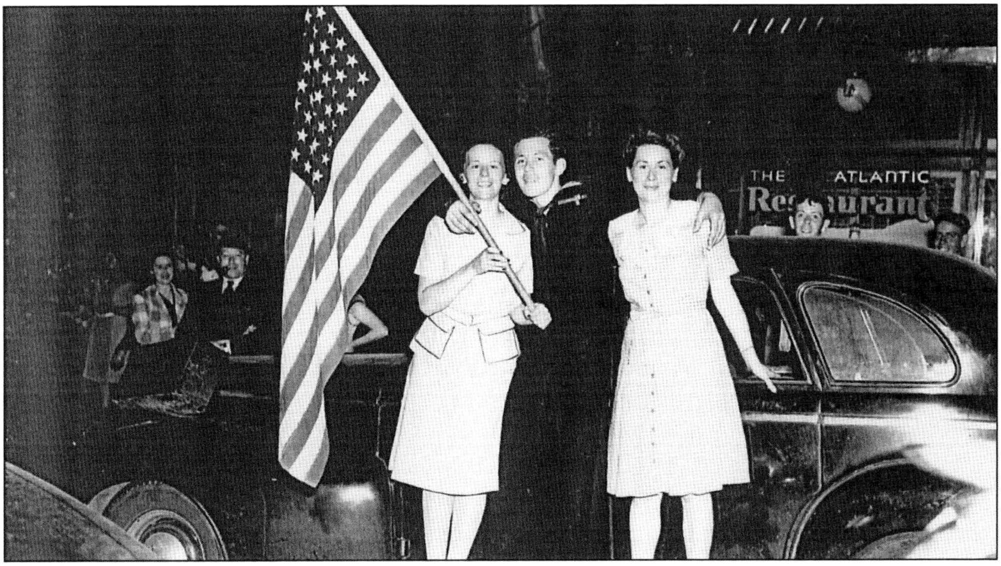

Main Street photographed on VJ Day, August 14, 1945. Was this really the end of four years of hardship, both for sailors (like the men pictured here) and the women and men here on the home front? Bangor's counterpart of the famous "Times Square kiss" photograph taken earlier in the day comes from the files of the *Bangor Daily News.* Ticker tape lay scattered in front of the celebrants, while people near the New Atlantic Restaurant looked on gleefully.

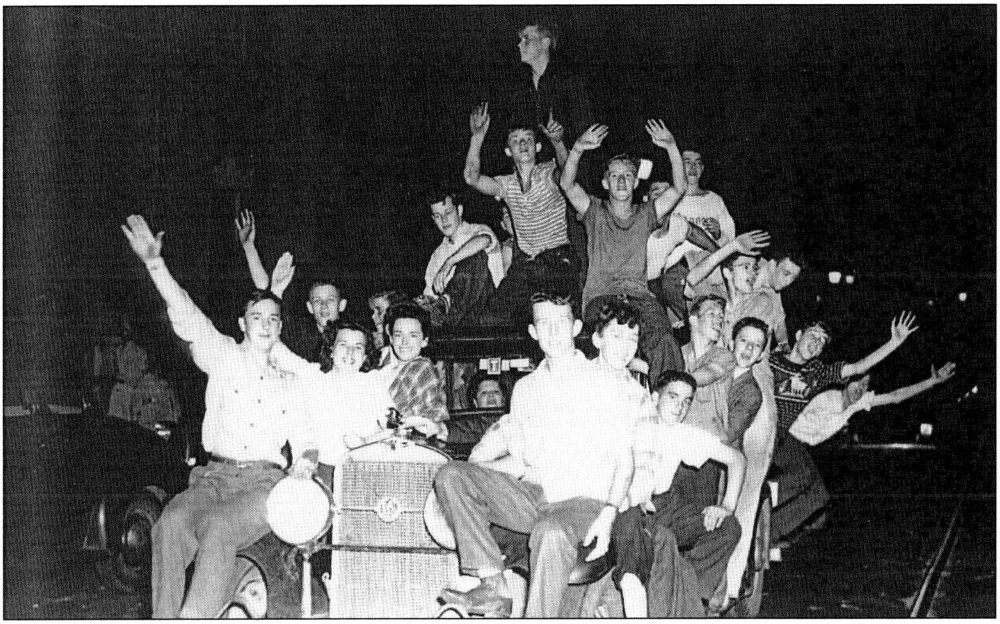

What might have been a scene from *The Grapes of Wrath* was photographed under far happier circumstances than the Steinbeck novel. Local young people who had pent up their emotions on VE Day in May, the end of only one phase of World War II, finally let loose in a ragtag victory parade in downtown Bangor. Some troops already returned home by this time joined in the celebration, while others didn't came back to the city for several weeks, or months. Still others never returned at all, having paid the ultimate sacrifice. Their portraits are contained in a Bangor book of honor displayed at the Bangor Public Library.

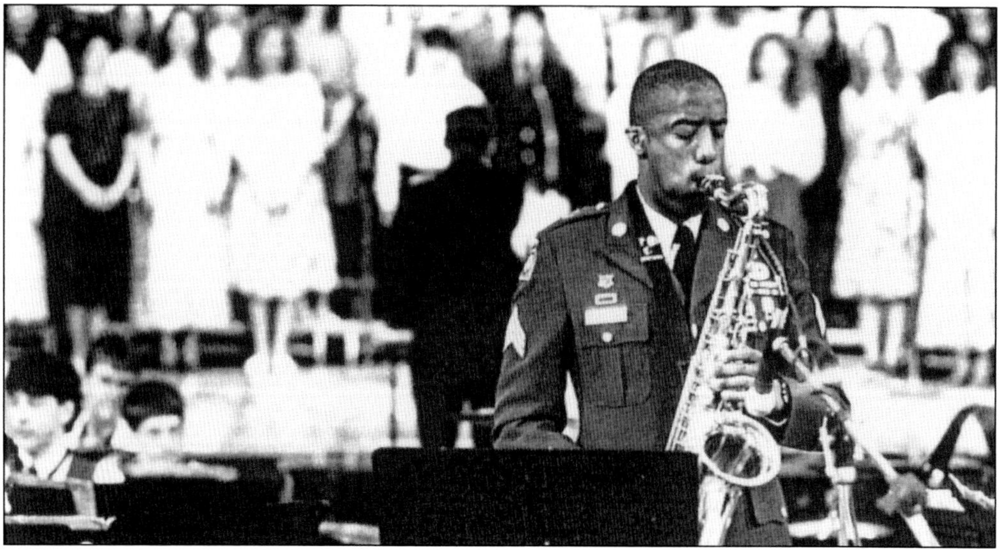

U.S. Army Sergeant Kevin Tillman of Fort Bragg, N.C., returning to the United States from duty in the Persian Gulf, galvanized a crowd of welcomers at the Bangor International Airport on March 8, 1991, when he played an emotional rendition of the national anthem on his saxophone. WLBZ-TV broadcast this first day of returning troop flights live, and by nightfall national television audiences were watching videotape of this historic moment. In April, Sergeant Tillman was invited back to Bangor to perform with music students at John Bapst Memorial High School.

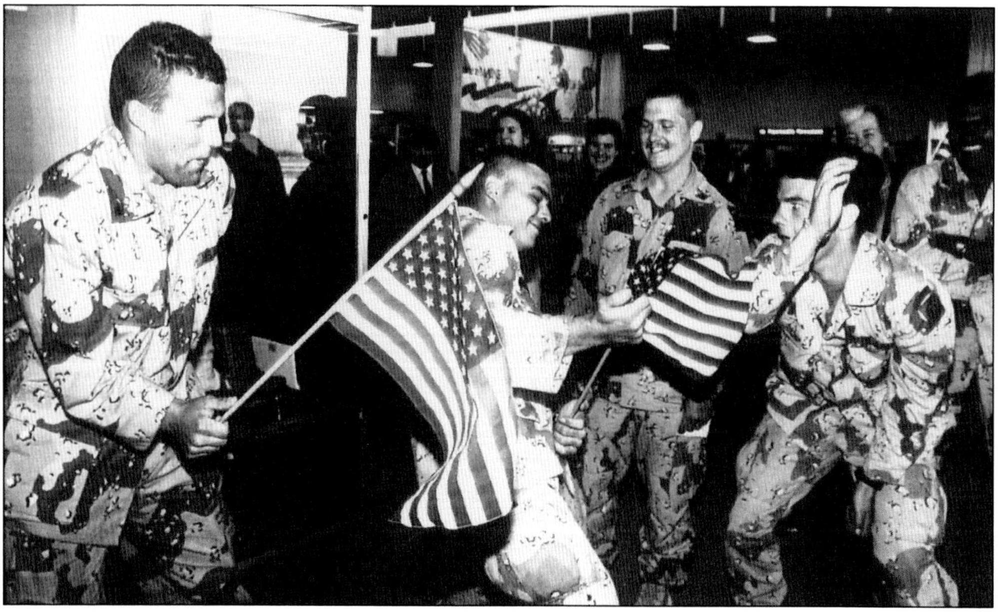

Early on the morning of March 8, the first soldiers to return home through Bangor dance in celebration in the domestic terminal of Bangor International Airport. Kevin Tillman arrived home the same day. In the coming months, men and women from all branches of service who had been on active duty during the Persian Gulf War were greeted by a large contingent of local airport greeters. Some airline pilots reportedly rerouted flights to Bangor for refueling so their passengers could join in the celebrations.

Seven

A Gallery of Portraits

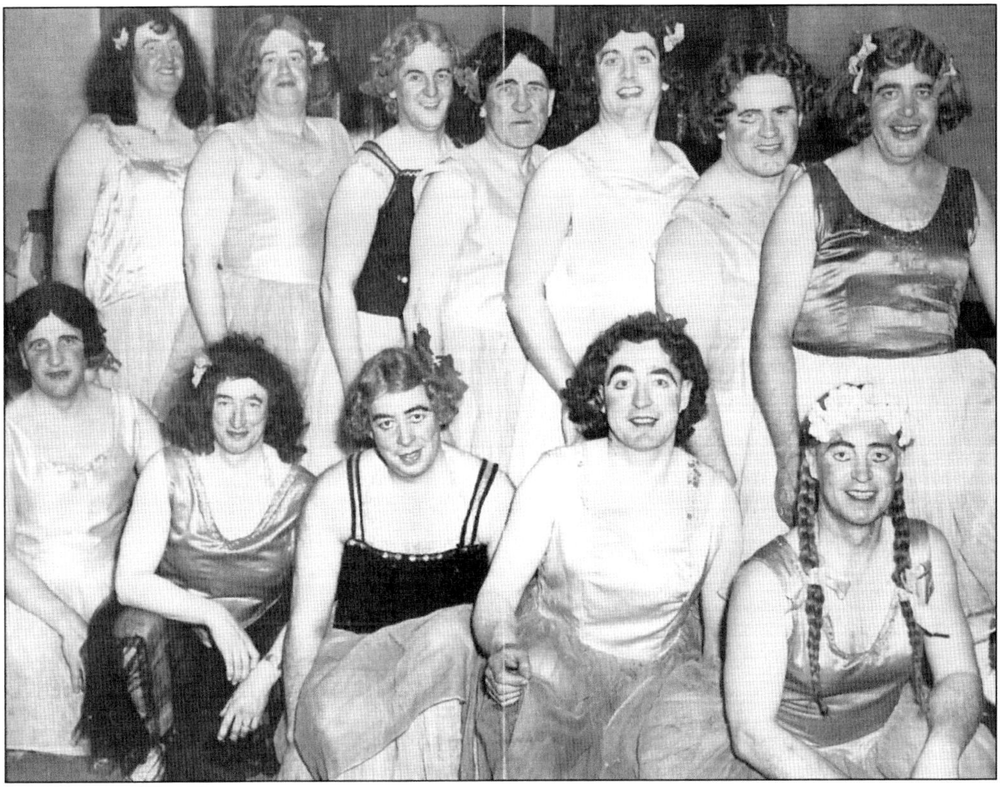

Who said local businessmen didn't have a sense of humor? Members of the Bangor Kiwanis Club performed in drag at the 1948 Kiwanis Kapers, held at the old Bangor Auditorium. From left to right are as follows: (front row) unidentified, Fred Jacques, Ken Day, Charlie Pooler, and Norbert X. Dowd; (back row) unidentified, John McIntosh, Jerry McLeod, Guy Albee, unidentified, Pete Furrow and Jack Carney. Mrs. John McIntosh made this photograph available to Pierre Dumont, who published it in his annual historical magazine, *Paper Talks*.

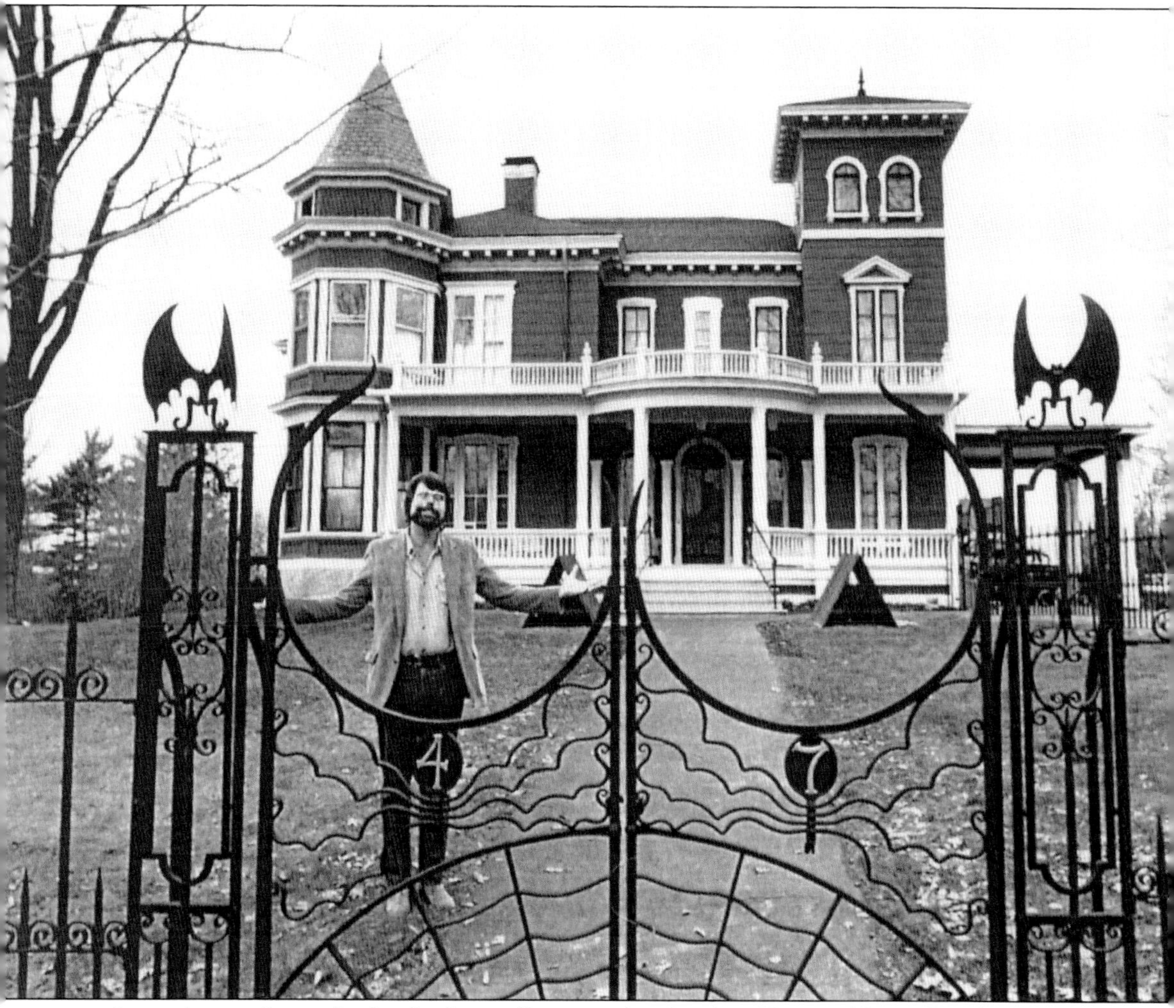

It was love at first sight the day best-selling novelist Stephen King and his wife Tabitha toured this old Victorian mansion on West Broadway. In 1979 he and his family moved in and began making extensive renovations. He even added the trademark iron fence in front of the home, custom made with bats and spiders. King had lived in other parts of the state, but moved to Penobscot County in the 1960s to attend the University of Maine. Many of his books, such as the massive *It*, were set in Bangor and written inside this old house. Of his home, King once wrote, "Of course we fell in love with the house we live in, and it has never disappointed us. Have we disappointed it? Disappointment probably isn't the right word. I think it *disapproved* of us at first . . . My oldest son was convinced there were ghosts in the turret towers (that idea was probably more due to the Hardy Boys than to parental influence) . . ."

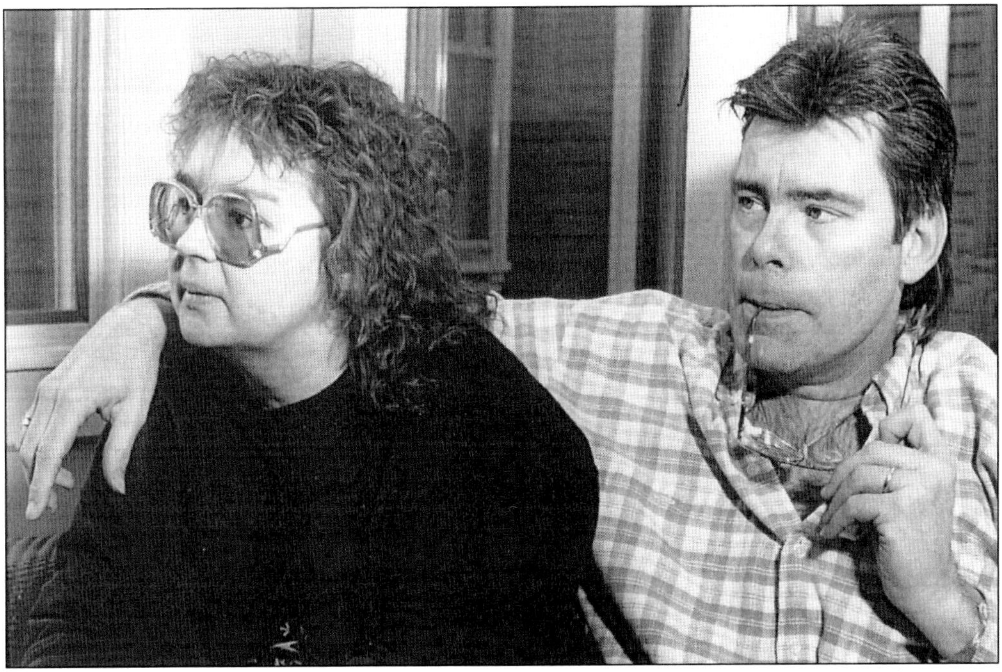

Tabitha Spruce married Stephen King before he was a world-renowned writer. Then came *Carrie*, King's first novel, sent to a publisher with Tabitha's strong encouragement. Sometimes people scare the Kings, such as in 1991, when this photograph appeared soon after an intruder broke into the Kings' home. Discreet security was added to the property not long afterward.

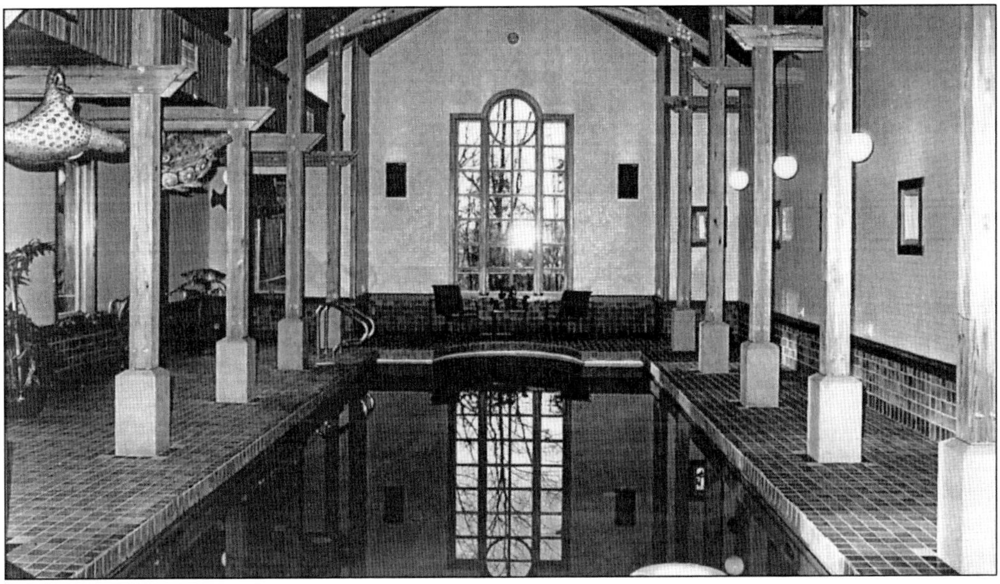

The Kings allowed photographer Bob DeLong a rare peek inside their mansion for a 1984 newspaper feature. This swimming pool and other improvements to the house were supervised by the couple. A published report in 1979 quoted Stephen King as saying that he and Tabitha had counted fourteen rooms in the house, but that the former owners had told him there were twenty-five. "The lady told me she'd counted all the rooms she'd had to clean," King said with a chuckle.

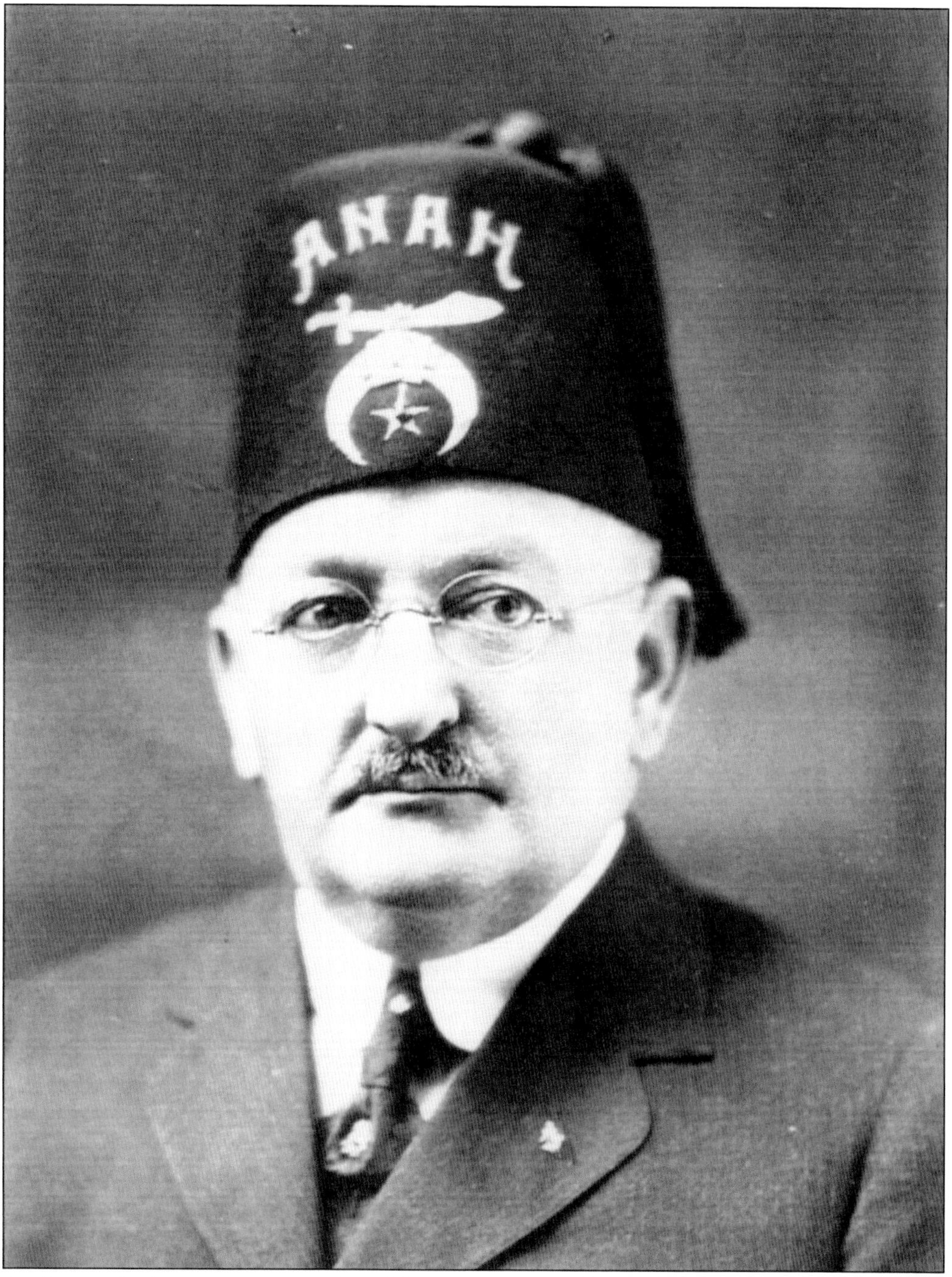

Dr. Eugene B. Sanger wore many hats. He was a trustee of Anah Temple of the Mystic Shrine, a 32nd degree Mason, a director of the Merrill Trust Company, a trustee of the University of Maine, and president of the Penobscot County Medical Association—to name but a few. His legacy in Bangor, however, is of a gifted surgeon long affiliated with Eastern Maine General Hospital (now Eastern Maine Medical Center). The son of a doctor, Dr. Eugene F. Sanger, E.B. was born in Bangor in 1871 and educated at Yale and Columbia. His residence at 42 Broadway is still standing.

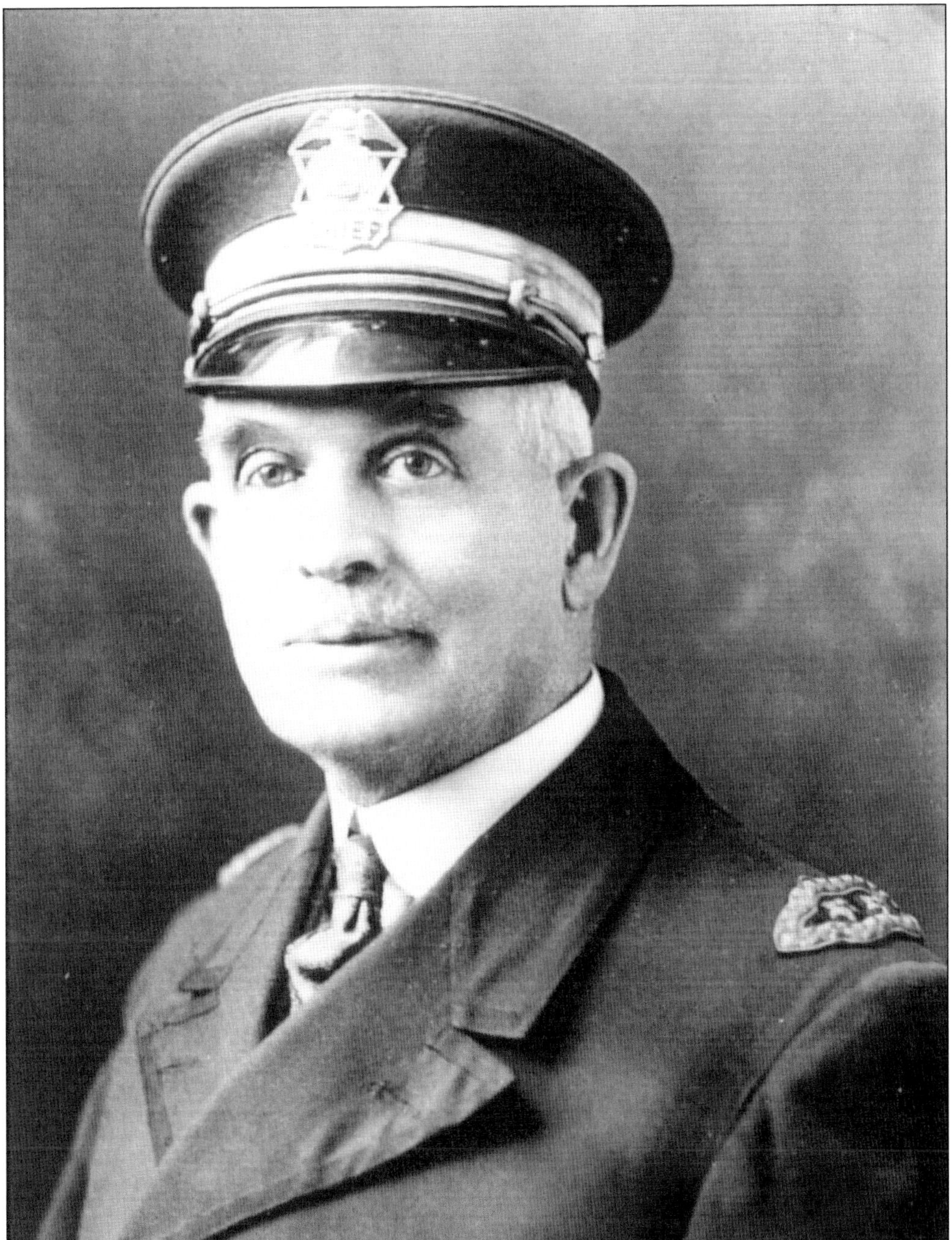

When Benjamin P. Sproul joined the Bangor Police Department in 1896 there were no call boxes on the streets, no motor-driven patrol, no modern mechanical aides to police efficiency. The waterfront swarmed with sailors and woodsmen; policemen patrolling this section needed high courage and physical endurance. Sproul was police chief from 1924–26, succeeding Calvin Knaide. According to a newspaper obituary on his death in 1935, "... those who made a business of transgressing the law knew better than attempt to take advantage of his good nature."

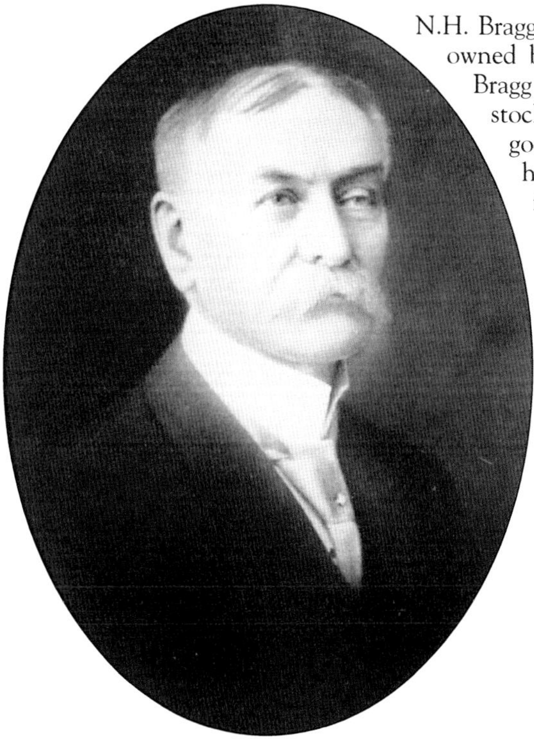

N.H. Bragg and Sons is one of Bangor's oldest family-owned businesses. Dixmont blacksmith Norris H. Bragg opened his business in Broad Street in 1854, stocking his store with iron, steel, and blacksmith goods. His sons, Charles Fred Bragg (pictured here) and N.E. Bragg, joined in the business in 1871. The firm survived the Depression, both world wars, and Urban Renewal relocation, updating its equipment and knowledge as needed.

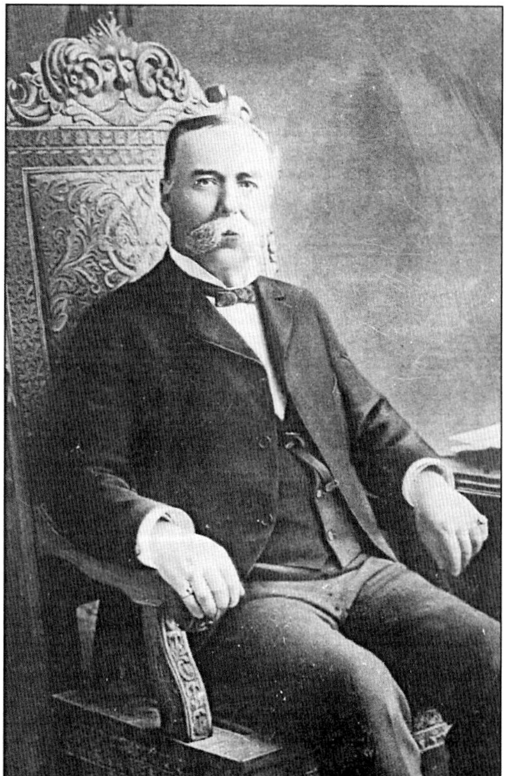

With his gift for oratory and a penchant for publicity, Flavius O. Beal was one of his city's best-known personalities in the late nineteenth and early twentieth centuries. Between 1892 and 1914, Beal was mayor for seven terms. As president of the state fair at Maplewood (now Bass) Park, he was the namesake of "Beal Weather," a legendary stretch of sunny summer skies believed to have resulted from this man's pull with the weatherman.

J. Edward Hand was rector of St. John's Episcopal Church on French Street in 1919. This was an important period in the history of the old church, which was rebuilt after the first building was destroyed in the Bangor Fire of 1911. At this time, Hand is listed as living at 11 Norfolk Street. Close inspection of this postcard-size portrait, selected from the Helen F. Parker collection, reveals a painted backdrop that resembles an actual bookcase; Reverend Hand appears to be reading a newspaper.

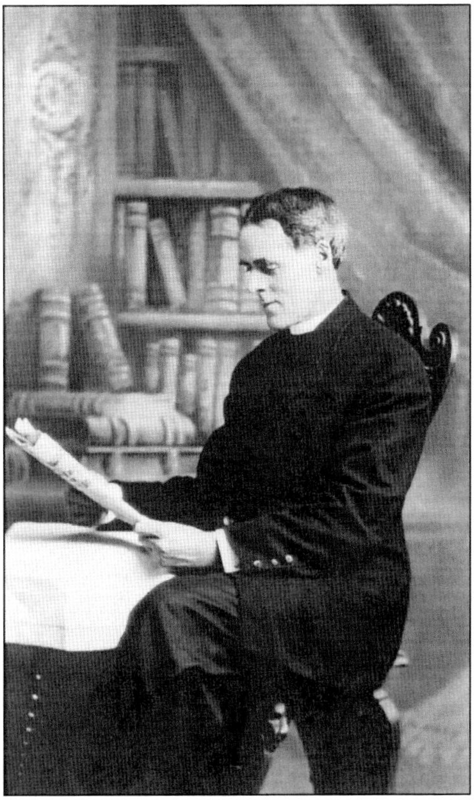

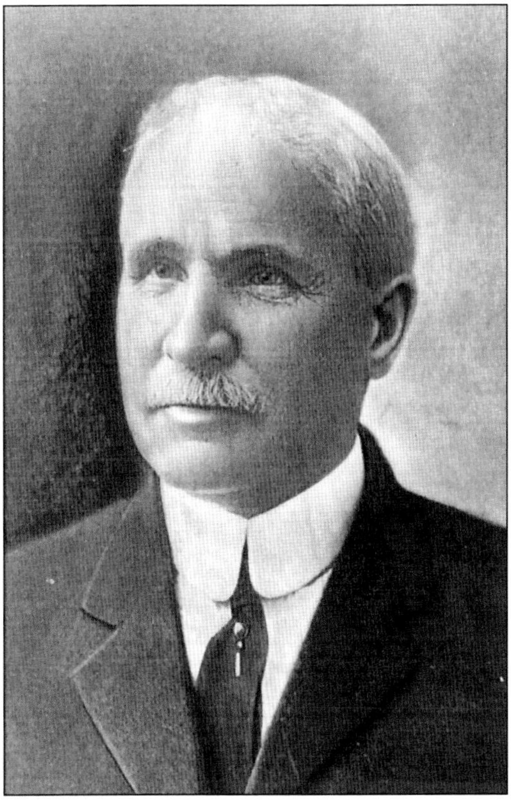

Bangor's man of the hour during the 1911 Fire was Mayor Charles W. Mullen. While the conflagration was raging and telephone service was out, he drove to Northern Maine Junction in Hermon to summon firefighting apparatus from other cities. Not long after the fire was extinguished, the Democrat rallied residents at a city hall meeting and helped raise $25,000, an enormous sum in those days, to aid the 375 people left homeless. By May 11 of that year, the relief fund had garnered more than $50,000.

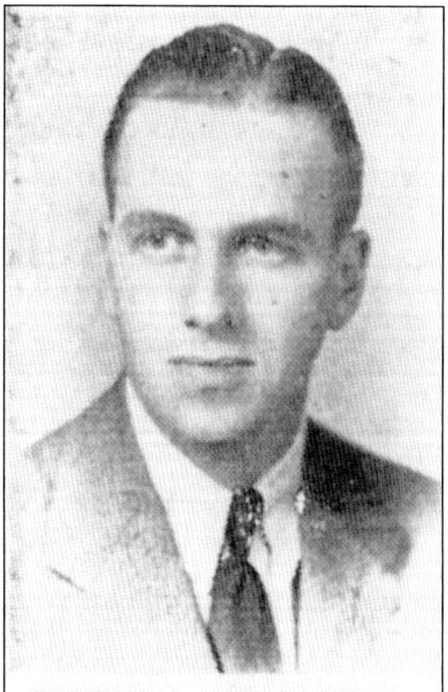

GORHAM A. LEVENSELLER
Senior Warden

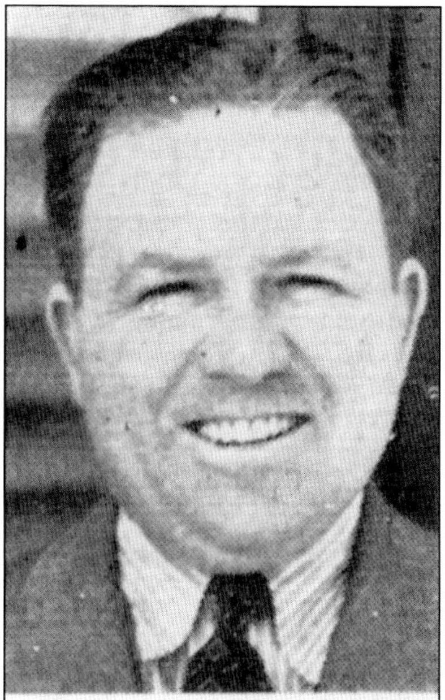

FIELDS S. PENDLETON, JR.
Senior Warden

More than five hundred air raid wardens had been selected by the summer of 1942. Each was trained and had specific duties assigned to them by Gordon D. Briggs, the man in charge of the wardens and the report center. Six air raid sirens were located throughout the city, the master siren positioned on the roof of the police barracks on Court Street. As much a morale-building measure as an actual security defense network, many of the system's wardens, such as the four shown here, were prominent citizens.

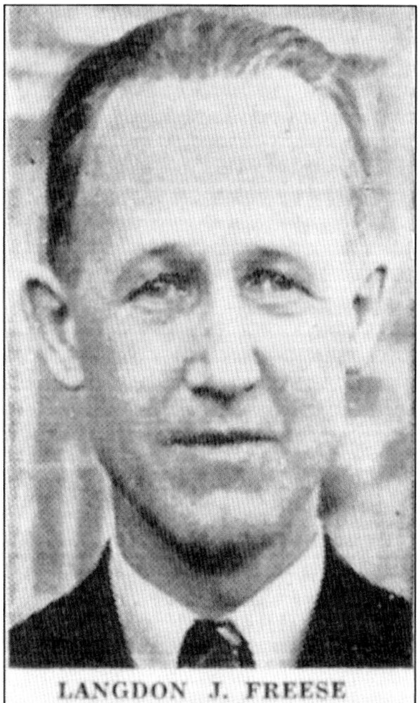

LANGDON J. FREESE
Senior Warden

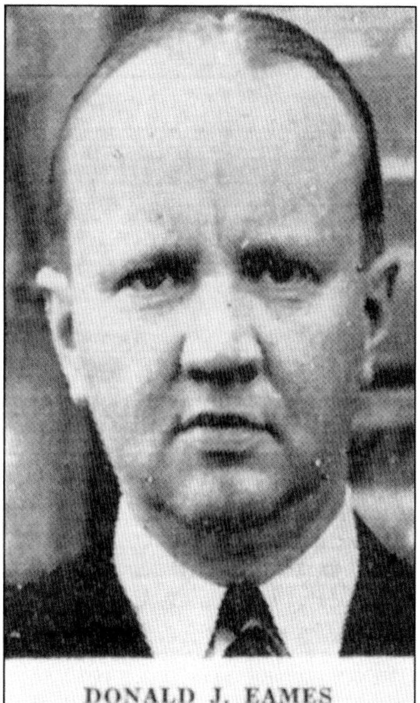

DONALD J. EAMES
Senior Warden

"Dear Mother and Father," this soldier may have written on the back of this 1916 picture postcard, "Thanks for seeing me off at Union Station on June 22 with Company G and the Machine Gun Company. Arrived at Texas a week later. Gee, it's hot down here. Waiting to fight ol' Pancho Villa." Fortunately, L. St. Peter of Orono and all the others in his unit were home by October after a war with Mexico was diverted.

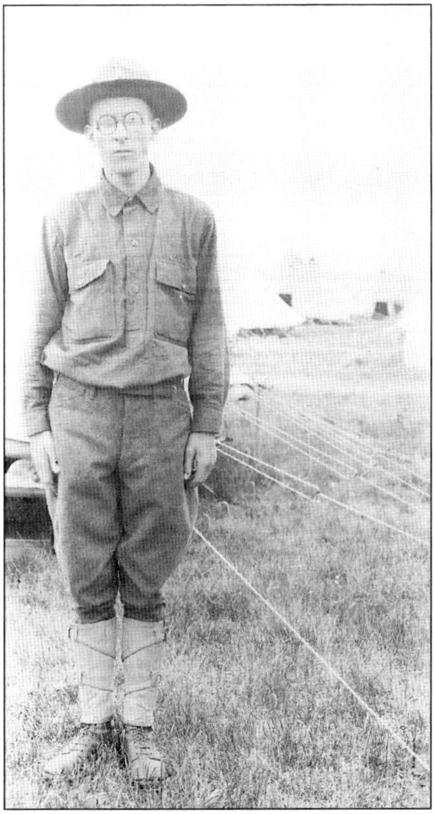

One cold morning in March 1941, the 152nd Maine National Guard field artillery band stopped at the old post office building while marching from the Bangor Armory to Union Station, where a train would take them to Florida in preparation for war. They are, from left to right, as follows: (front row) Joseph Dinsmore Jr., Francis Shaw, and Paul Monaghan; (second row) Alden Goode, John Kelley, Robert Wood, Roland Luce, and Spotford Avery; (third row) Ward Shaw, Oscar Grant, George Lougee, Paul Ford, and Tubby Giroux; (fourth row) Walter Wyman, Bernard Beach, John Riley, Frank Wyman, and Robert Rosie; (fifth row) Russell Springer, Edward Andrews, John Roberts, and unidentified; (back row) Robert Clark, George Chase, and Samuel Wyman.

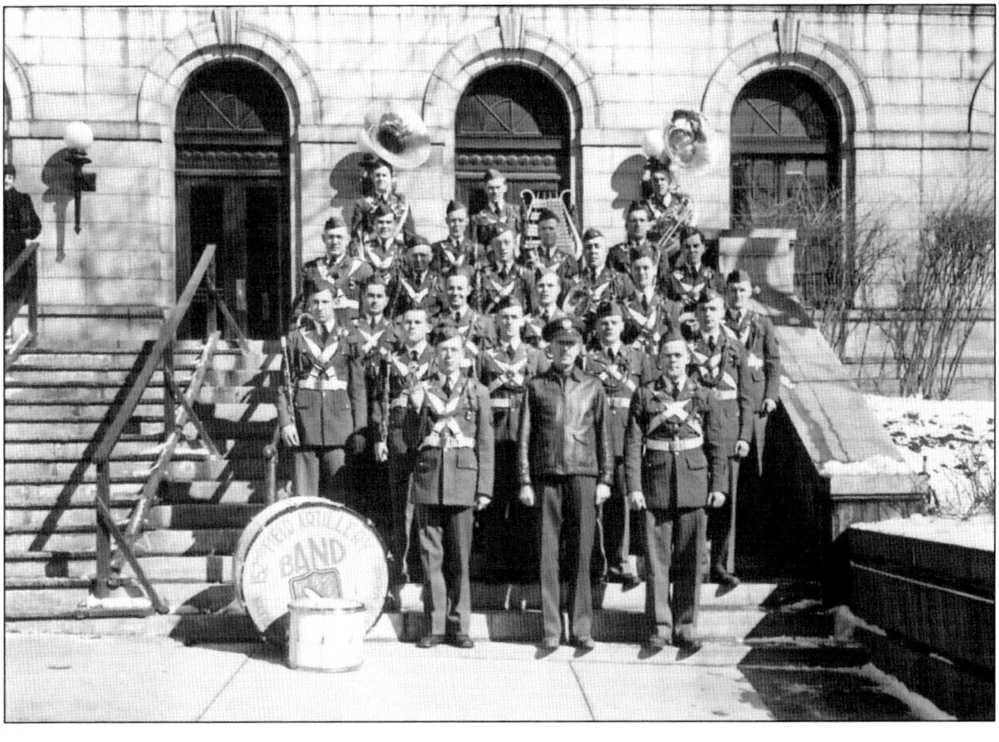

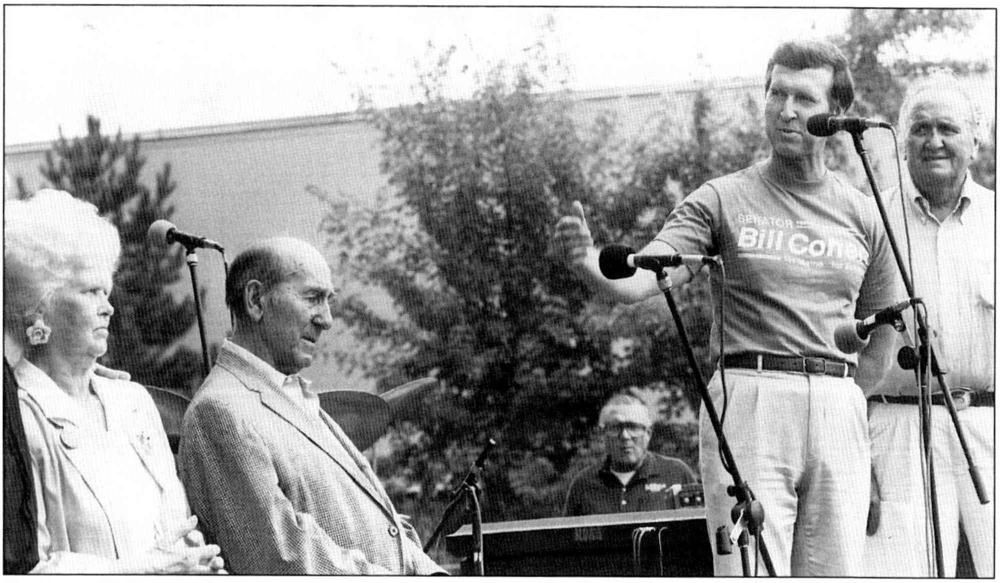

Senator William S. Cohen, a Bangor native, mixed re-election politics with a birthday celebration in the summer of 1990. Returning to his alma mater, Bangor High School, Cohen was the guest of honor at an informal public gathering that also featured his parents (far left), Clara Cohen and her husband Reuben, a baker. Veteran newspaper columnist Ralph "Bud" Leavitt (right) served as the master of ceremonies. Bill Cohen began his political life as a Bangor city councilor, advancing to election to the U.S. House of Representatives and, later, the Senate.

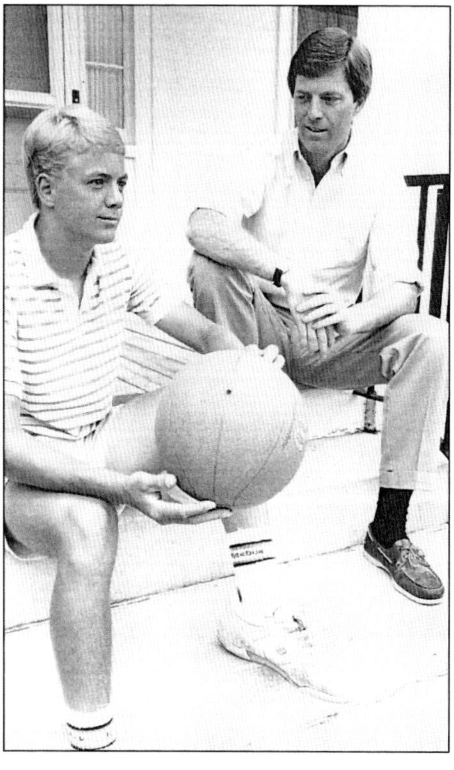

Peter Alexander McKernan's life was too brief. The only child of Governor John R. McKernan died of heart failure in 1991, while attending Dartmouth College in New Hampshire. The twenty-year-old, shown here with his famous father, was eulogized as an all-around good kid with no pretensions. "During the past eight days, I've come to realize the importance of friendship," recalled Peter's roommate, Adam Berkowitz, at the Bangor funeral. "I don't think Peter ever realized how many people loved him."

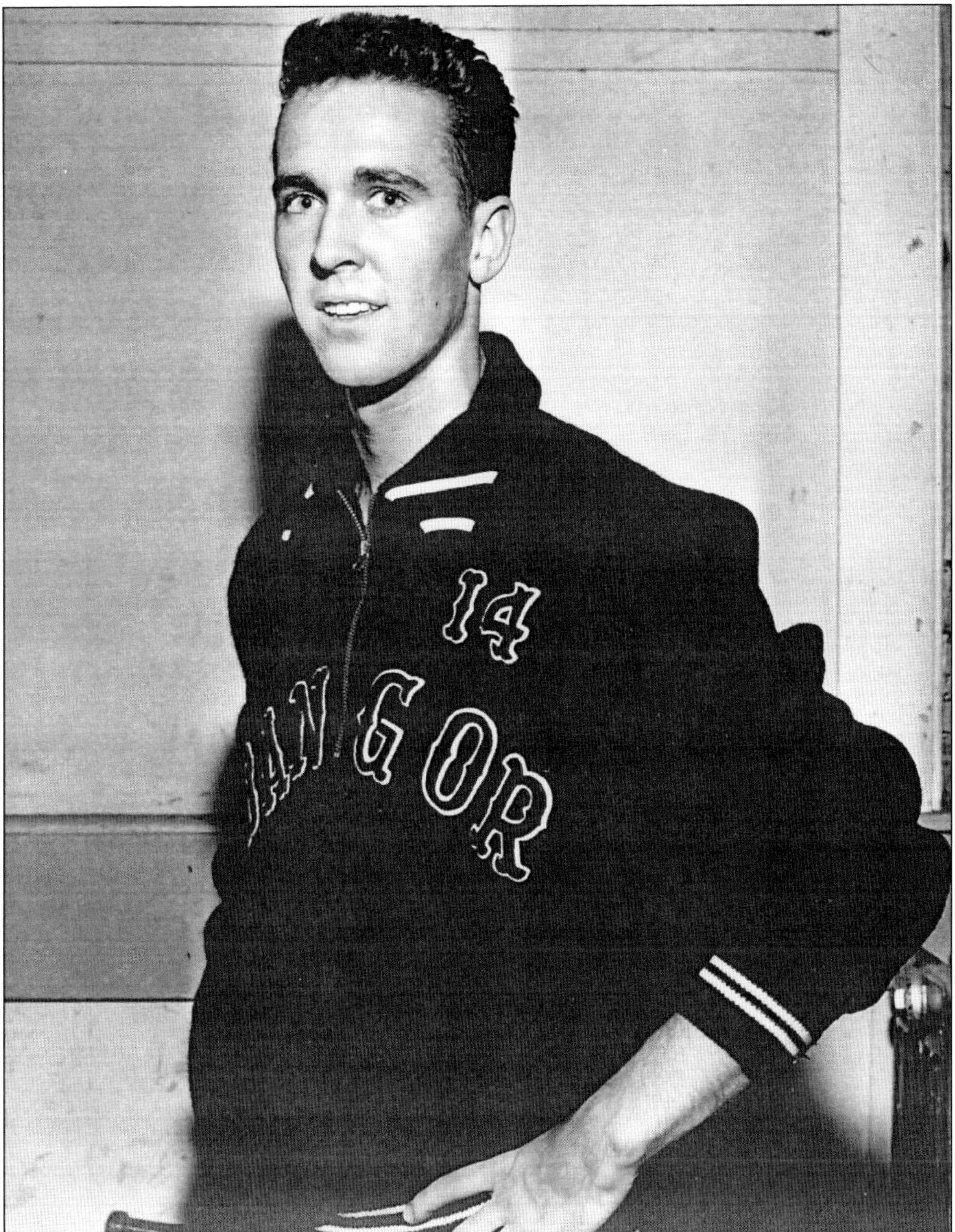

Bill Cohen was a rising star even in December 1957, as he played for Bangor High School in the annual basketball tournament. The future senator and U.S. secretary of defense was an outstanding athlete and honors student. And these were the eyes of a budding poet. His poems (and novels) have been published and his love of the language was evident in many Senate floor speeches. Recalling the loss of Bangor's ethnic mix in his old neighborhood, Hancock Street, he wrote in 1991, "The tide of history has pulled them all away, and yet, in my mind's eye, I still see the people, hear the voices that filled my past, and so the past lives within me."

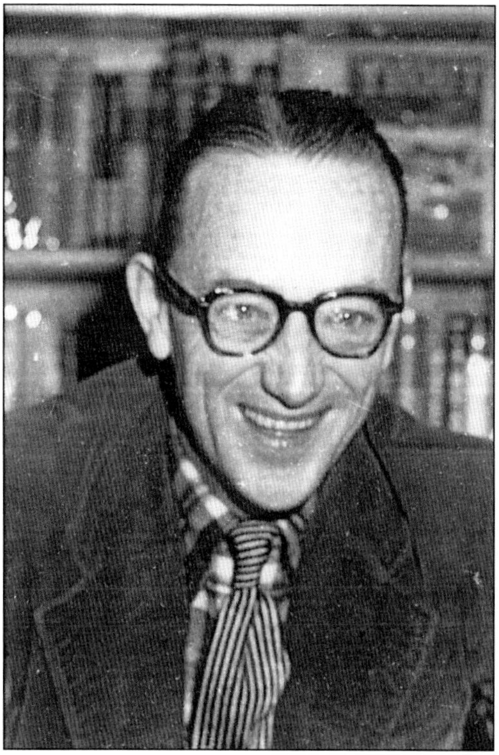

There will never be another Bill Geagan. The Bangor author, artist, and newspaper columnist was lauded as a pioneer of outdoor writing on his death in 1974. "Although considered a sensitive and shy man," read one obituary, "he never feared anything, and asked only to be with nature's things." Readers can enjoy his three books, which brought him a national audience: *Nature I Loved*, *The Good Trail*, and *Seed on the Wind*.

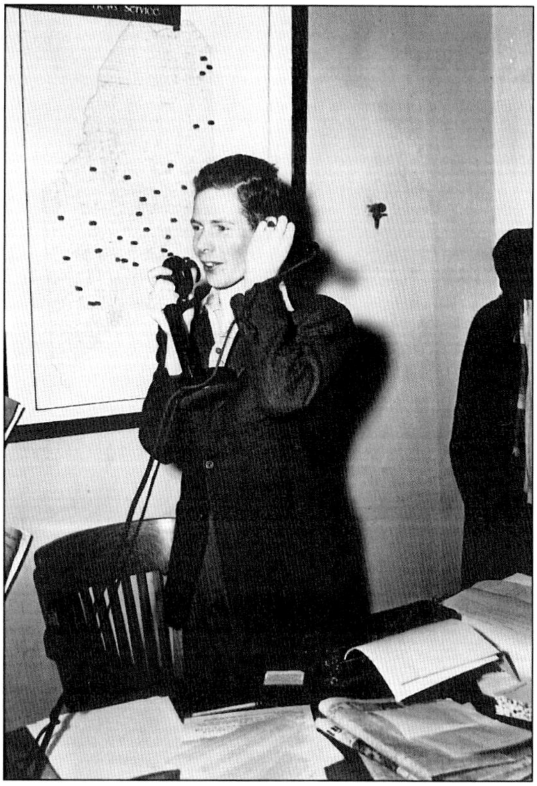

Young Joseph Eaton was the news editor of station WLBZ from 1940 to 1950. Behind him is a map which featured blinking lights that related to field correspondents (reporters) of the Maine Radio News Service. Eaton succeeded Edgar Welch, the station's first newsman in the 1930s. The first radio broadcast in Maine originated from a studio and tower in the First Universalist Church in Bangor; another tower was positioned atop the nearby Graham Building.

Albert J. Cole, born in Lowell, Maine, in 1893, started a modest business with teams of horses and finished with Cole's Express, the state's largest carrier of general freight, based in Bangor. Three years after "Allie" Cole's death in 1955 a memorial gymnasium at the Bangor-Brewer YMCA was erected in his name with this inscription on a bronze plaque: "Dedicated to the memory of an orphan boy who through faith in God, courage and hard work rose to prominence in civic and business affairs, an example for the youth of today."

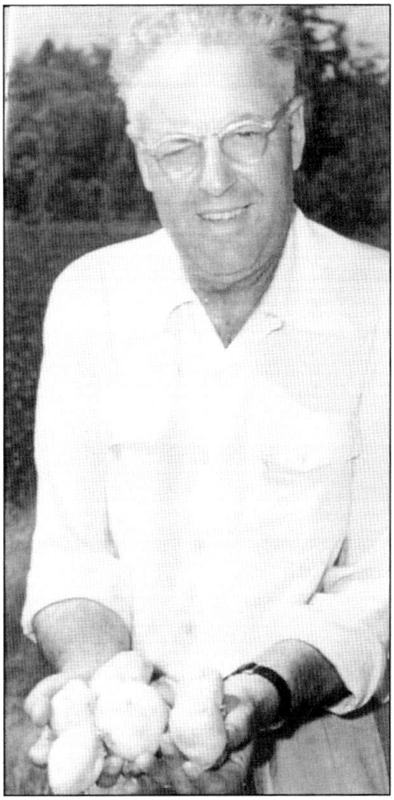

Men and women employees of the Burr Printing Company had printer's ink in their blood. They were expected to know every aspect of the business, from typography to inks and papers. Thomas W. Burr bought out an existing business in 1879, finally incorporating the Columbia Street printing and advertising company in 1902. This photograph dates to the 1920s. Later, the company moved to new quarters on Franklin Street, and after that, Central Street.

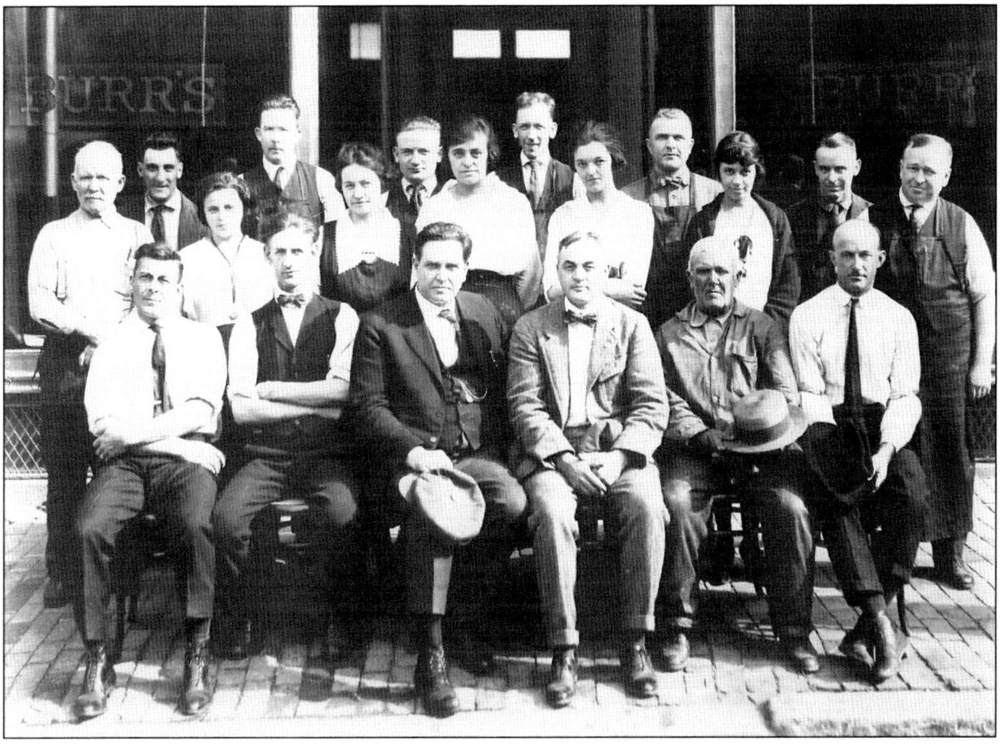

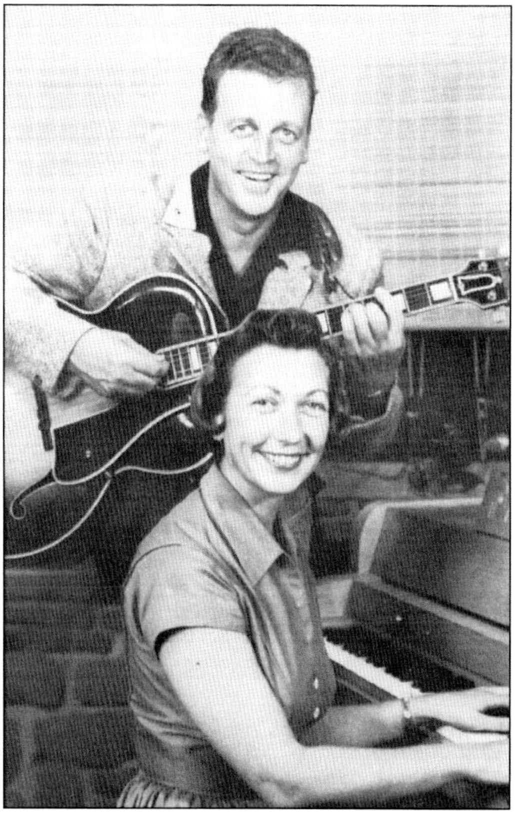

Al and Aileen Rawley brought a smile to the breakfast table each morning with a chat-and-music program on WTWO-TV, later to become WLBZ-TV. Pictured here in August 1957 at the beginning of their lengthy career at Channel 2, the couple eventually retired with a combined service of eighty-five years in broadcasting. The Rawleys and another local TV favorite, funny man Eddie Driscoll, performed live in those days. No second-chance videotaped performances for them.

The year was 1962, the place, WABI-TV's Studio City, where Channel 5's first news director, Dan Connelly, and cameraman Ron Cook are broadcasting live election night returns. The major candidates were Maynard Dolloff (Democrat) against John Reed (Republican) for governor, and William Hathaway (Democrat) versus Clifford McIntire (Republican) for the 2nd District House seat. Reed and Hathaway were the winners. Channel 2 and 5 news programs are still competitors in the coverage of local and statewide news.

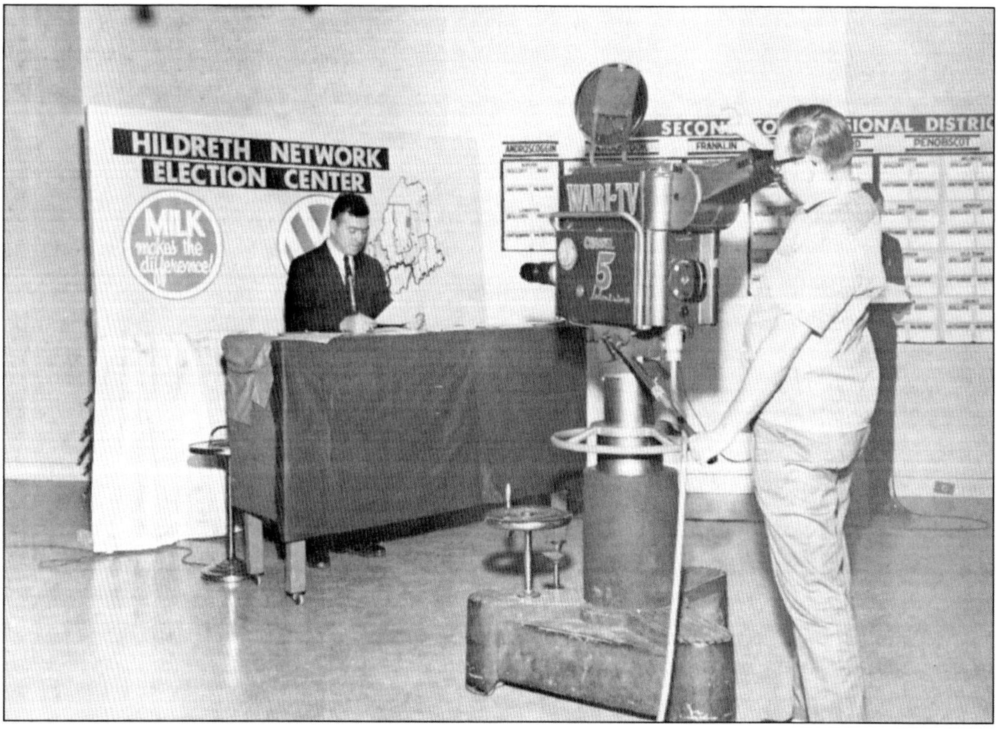

Eight

Delving into Downtown

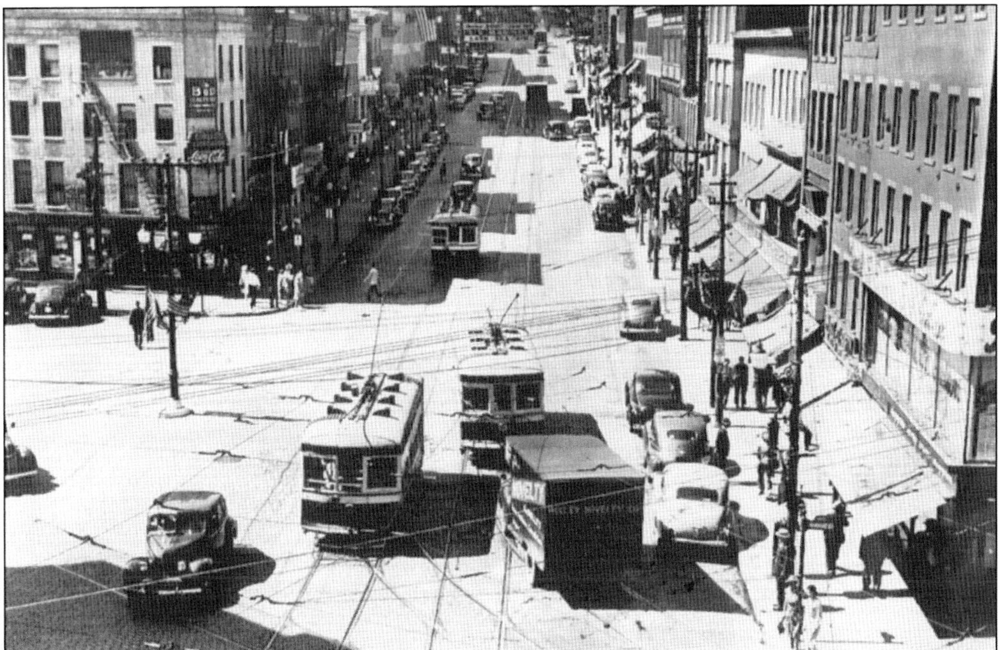

West Market Square and Main Street were still paved with cobblestones when this 1940s newspaper photograph was taken, and trolleys still made their regular runs up and down the street and to surrounding towns and neighborhoods. A flag flew near a long banner announcing a morale-booster war drive and people had time to stop and chat on the city's sidewalks. The pharmacies on the corners at the left and right were downtown fixtures for many years. So were upstairs businesses such as the B&D Beauty Shop at left, over Sweet's Drugstore. Today much upstairs space remains unused, forbidden because of fire rules and a diminished interest in even ground-level space.

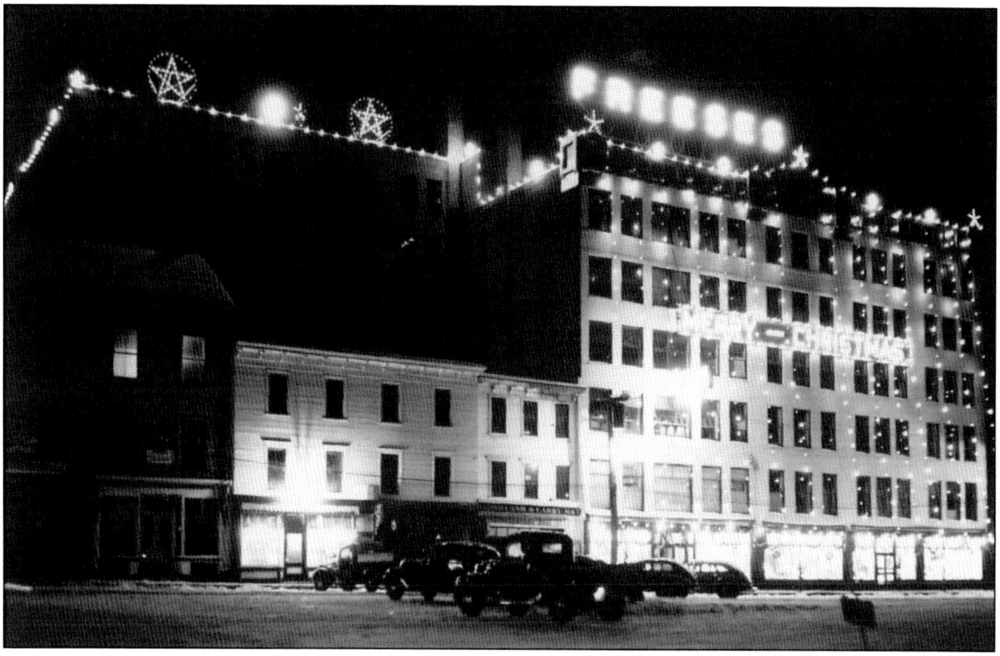

A. Langdon Freese started his business in September 1892 in a 19-by-60-foot store with one window on Main Street. At first he sold suits and coats, but he eventually purchased the downtown millinery business of Smith and Scott. In 1906 he expanded into larger quarters, something he would do again several times in the coming decades. At the time of his death in 1953, Freese's was known throughout New England as a wondrous "Fifth Avenue in Maine."

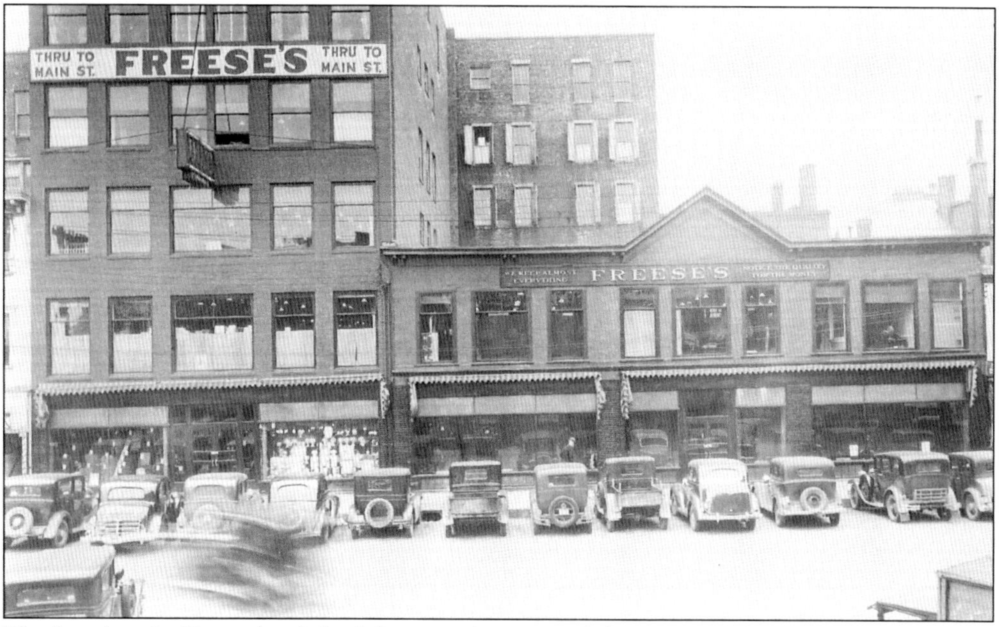

The fact that the Freese family had the capital to expand their store spoke volumes about where frugal shoppers were spending their money during the Great Depression. This photograph, taken on March 27, 1936, from the Pickering Square side of the store, was published just as the two-story wing on the right was to be raised to six, a total expansion of 14,400 square feet.

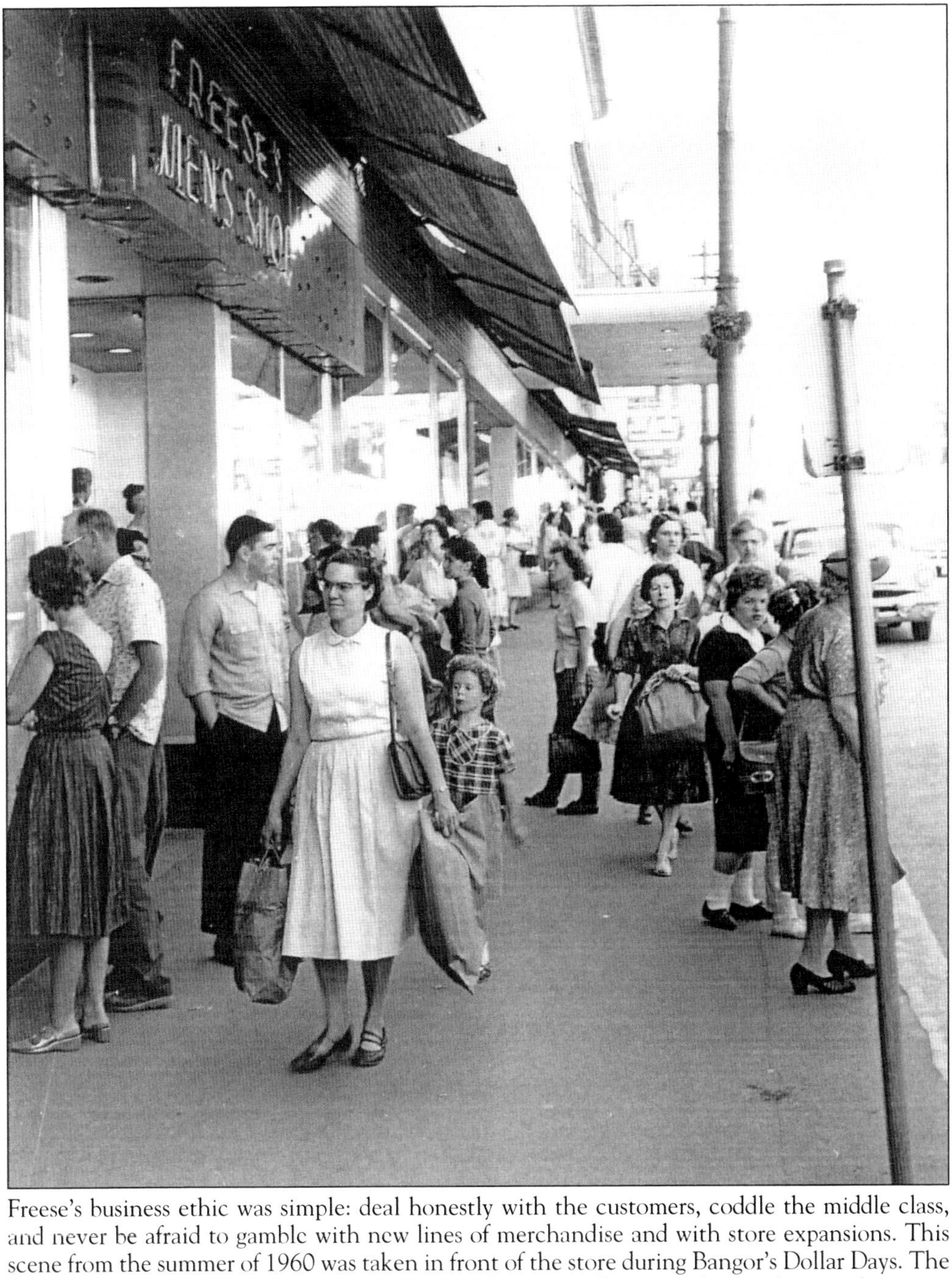

Freese's business ethic was simple: deal honestly with the customers, coddle the middle class, and never be afraid to gamble with new lines of merchandise and with store expansions. This scene from the summer of 1960 was taken in front of the store during Bangor's Dollar Days. The publicity gimmick drew thousands of shoppers downtown for a grand prize drawing for a new station wagon. Freese's was sold to the Gorin's chain in 1957, which later opened a branch store at the Airport Mall.

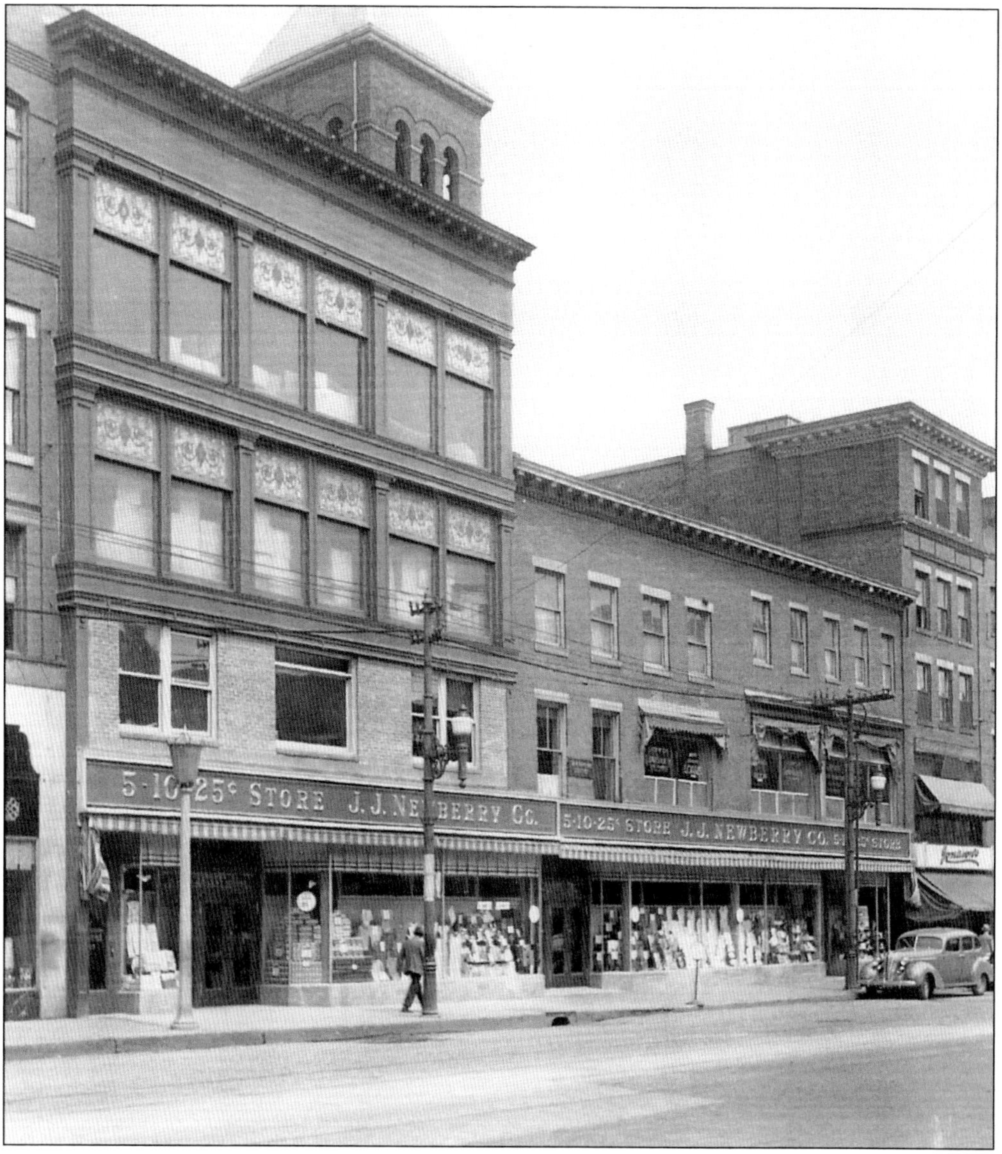

Do you remember when the J.J. Newberry Company took up two entire storefronts along lower Main Street? This 1940s scene from the Dan Maher photographic collection shows a variety of merchandise displayed in the windows. The affable Leo Mouradian managed the five-and-dime store for twenty-eight years. Also a favorite with downtown shoppers was Jonason's restaurant, located next to the Newberry store.

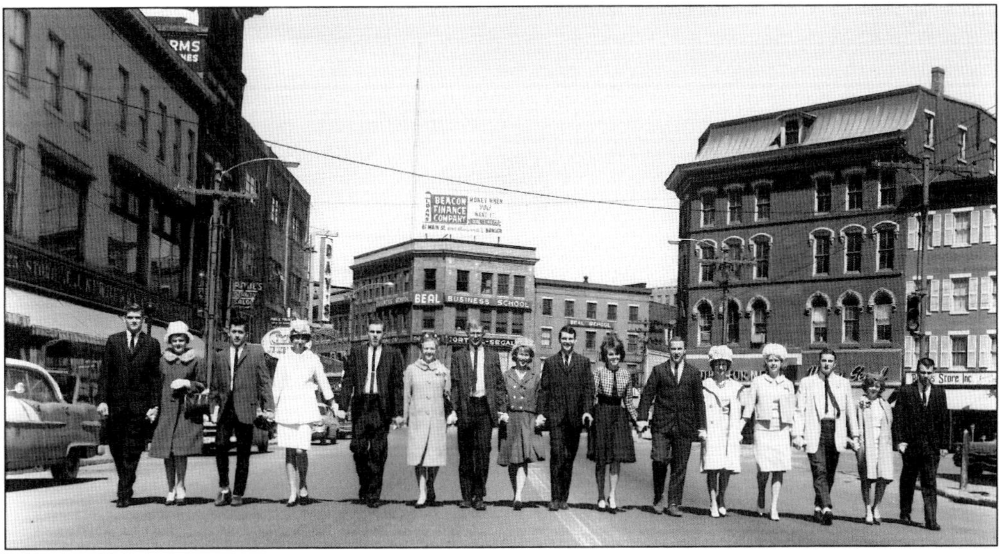

Sixteen people dressed in their Easter Sunday best fan out across Main Street on April 14, 1963, to pose for a unique newspaper photograph. From left to right are Mr. and Mrs. Edward McClure, Richard Spinney, Sally McCready, Sam Parker, Gretchen Goodwin, Whit Russell, Judy Johnson, Edward Farwell, Ann Rathbun, Sandy MacPherson, Judy White, Nancy Robertson, Paul MacPherson, Andrea Campbell, and David Eaton.

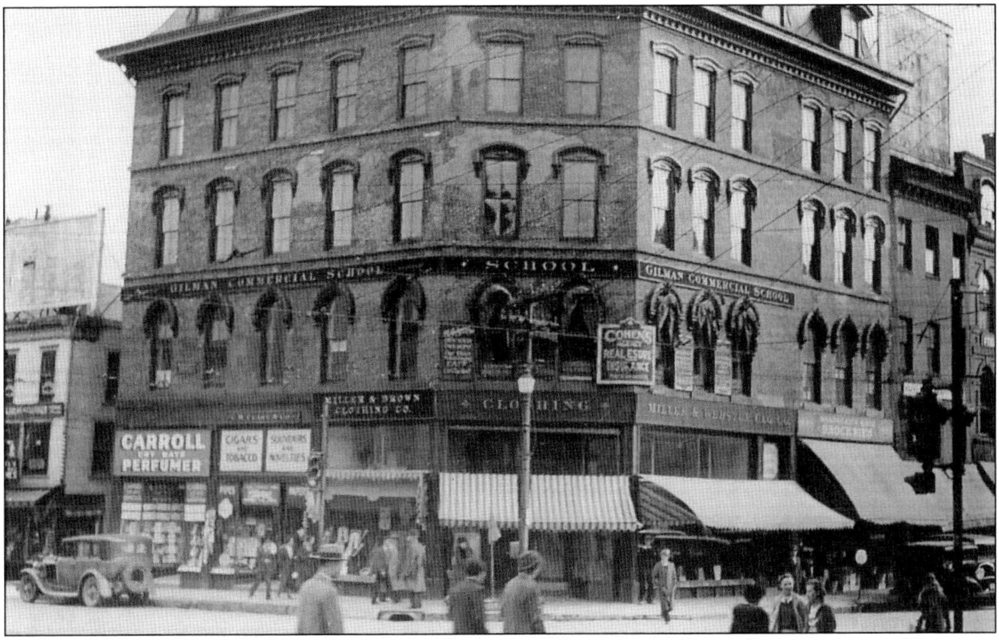

The Wheelwright and Clark Block was built in 1859 and always has been an important location, situated at West Market Square. Historian Deborah Thompson writes that the five-story building was designed of irregular shape to conform to the corner lot on the square. Miller and Brown and Miller and Webster clothiers were located on the ground floor when this picture was taken in the 1920s, and around to the left were Clare's Tobacco Company and Carroll Perfumer. When Henry Segal closed his men's clothing business in 1980, it was the first time since the building's construction that a clothier hadn't occupied the first floor.

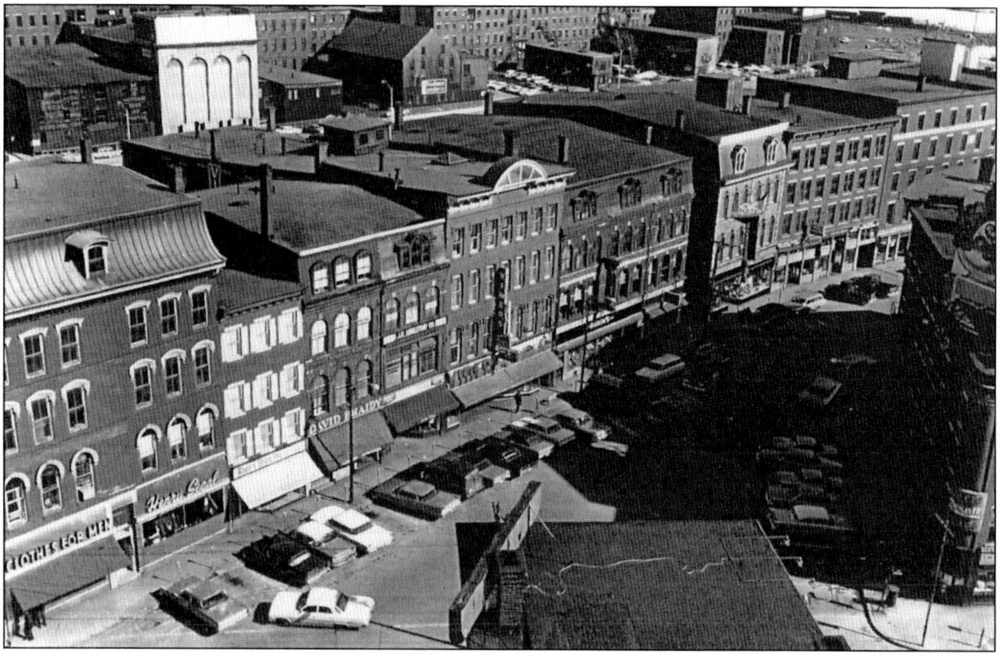

Broad Street in the early 1960s, as seen from the city hall bell tower, was a string of locally owned businesses that stretched all the way to the river. Urban Renewal demolition interrupted this flow of business blocks, beginning with the historic old Home Furniture Company block (at right center). Sharp eyes will pick out these businesses along Broad Street: Henry Segal clothes for men, Rogers Store Incorporated, David Braidy clothes for women, the Viner Music Company, and the Dakin Sporting Goods Company.

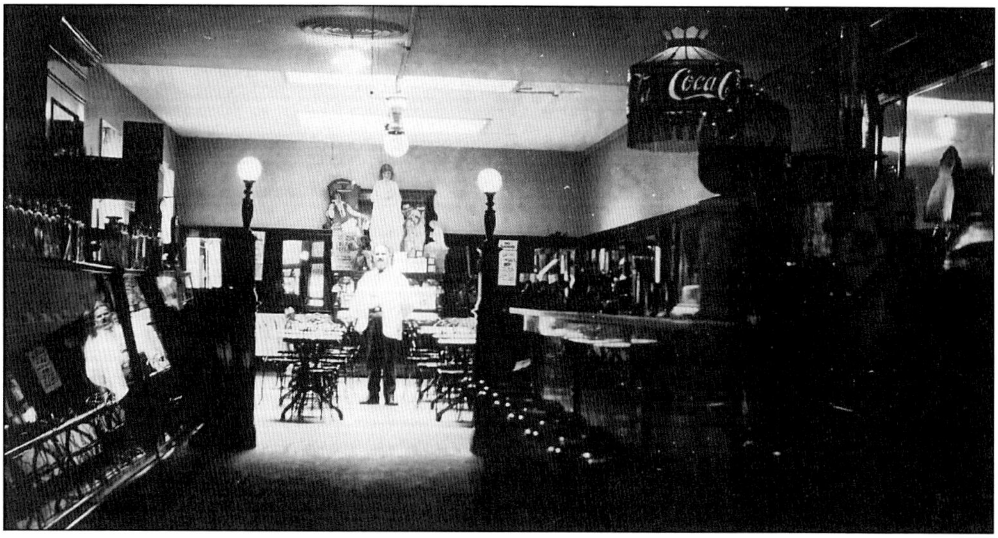

The patriarch of Bangor's Greek colony was a well-known downtown personality for decades. Born in Greece, George N. "Papa" Brountas immigrated to America, at first selling merchandise off a wagon that he pushed around town. He started his own business on Main Street in 1903, and his candy store eventually became Brountas Restaurant, one of the city's most fondly remembered eateries. Pictured in his business around 1912, Papa was the father of one son and seven daughters. He died in 1962.

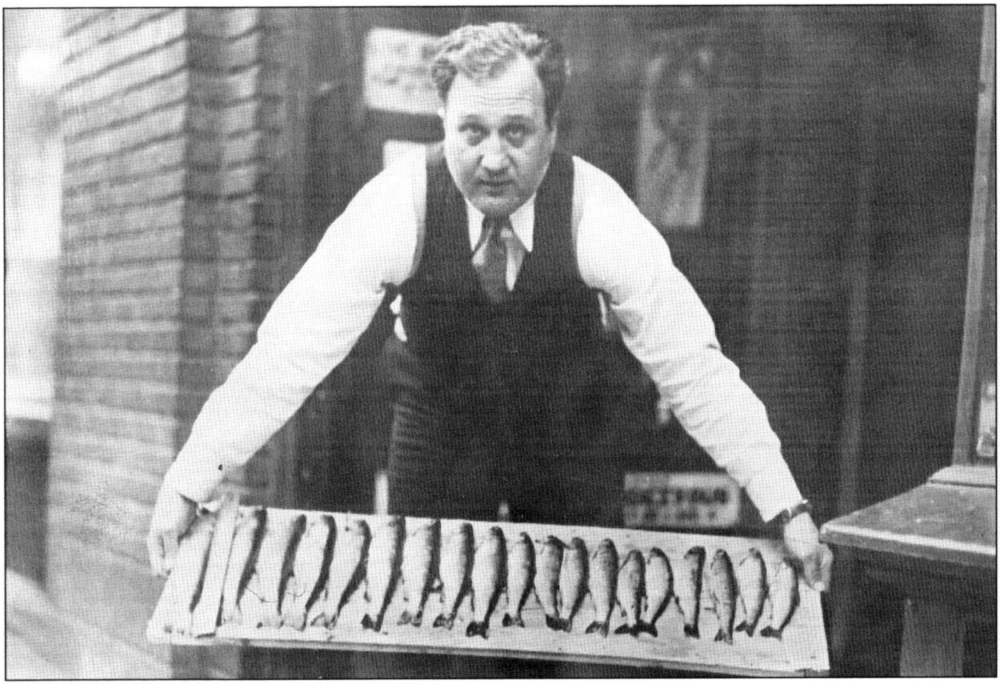

Everett S. "Shep" Hurd, the owner of the Dakin Sporting Goods Company at 25 Central Street, was an enduring downtown businessman. In 1924 he bought out Eugene Dakin's interest in the business, built it into an impressive retail and wholesale enterprise, at one time supplying more than 250 schools in Maine with athletic equipment, and eventually moved to a larger store on Broad Street. In October 1937, around the time of this informal snapshot, Hurd furnished a tip to police that resulted in the shooting deaths of Alfred Brady and another gangster outside his store (see pp. 65–7).

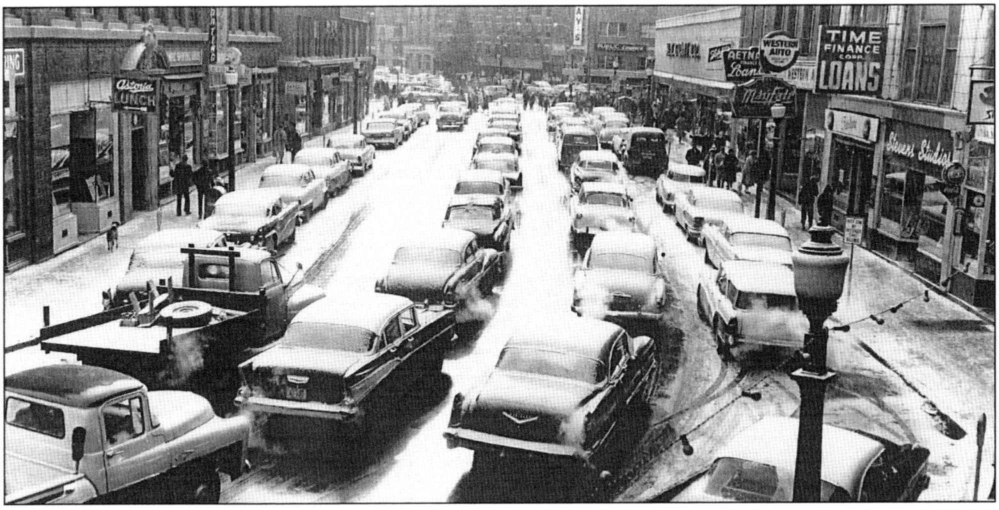

Christmas shoppers drive around and around Central Street on December 13, 1958, searching for a place to parallel park. And then, decisions, decisions. On this street alone, these businesses were among those that beckoned: Olympic Sporting Goods, Brockway Floral, Western Auto, Stevens Studios, Sirabella Studios, and the W.T. Grant Company. The Mayfair and Astoria restaurants served good food and provided a resting place for the weary.

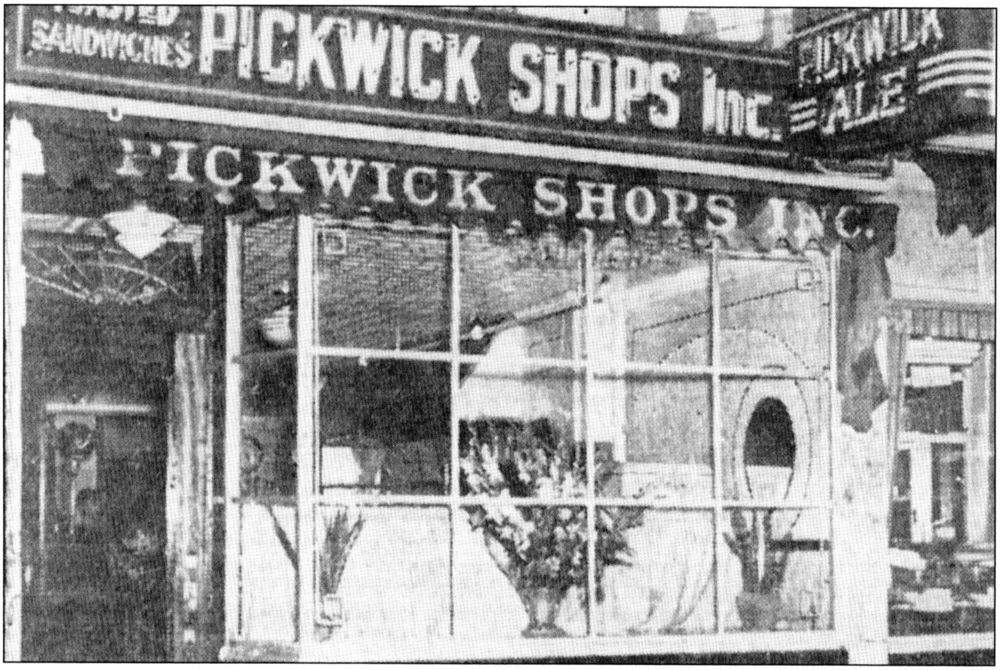

Before he opened the legendary Pilots Grill in 1940, Paul Zoidis ran the Pickwick, an all-night hamburger shop located at 22 Hammond Street. A three-egg breakfast with bacon, hash browns, and hot biscuits cost only 30¢. Sportswriter Bud Leavitt frequented "The Pick" and reminisced in 1990, "Each night, before and after the boxing and wrestling cards (at the Chateau across the street), the crowds met at the Pickwick. A nightcap then was coffee and a slab of homemade banana pie with a three-inch topping of whipped cream," all for 13¢. H.R. Stanhope and M.L. Leach owned the remodeled Pickwick after a fire in 1942, when this picture was published.

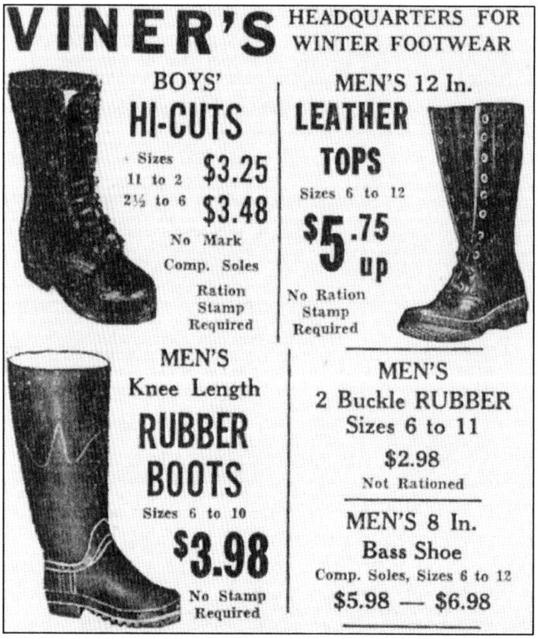

The Viner brothers operated a shoe factory in Bangor and had a retail shoe store on Pickering Square. Wartime prices seem low by today's standards. Sam Viner and his family later graduated to selling musical instruments, records, and sheet music on the square, eventually expanding to larger quarters on Broad Street.

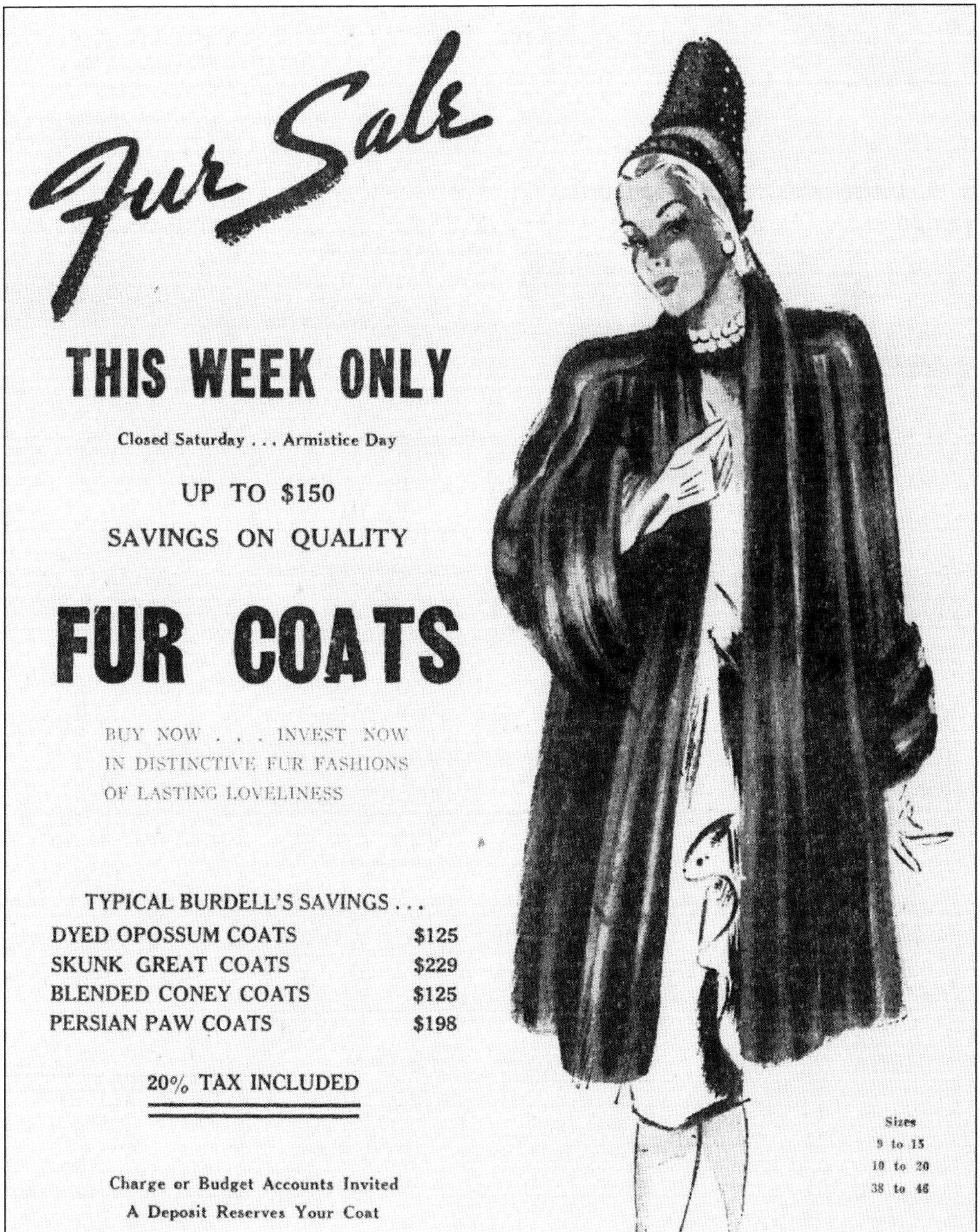

Changing fashion tastes and new attitudes in animal rights would render advertisements like this inappropriate today, but in November 1944 there was nothing out of place about a woman shopping for a dyed opossum coat, or a skunk great coat. Burdell's was long a favorite for fine women's clothing. Also popular was the Maine Fur Company at 66 State Street, which advertised itself with a trademark black bear walking across an outline of the state of Maine, with the motto "Furriers exclusively since 1901" printed underneath.

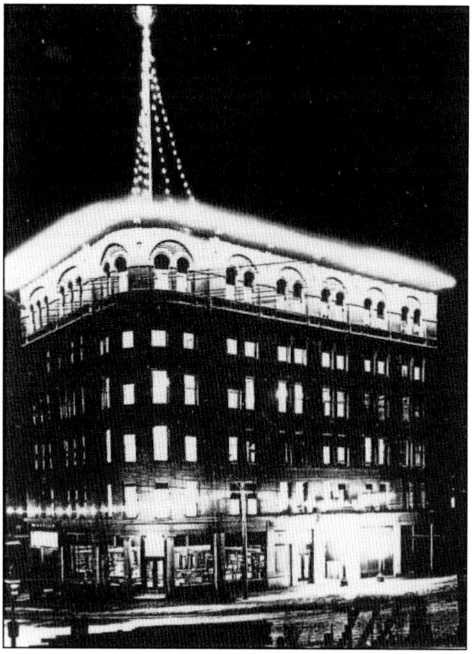

The Graham Building at night, shown here in *c.* 1925. This handsome block at Harlow and Central Streets rose out of the ashes of the Great Fire of 1911, which burned much of this section of downtown. The general offices of the Bangor and Aroostook Railroad were located upstairs for many years. On the first floor was the waiting room of the Bangor street railway, and later the Post Office Pharmacy.

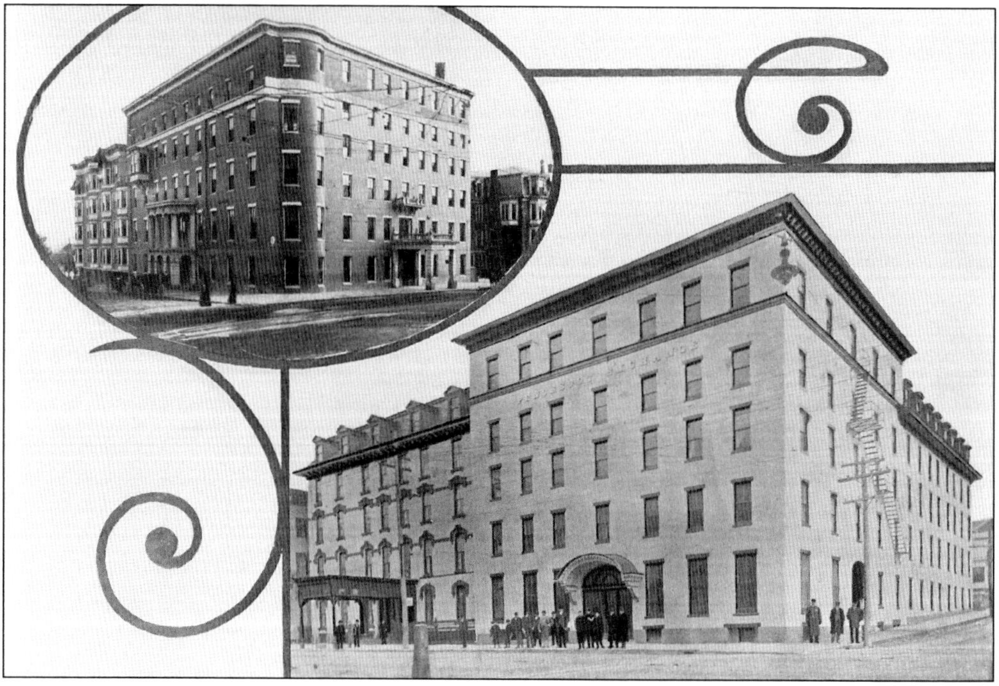

Bangor's two finest hotels accommodated many thousands of guests during the years they ruled downtown. The Bangor House (top) at Main and Union Streets opened in 1834 to immediate acclaim, putting up the rich and famous, and the ordinary traveler as well, for over a century. During many of the same years, the Penobscot Hotel was a fixture on working-class Exchange Street, catering to theater performers (the Bijou and Park Theaters were nearby), railroad travelers, and to an occasional celebrity such as Howard Hughes. Unlike the Bangor House, which has a new life as an apartment complex, the Penobscot was demolished in the 1960s.

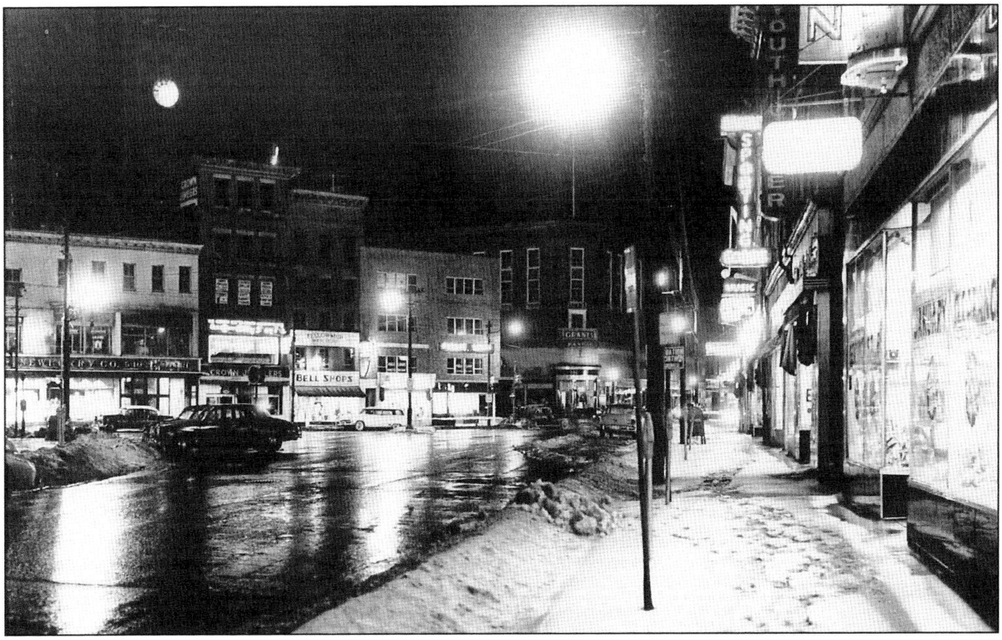

Photographer Dan Maher loved to take his camera out onto Bangor's wet, glistening streets at night and snap away. This study of West Market Square in the 1950s reveals the lighted clock tower of city hall (top left), the W.T. Grant building in the distance (center), and Dakin Sporting Goods (right). At the left is the J.J. Newberry Company in a wooden block that was razed because of a building ordinance that bans such construction downtown.

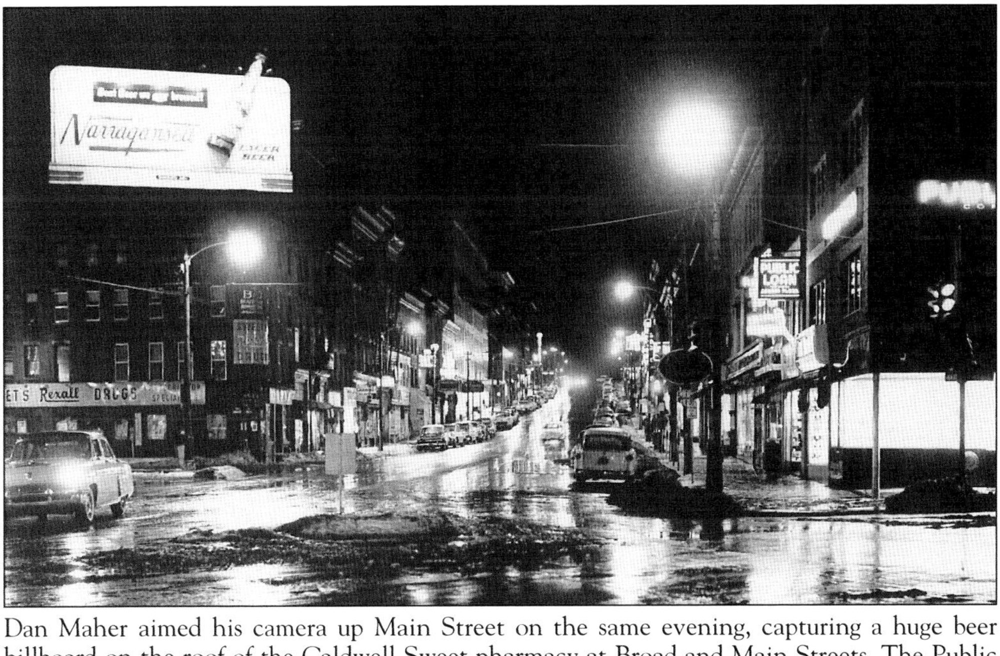

Dan Maher aimed his camera up Main Street on the same evening, capturing a huge beer billboard on the roof of the Caldwell Sweet pharmacy at Broad and Main Streets. The Public Loan Company is across the street. This part of downtown survived the ravages of the 1911 Fire, and as a result, some of the blocks date back to pre-Civil War times. The left side of the street, in particular, is a fascinating study in architectural styles.

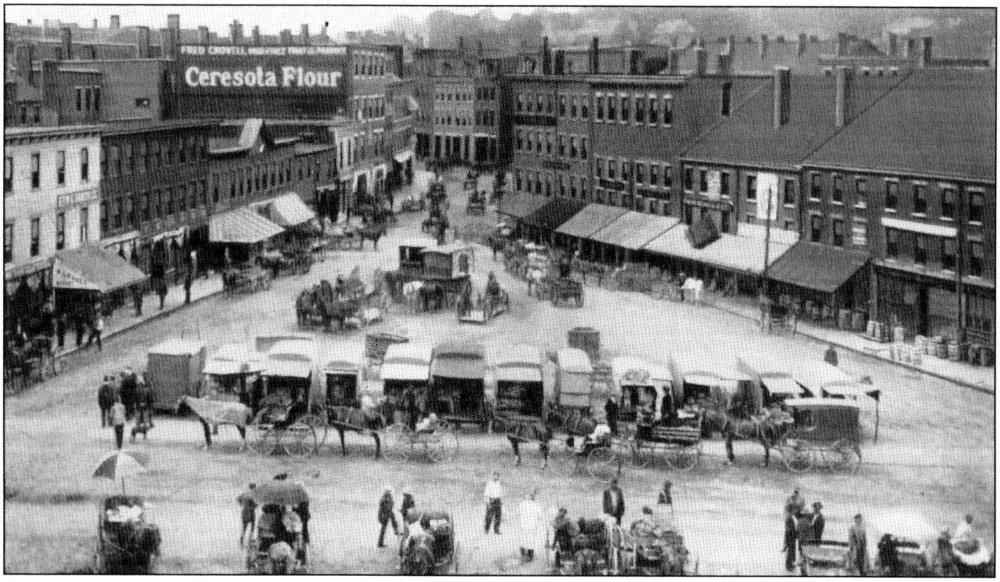

Every morning, often before the sun had even risen, merchants drove their wagons into Pickering Square and set up shop for the day. This was a very busy section of town, owing to its closeness to Main Street and other downtown districts. Many shoppers went to this square on foot. Today it is known as Pickering Plaza, a bricked park that showcases musicians and other entertainment in the summer. A large parking garage overlooks the area.

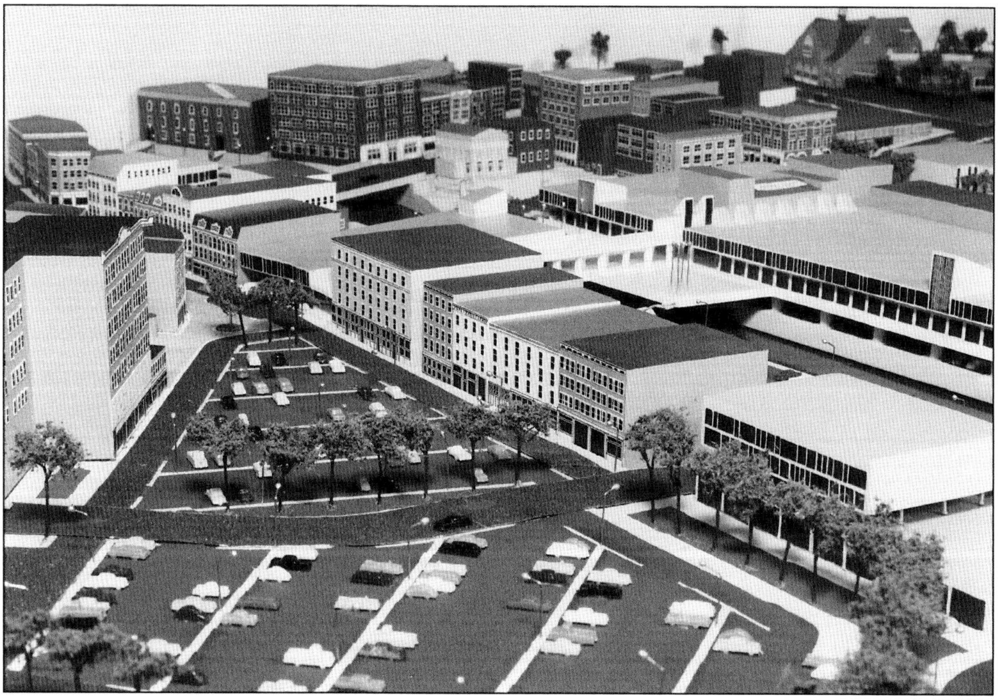

A scale model of the proposed new Pickering Square in modern times, created during the 1960s Urban Renewal era, isn't really close to today's plaza area. Pedestrians, not cars, occupy most of the square, and the large building at the right—a planned convention center, perhaps?—was never constructed. Bank buildings and the parking garage dominate the area today.

Nine

Women and Children First

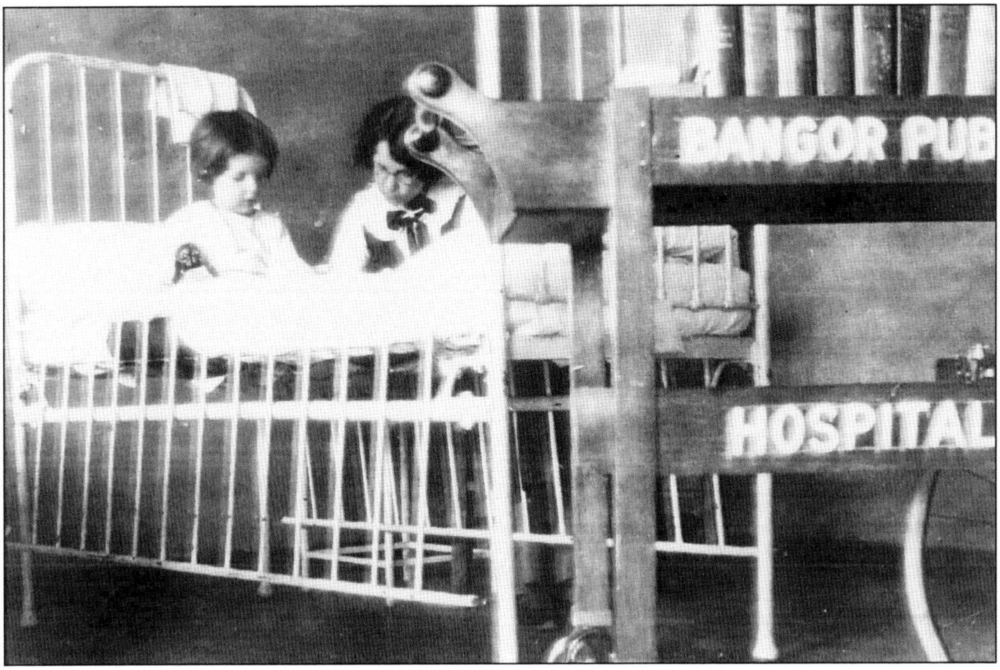

The Bangor Public Library book wagon began appearing at the old Eastern Maine General Hospital in 1925 as part of the library's extension service, founded the year before. Money from the Hill Fund was used to purchase books and magazines for patients like this young girl, shown with Pauline E. Tartre, director of the extension service. Miss Tartre began visiting the hospital once a week, increasing her visits to twice weekly to meet the demand. "Small girls enjoy reading stories which tell of the adventures of other little girls," noted a newspaper story. "For the tiny children there is a wide assortment of picture books." Boys preferred the stories of Richard Haliburton, and those dealing with sports.

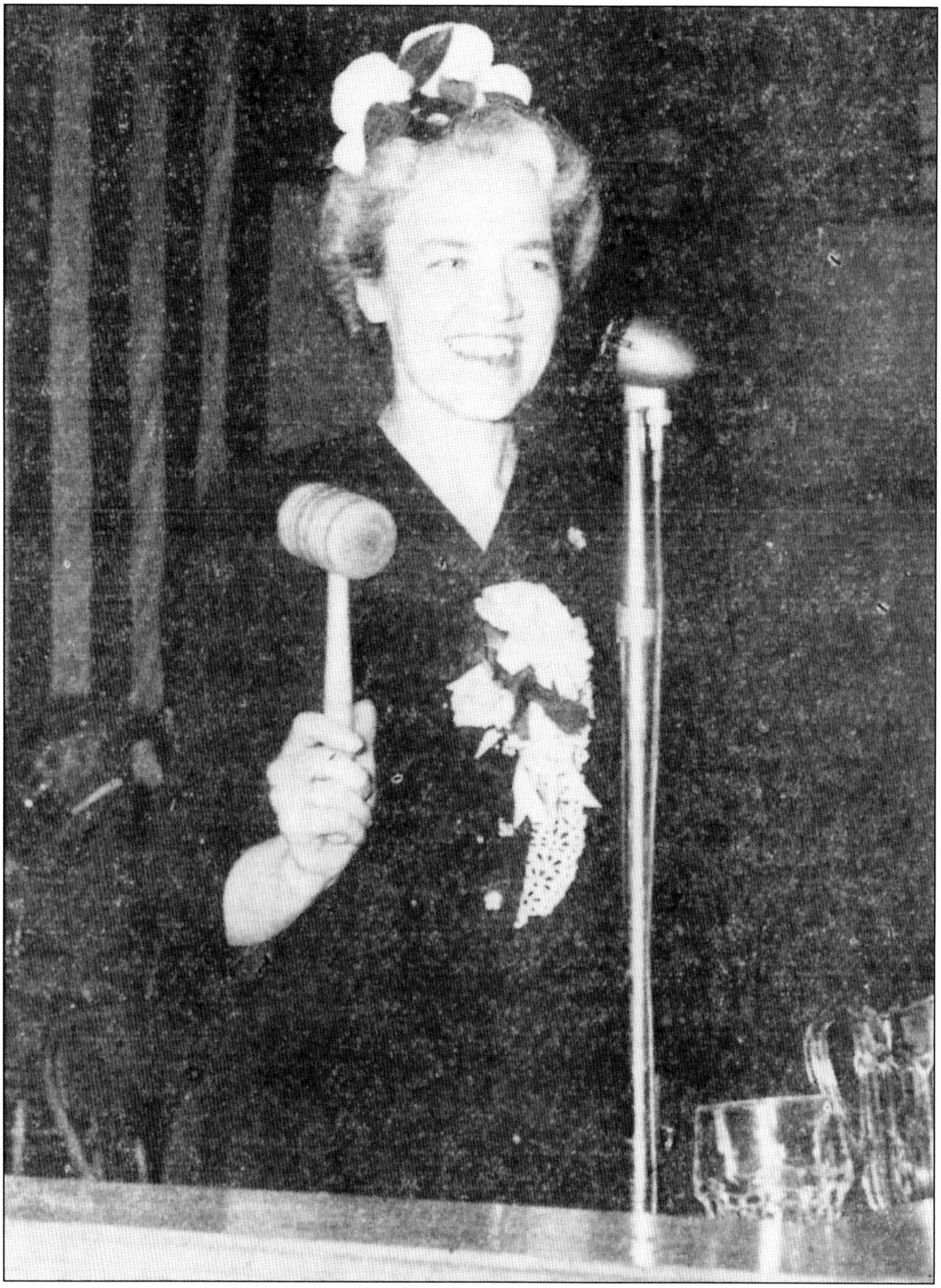

U.S. Representative Margaret Chase Smith raises the gavel and calls the Maine State Republican Convention to order in April 1944. The setting was the old Bangor Auditorium, which was filled with 1,685 delegates attending the opening ceremonies. Mrs. Smith was reported to be the first woman in Maine, and possibly the nation, to have achieved the honor of gaveling in a state political convention. She went on to be elected to the Senate, where she was long remembered for her faithful service and for the single red rose which she kept on her desk.

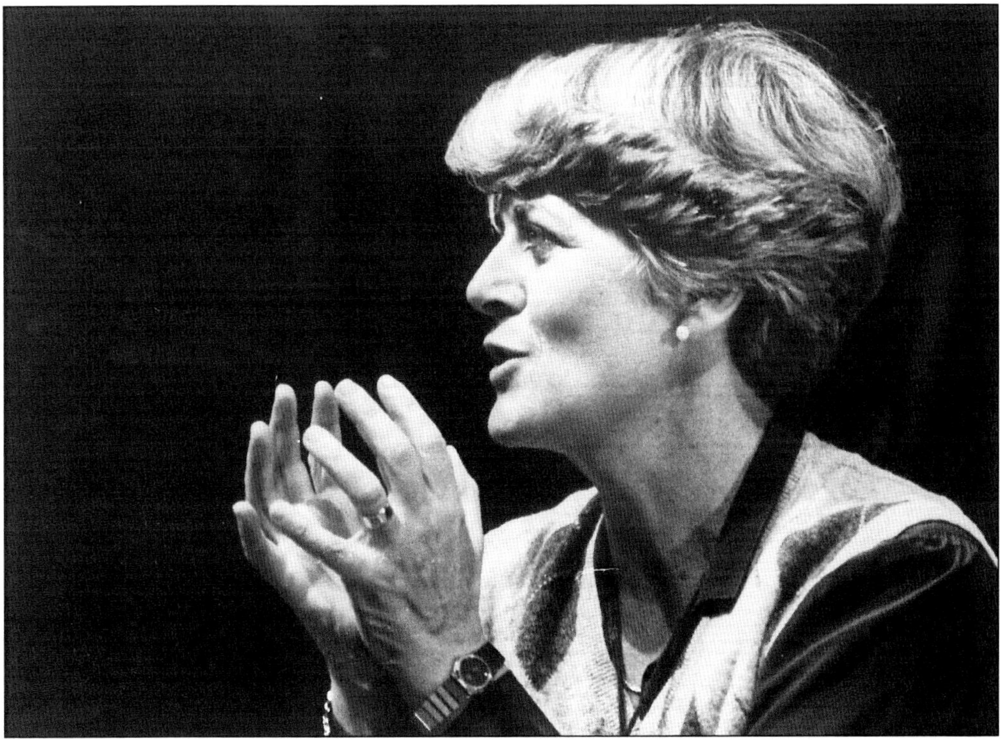

An overflow crowd at Bangor High School had an opportunity to see Geraldino Ferraro, Walter Mondale's running mate in 1984, up close and personal. The Democrat sat on the edge of the stage at the school's Peakes Auditorium and fielded questions from the audience, while outlining her strategy for victory (which wasn't successful, as she and Mondale lost to Ronald Reagan and George Bush in the November election). Ferraro was the first woman in American politics to run as a vice-presidential candidate.

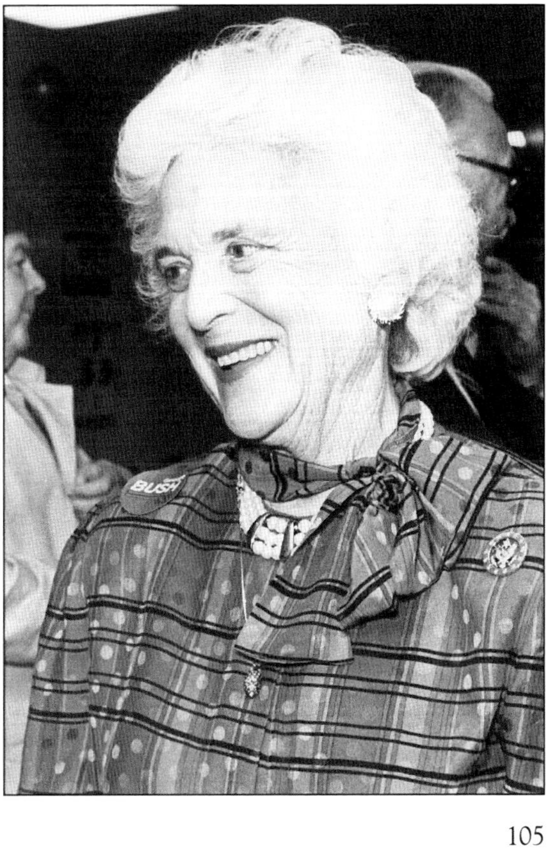

Barbara Bush has visited the city on several occasions. Here she campaigns for her husband, George Bush, appearing at a function held at the Holiday Inn on the Odlin Road. Most recently, the Bushes and Colin Powell spent a night in 1996 at the Ramada Inn when their flight bound for Europe developed mechanical problems. Early the next morning, George walked the 2 miles to the airport terminal, while Barbara and Colin chose to ride.

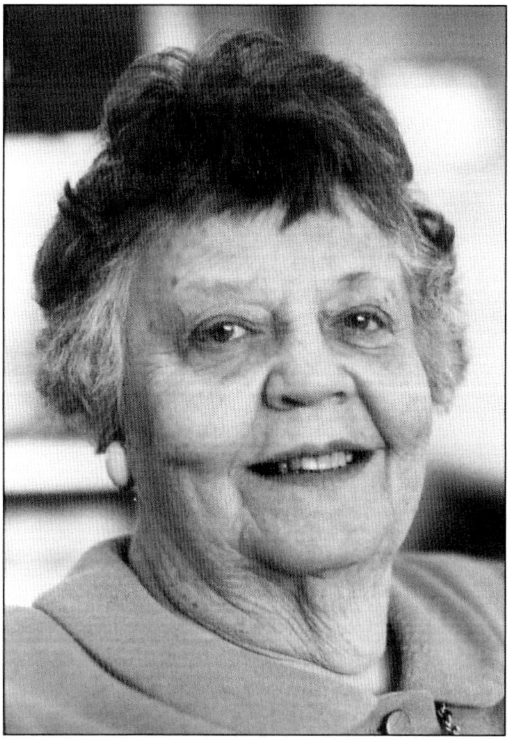

Lillian Wall (1904–1984) didn't let a physical disability (polio) stop her from improving the lives of the countless young students she taught in the Bangor school system. Her school for disabled children opened in 1935, and she also was a nationally recognized speech therapist. One of the Massachusetts native's favorite mottos was "Handicapped need self-respect."

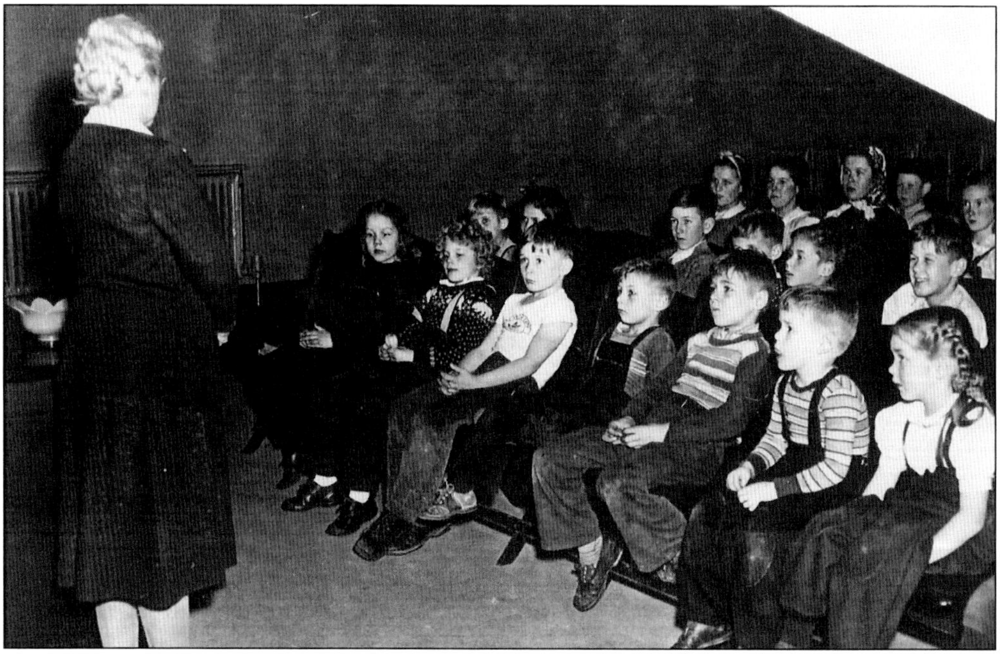

When Alice Wetherell Rice retired as the Bangor Public Library's children's librarian in 1953, a schoolboy reportedly asked, "Does this mean the library will have to close its doors?" Of course, the answer was no, but Mrs. Rice's contributions to the education of the young during her many story hours are legendary. The city's first children's librarian was succeeded by Helen Wheeler, and, in 1972, by Nancy Nichols.

Mary Savage Snow (1857–1924) is best known for the elementary school on Broadway that was named for her three years after her death. Few know the real story of this gifted woman, who advanced from being a grammar school principal to a school superintendent in the late nineteenth century. She also organized the Bangor Teachers Training School, the first such institution in Maine.

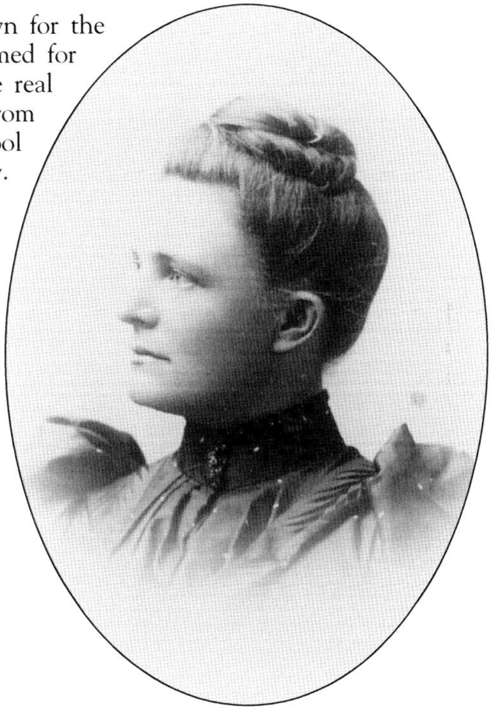

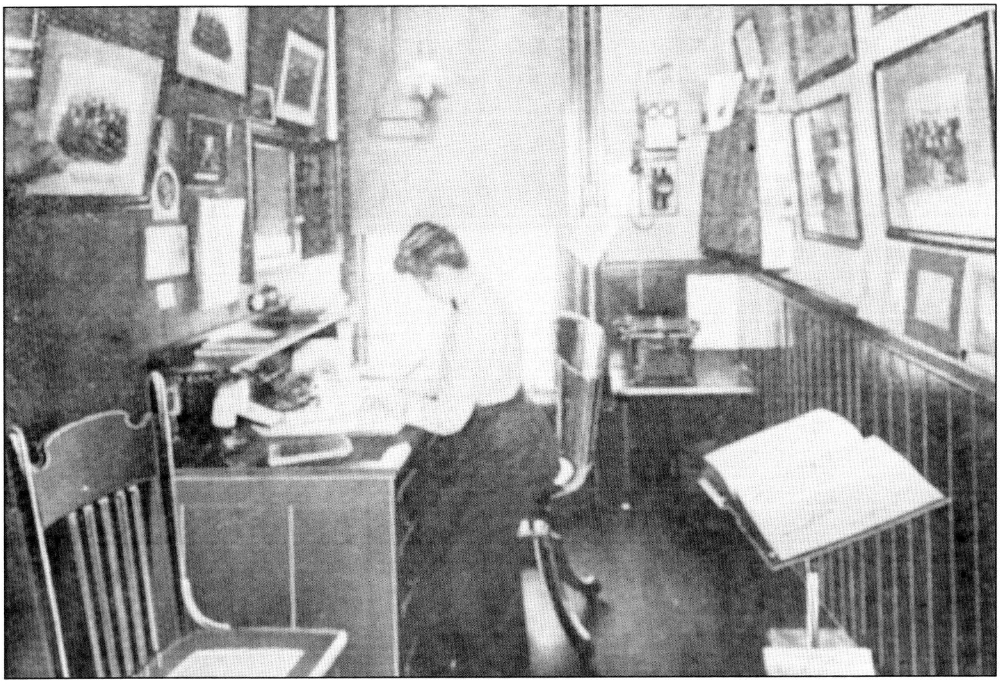

Another pioneer woman in local education was Miss Mary Beal, seen here in 1906 at her "school of shorthand and typewriting." At first the Norway, Maine native was affiliated with the Bangor Business College but later opened her own school in rooms on Columbia Street. The school was located at 9 Central Street for nearly forty years, eventually relocating to the former city farm buildings on lower Main Street.

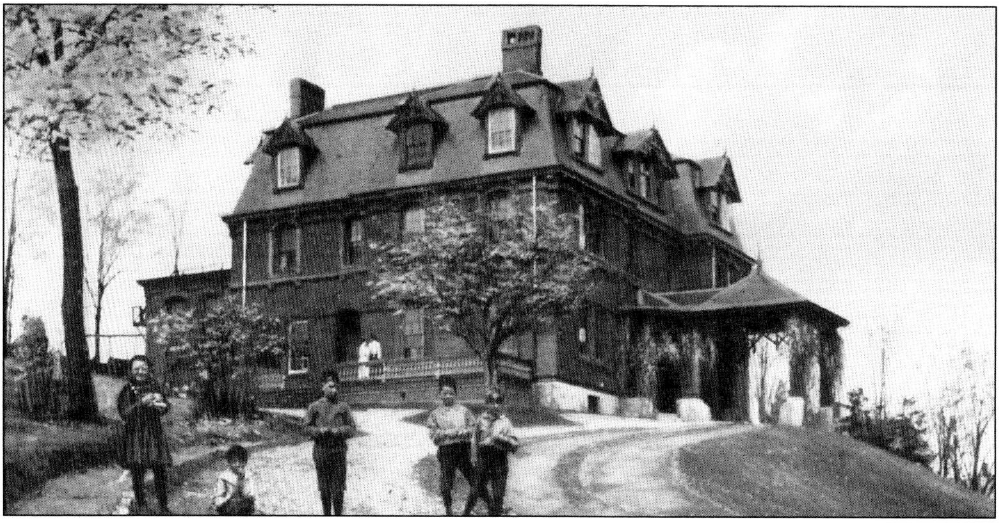

The Bangor Children's Home, high atop Thomas Hill near the Bangor Standpipe, was dedicated in 1869. It was the culmination of the city's generosity of spirit during the last century and housed as many as fifty children during World War II. Although many generous citizens opened their pocketbooks to keep the home going, it closed in 1975, as foster homes began caring for more of the needy children. It was converted to the Hilltop School and day care center.

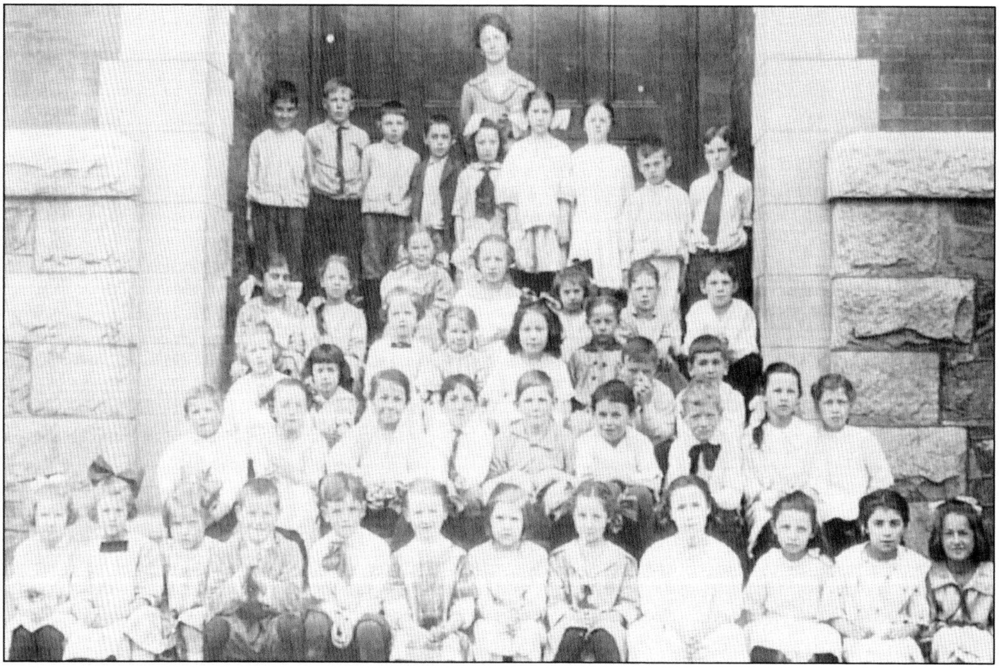

School portrait day was always an exciting occasion to dress in your finest and cleanest clothes and smile pretty for the photographer. This picture was believed to have been taken at the Hannibal Hamlin grammar school at Union and Fourth Streets. Future sisters-in-law Therma Perry and Ruth Fox are somewhere in the photograph. Ruth went on to become a veteran school teacher, especially remembered for teaching in Old Town, and in eighth-grade social studies at Garland Street Junior High School in Bangor.

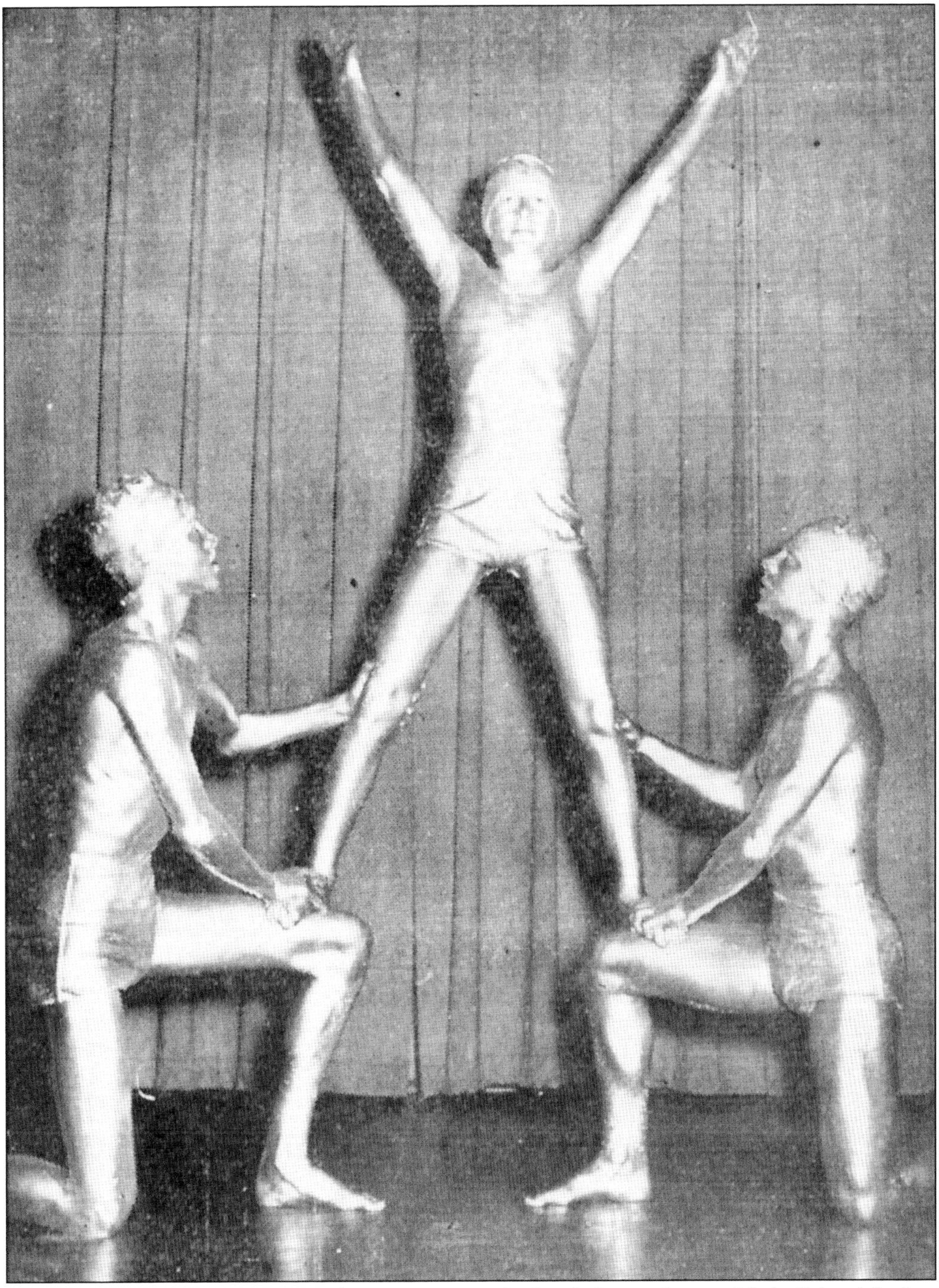

Human tableaus were an annual attraction at Garland Street Junior High School before health concerns ended the practice. Boys from the school's physical education classes, having coated themselves with red paint, appeared to be cast in bronze when viewed under specially prepared lighting. This 1942 performance featured, from left to right, James Prentiss, Harrison Homans, and Dick Faulkingham striking a silent pose. Another trio depicted the center jump in basketball.

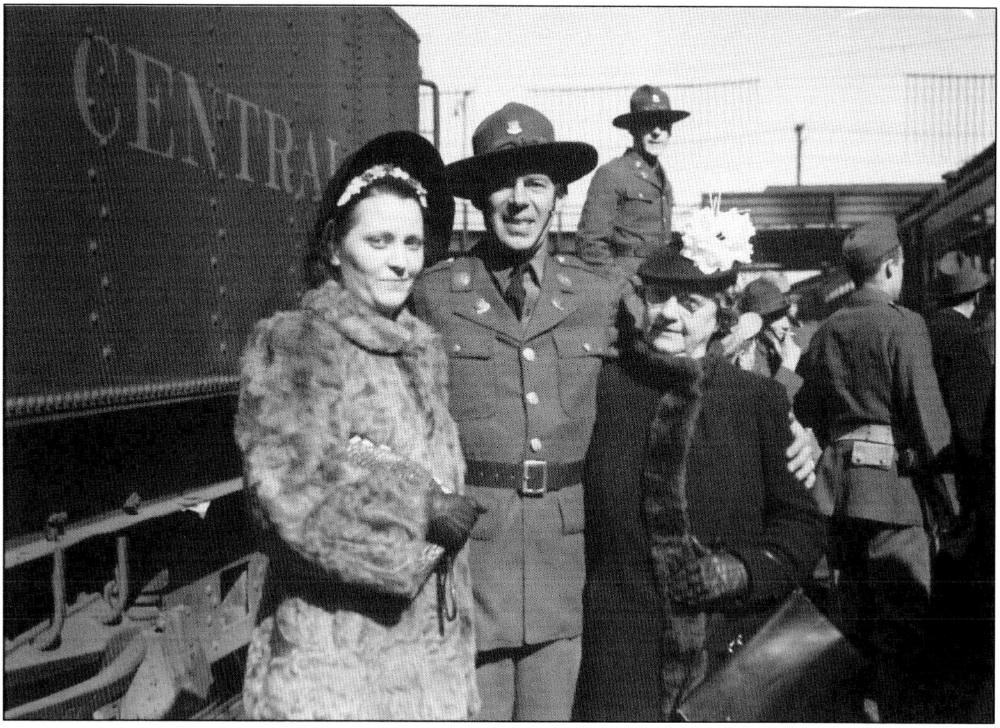

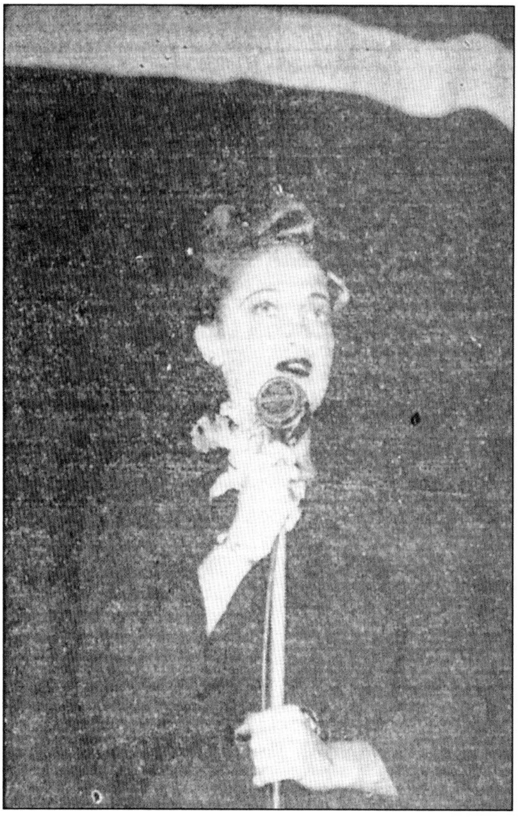

The names of this trio have been lost to time, but with a little imagination, one can guess the circumstances. Several hundred men from the Army National Guard left Union Station in March 1941 for duty that would for many include overseas combat. Mothers like the woman at the right, and young wives like the woman on the left, bid loved ones goodbye. Everyone tried hard not to cry. A few actually succeeded.

Movie star Dorothy Lamour hosted a War Bond rally at the auditorium in 1942. Having been credited with selling more than $24 million worth of bonds during her three tours across the nation, Lamour filled the Bangor Auditorium with eager contributors like Captain Calvin Knaide, who presented her with a $1,000 check from the Bangor Police Relief Association. The actress' visit is recounted in whimsical fashion in a story by Maine essayist E.B. White.

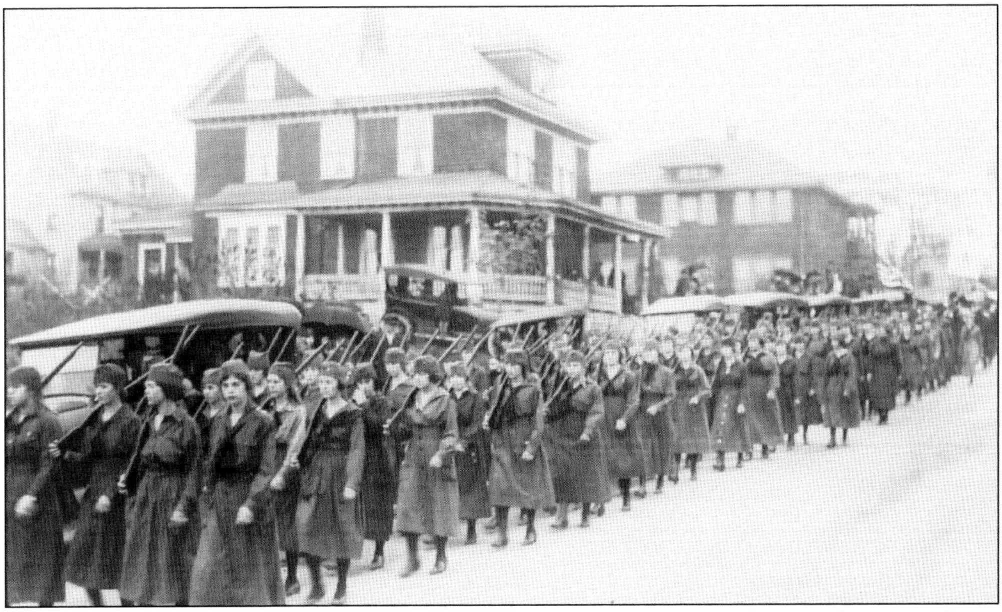

Look closely and you'll see that these troops are women, not men, marching in formation down Somerset Street. World War I saw service by many women, both at home and abroad. Some were nurses. Study the young faces of these people; many look no older than teen-agers. The photograph's date isn't known, but the weight of the clothing and the leafless trees suggest it was taken on the original Armistice Day, November 11, 1918, when the "war to end all wars" actually ended.

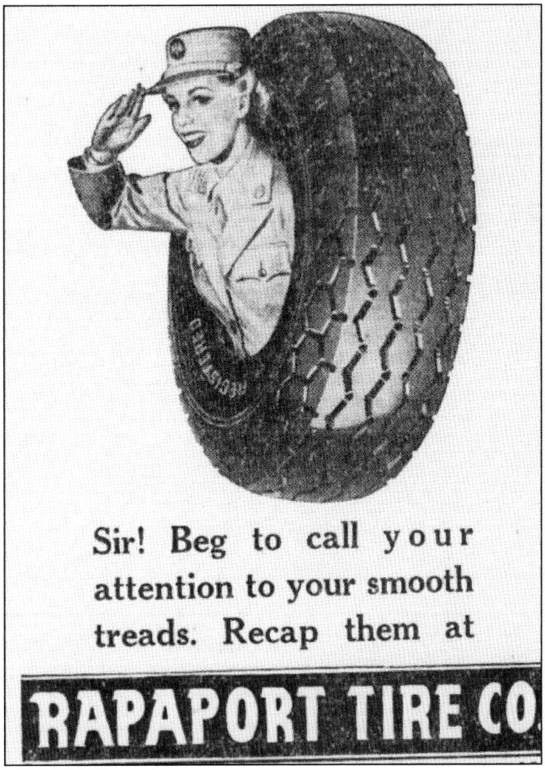

World War II was drawing to a close in January 1945, but newspaper advertisements such as this were still needed to boost morale and conserve on war materials. By then, Americans were used to seeing women in uniform. In fact, they were often used as promotional props. The Rapaport Tire and Auto Company remained on Oak Street for decades after the war's end.

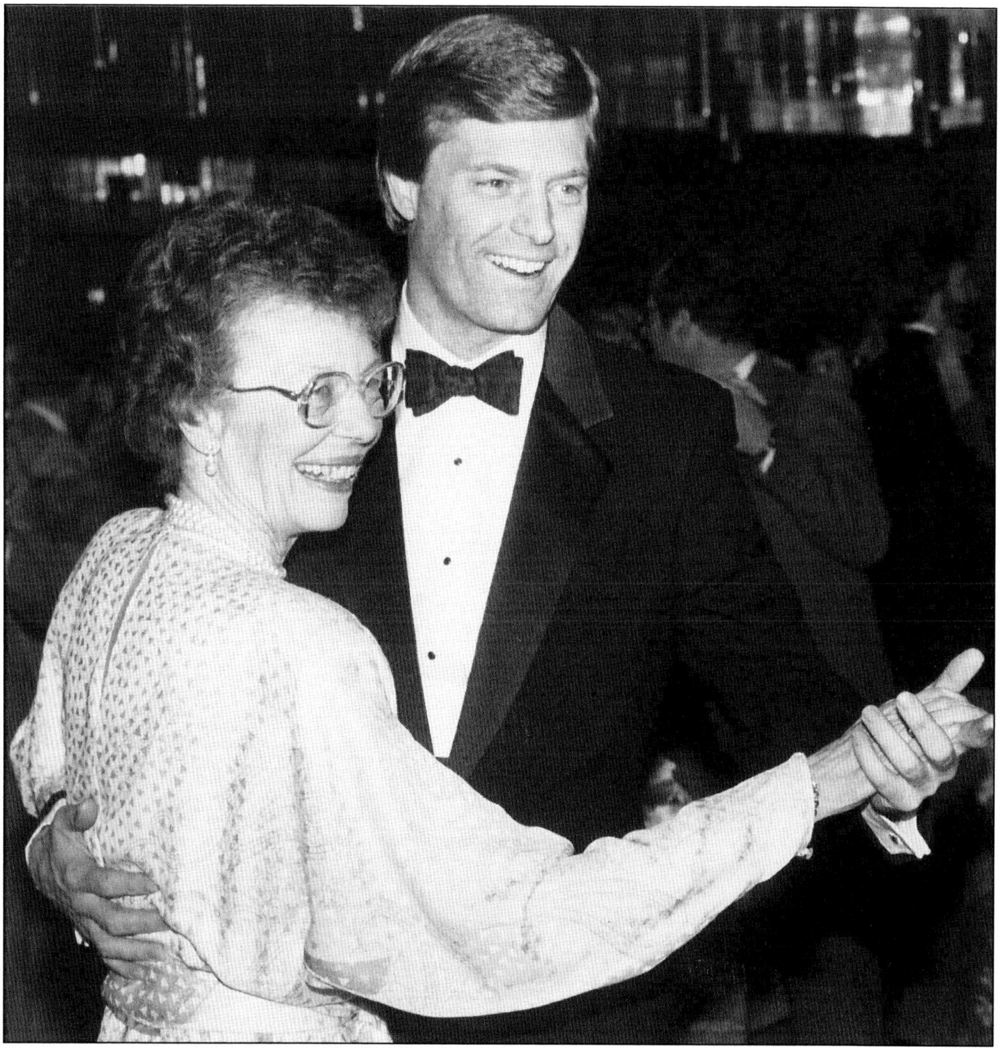

John R. McKernan Jr. and his mother Barbara share a dance at an inaugural ball in Augusta when the Bangor native was governor. Barbara watched proudly as her first-born son was elected to the Maine Legislature, then went on to Washington as his state's First District congressman. "Jock" was twice elected governor, during which time he married U.S. Representative Olympia Snowe, a future senator. In 1964, when Jock was fifteen and his brother Bobby was eleven, Barbara (Guild) McKernan, at age forty-four, was widowed suddenly. She went on to publish two Old Town newspapers, and was elected to the Bangor City Council. She has been described as a "politician, publisher, gardener, golfer, marketer, and mother."

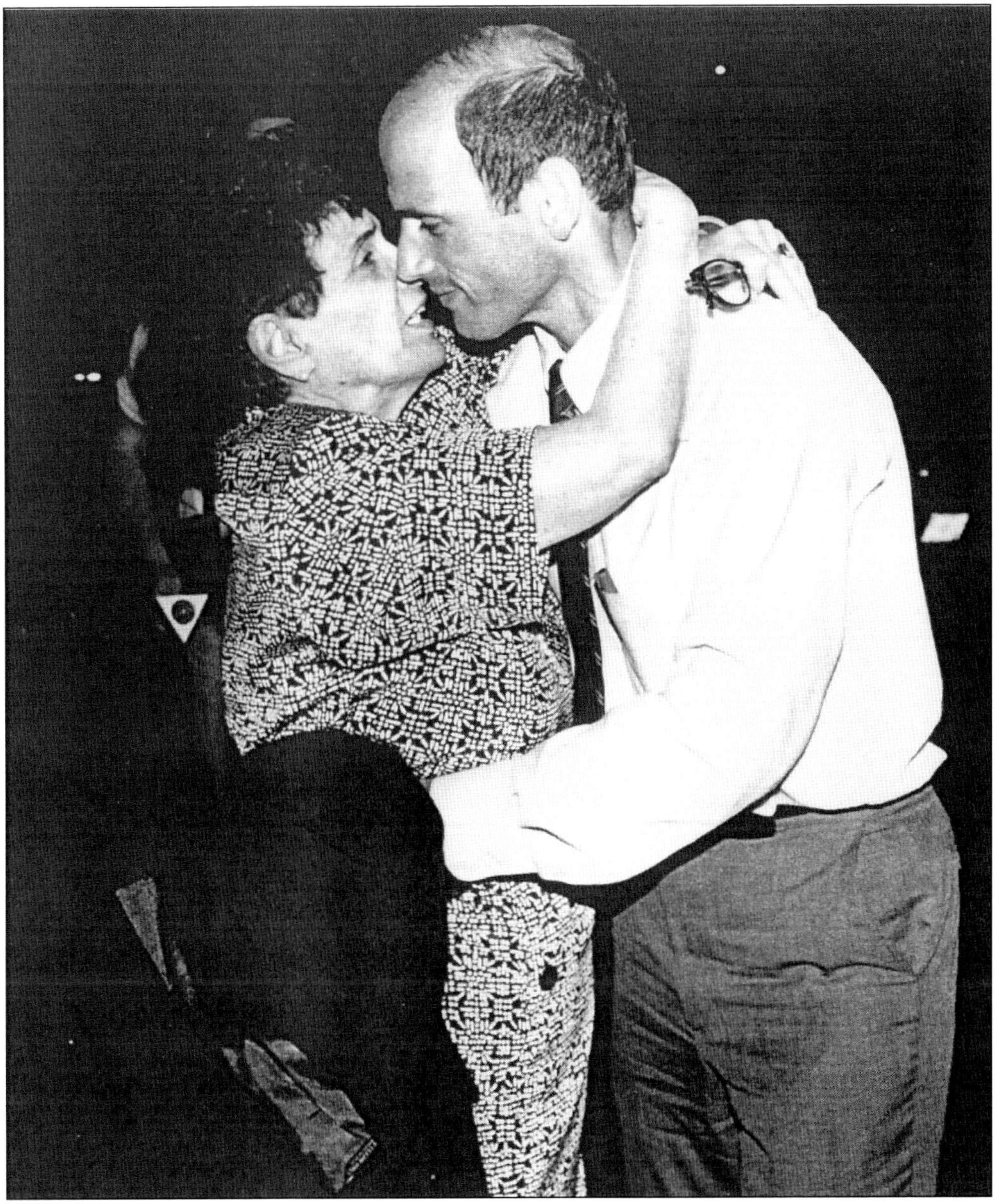

Another mother and son celebrate political victory in Bangor on the night of June 14, 1994. John Baldacci (right) and his mother Rosemary appeared at a party in his honor after he won the Democratic primary race for the Second District to the Congress. Rosemary celebrated again in November when Baldacci won the House seat, continuing a family tradition in Democratic politics that included his late father Robert, and Robert's brother Vasco. Mrs. Baldacci, the mother of eight children, is the namesake of Momma Baldacci's, an Italian restaurant that succeeded the family's Old Baltimore restaurant "under the bridge" in downtown Bangor.

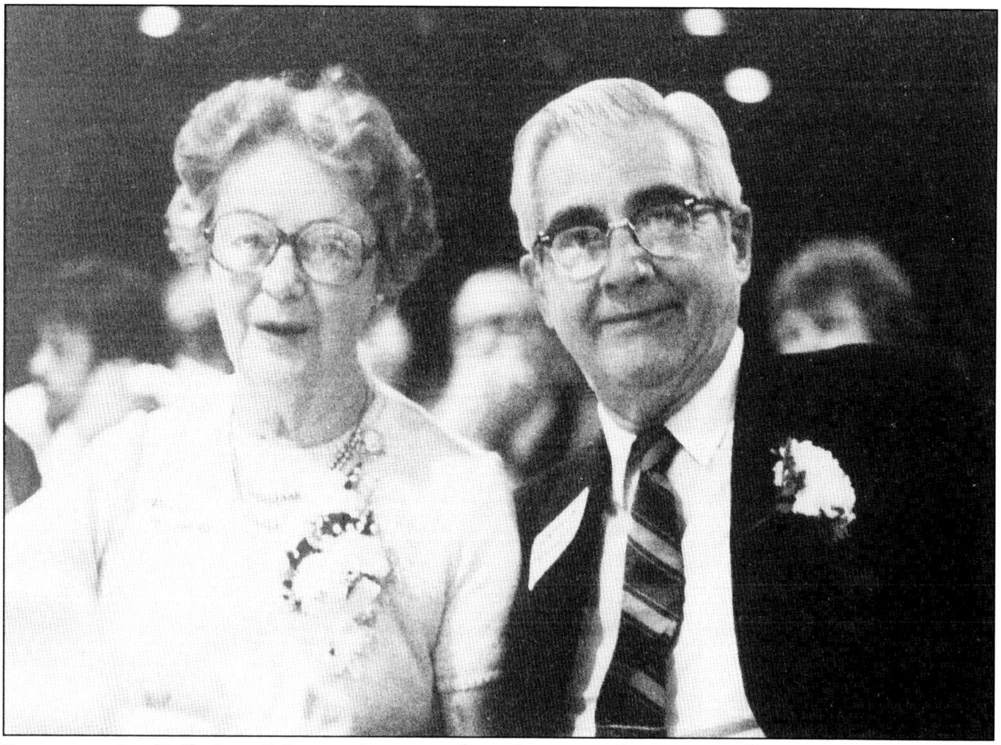

Bangor native Polly Lynch began dancing when she was only sixteen. She went on to become a professional dancer, choreographer, dance teacher, and publicist. Along with her husband and business partner, Arthur, Polly Thomas operated a school of dance in an old home on lower Broadway. She could be a strict teacher, but was always fair and never mean.

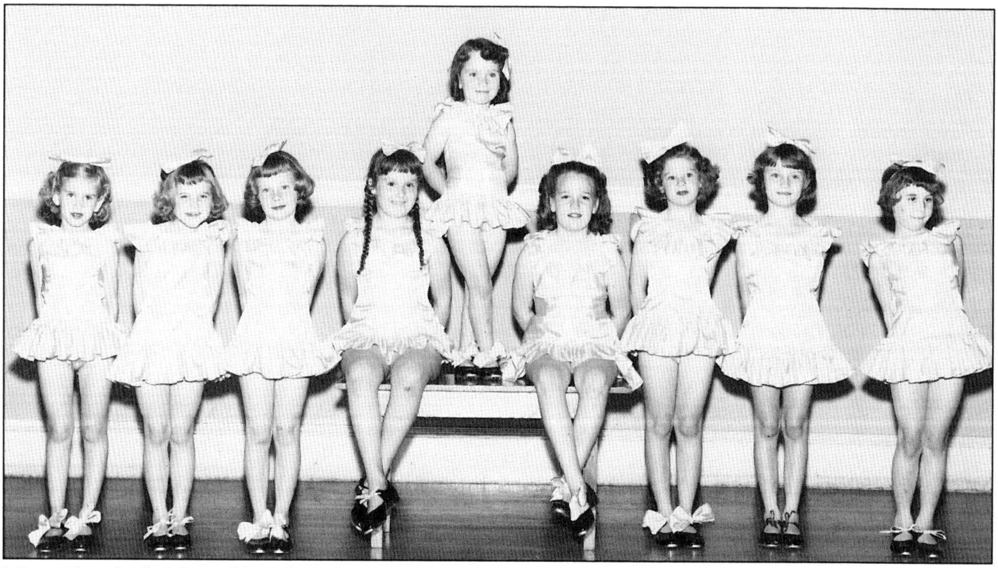

Many local children like those pictured here in the early 1950s studied under the tutelage of Polly Thomas and other Bangor dance teachers. Thomas even staged performances of Tchaikovsky's *Nutcracker*, still a perennial favorite with audiences. Studios for tap dancing, and later gymnastics, have also attracted young students.

Ten

What We Lost, What We Saved

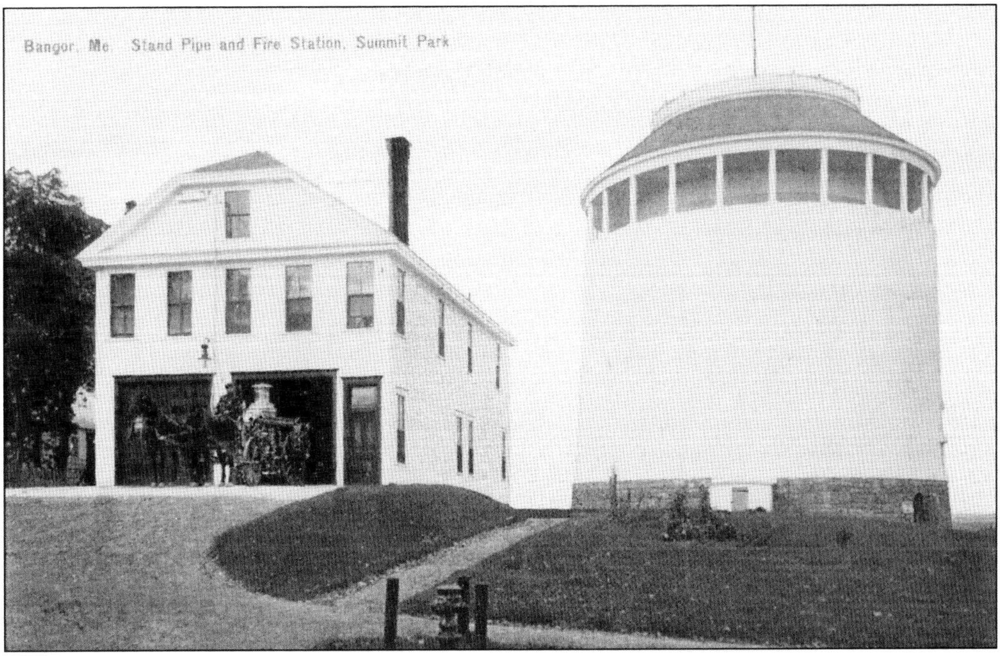

The Bangor Standpipe, the large circular tower at the right, is a survivor. The Thomas Hill Hose House to the left is not. In fact, the fire station has been missing for so many years it's hard to imagine Thomas Hill and Summit Park with it still being there. Both structures were built in 1897 (the Standpipe being completed in 1898). At first, this seemed like a fine place for a firehouse, close to the West Side neighborhoods, but in the days of horse-drawn fire apparatus, hills were torture for the animals. The station was eventually demolished but the gleaming white water tower and the Joseph Low House nearby, both well restored, continue to connect the city with its rich past.

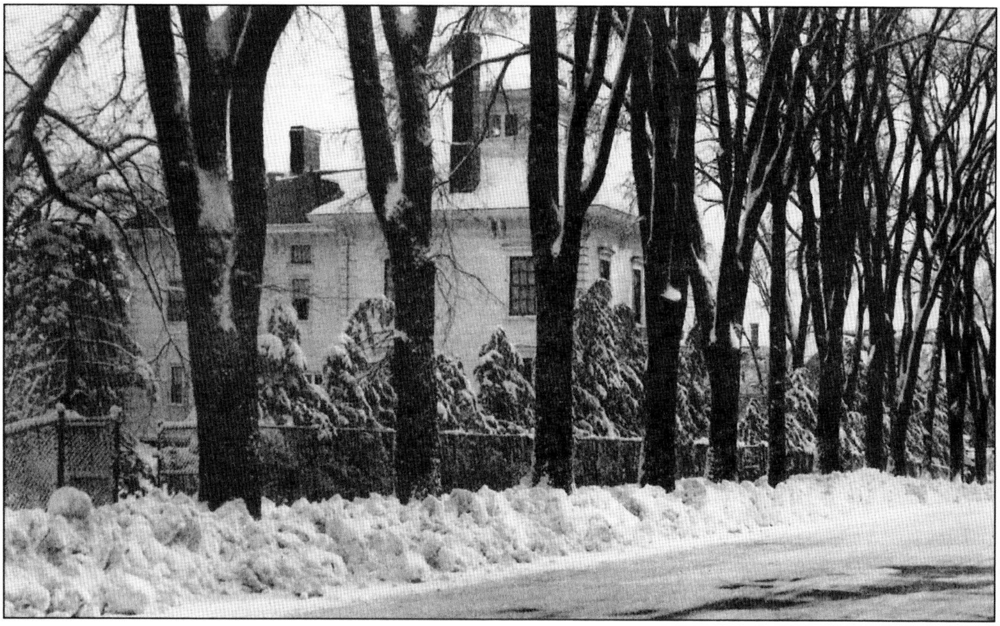

Marion J. Bradshaw, a professor at Bangor Theological Seminary, photographed this scene in the winter of 1944 for his book, *The Nature of Maine*, maybe never imagining the extent to which Union Street would change over time. While the large Victorian house (built in 1854, the Joseph C. Stevens House has been a funeral home for years) still stands, the long row of stately elms has vanished, victims of the Dutch elm disease that has ravaged all but a few of the city's elms.

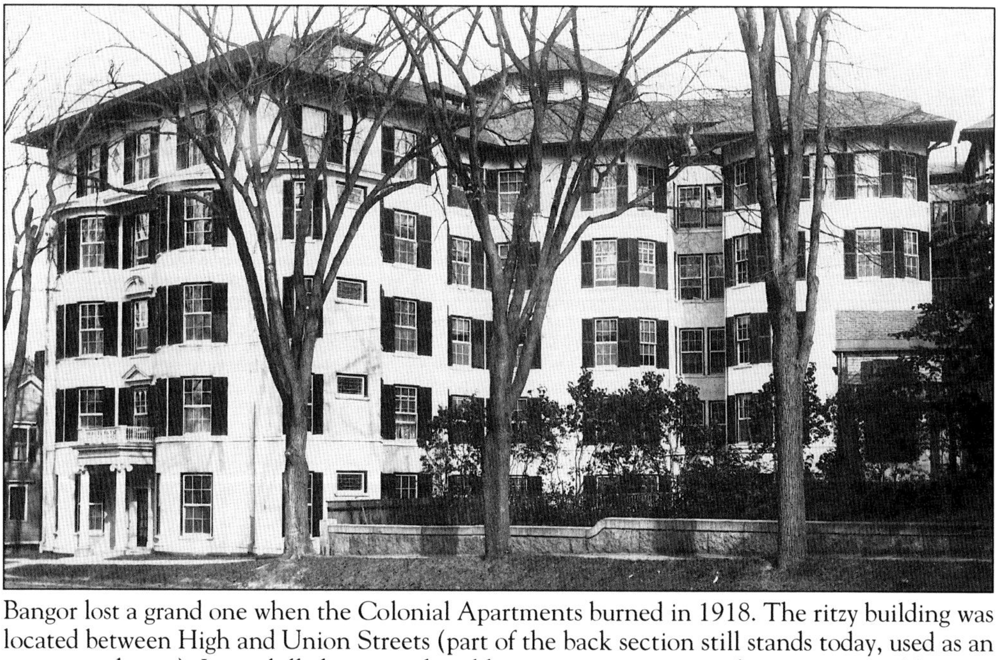

Bangor lost a grand one when the Colonial Apartments burned in 1918. The ritzy building was located between High and Union Streets (part of the back section still stands today, used as an apartment house). It was billed not as a hotel but an apartment complex containing fifty-nine suites of two to five rooms and a dining room where residents took their meals. Even before the fire, the business was failing as the concept didn't catch on in such a small city.

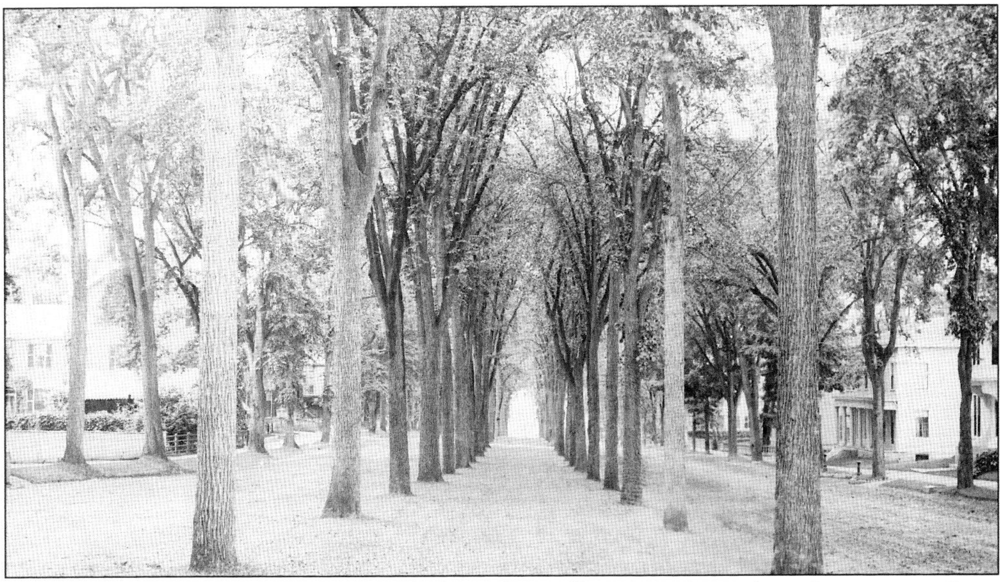

Once, a canopy of elm trees extended along the mall on Broadway, from Somerset to State Streets. Carefully planted in perfect symmetry by nineteenth-century planners, the elms are all gone today. Disease claimed these trees, like so many others in the city. At one time the city undertook a spraying program. Crews would fire high-pressure insecticides at the trees. But under protest from residents with environmental concerns the practice was abandoned. After that even healthy elms were destroyed to stop the spread of the Dutch elm beetle.

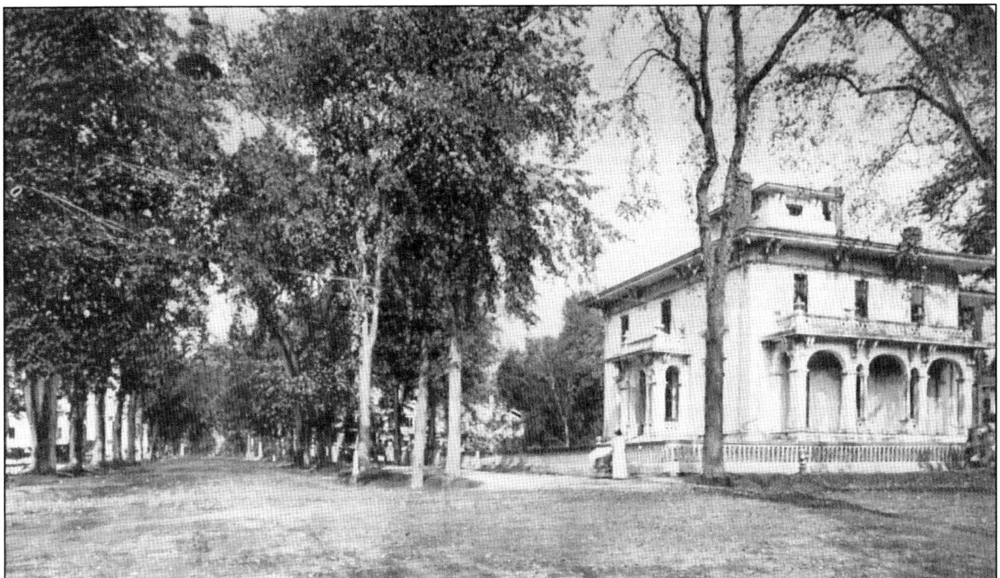

The trees aren't all that are missing from this picture. Bangor also lost a lovely old mansion at Broadway and Somerset Streets. It was built for Ephraim Paulk in 1854, the same year it was valued at an astonishing $10,000, a lot of money in those days. Two other notables also lived here in the nineteenth century: bank president George K. Jewett, and Charles Stetson, a prominent lumberman. The house's crowning glory was its ornate trim, making it seem even larger than it was. It was demolished in 1968.

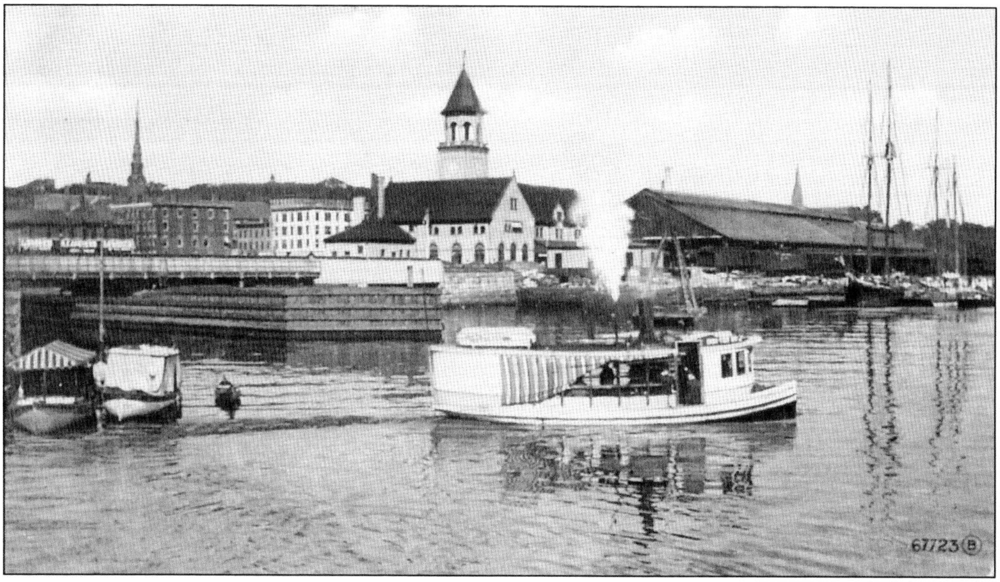

This 1922 penny postcard shows the City Point area of Bangor that once stood on Exchange Street and part of Washington Street. Fondly remembered today, in its own time—dating well back into the 1800s—it was a wide-open conglomeration of bars, brothels, boarding houses, hotels, and legitimate businesses. In the middle of it all was Union Station, built in 1907, a victim of the 1960s Urban Renewal demolition era. One of the *Bon Ton* ferries steams by, leaving in its wake a canoe and two smaller vessels at the left. Schooners are tied up to a Bangor wharf at the right.

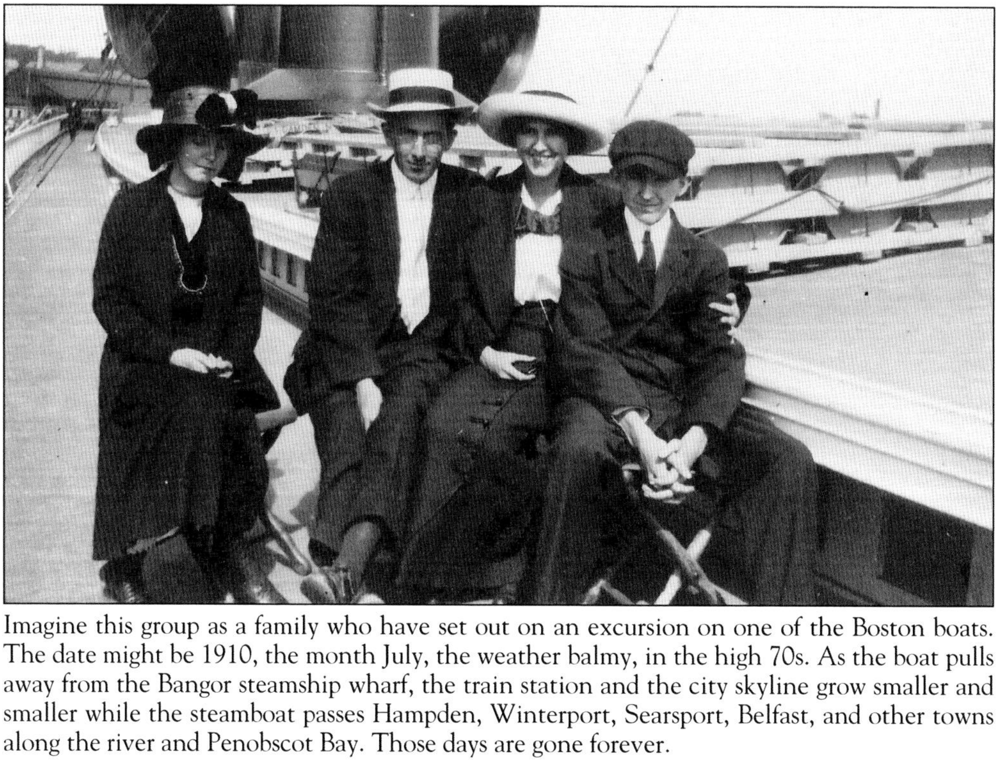

Imagine this group as a family who have set out on an excursion on one of the Boston boats. The date might be 1910, the month July, the weather balmy, in the high 70s. As the boat pulls away from the Bangor steamship wharf, the train station and the city skyline grow smaller and smaller while the steamboat passes Hampden, Winterport, Searsport, Belfast, and other towns along the river and Penobscot Bay. Those days are gone forever.

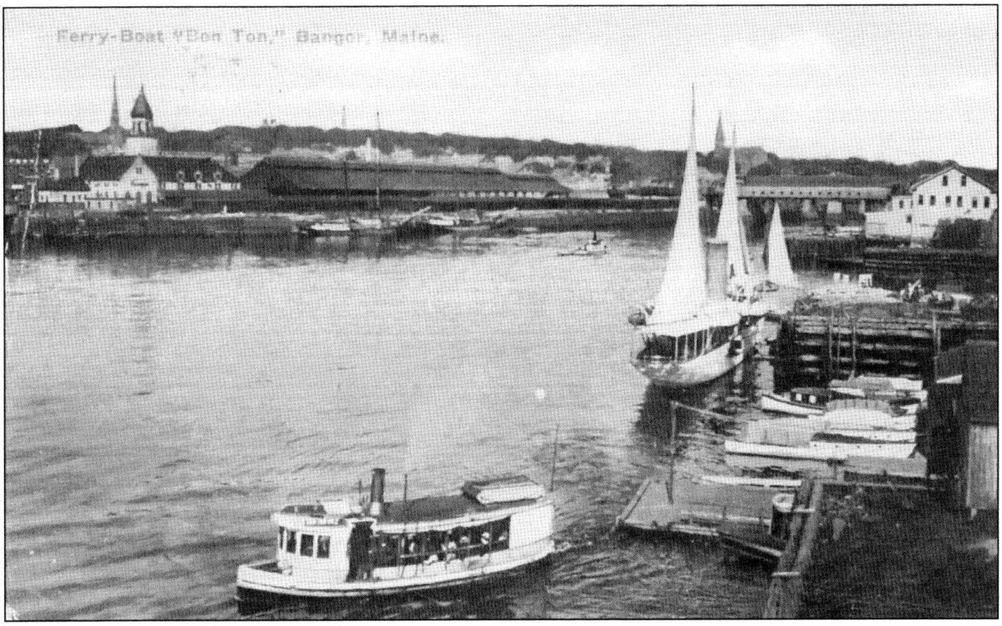

So many things in this early picture postcard don't exist today, it's hard to know where to begin identifying them all. The stately Union Station was razed in 1961 (its bell tower is at the far left, to the right of a church spire); part of the long wooden covered bridge that connected Bangor with Brewer (right) washed away in 1902, and the rest was removed in 1912; and the vessels on the river—the lovely yacht and the steam-powered *Bon Ton II*—will never again grace the Penobscot.

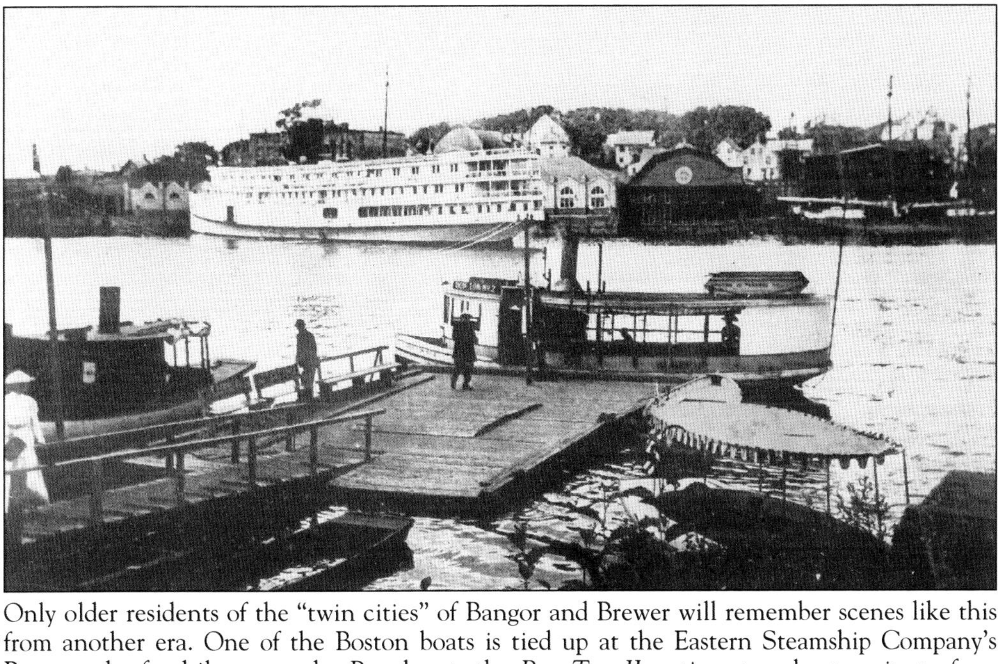

Only older residents of the "twin cities" of Bangor and Brewer will remember scenes like this from another era. One of the Boston boats is tied up at the Eastern Steamship Company's Bangor wharf, while across the Penobscot, the *Bon Ton II*, a tiny steamboat, waits to ferry passengers over to Bangor. The last of the Boston boats ended with the *Belfast*'s final run in 1935, and the last of the three *Bon Ton* vessels burned in 1939.

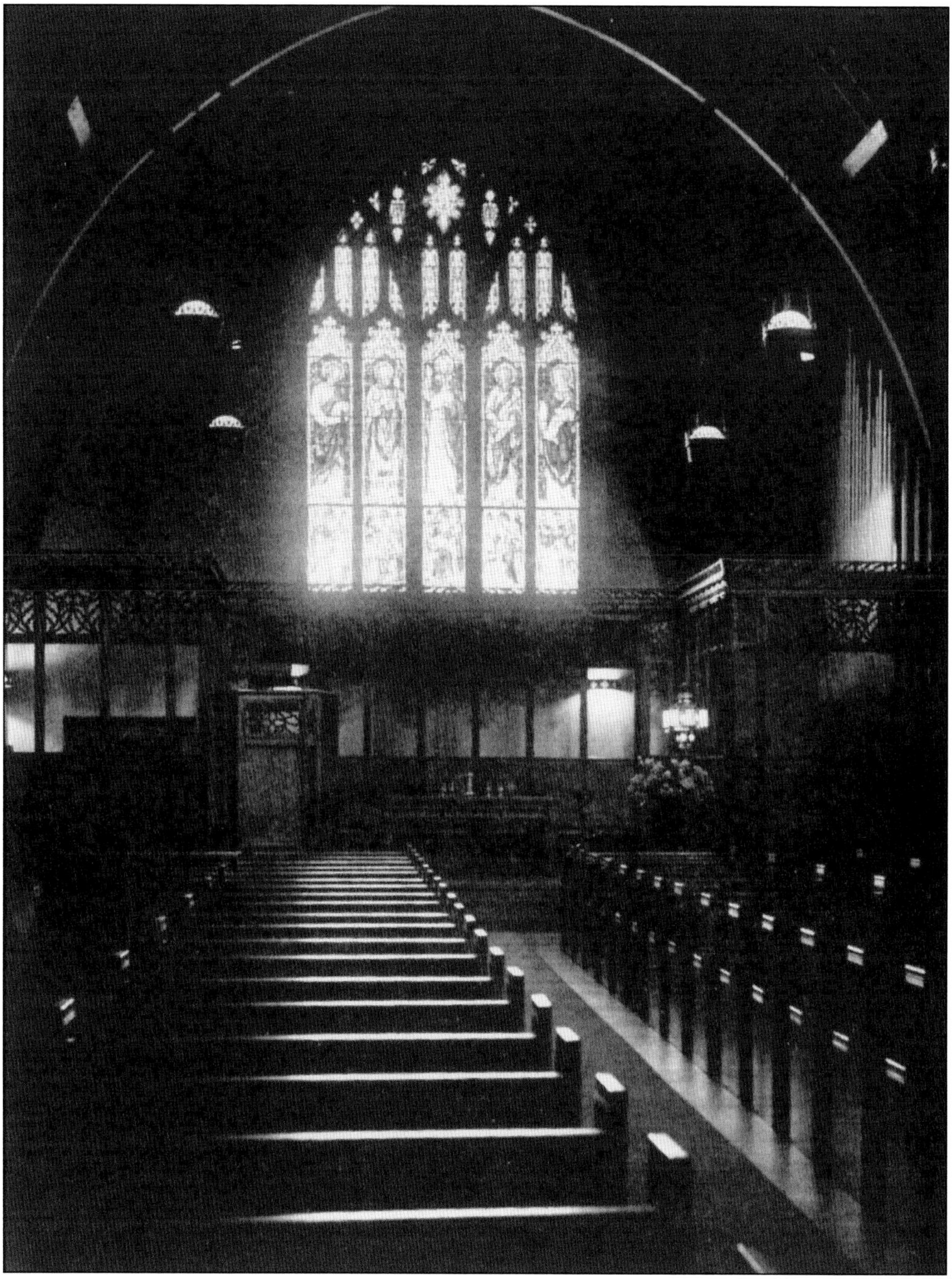

The interior of All Souls Congregational Church has inspired generations of worshippers since it rose from the ashes of the 1911 Bangor Fire. Theologian Marion J. Bradshaw took this study of the church in 1941 and wrote these words in his book, *The Maine Land*: "[The church] . . . is the artistic creation of Ralph Adams Cram, the recognized leader of the Gothic Renaissance in American religious and academic architecture. The windows from the Connick Studios include some of the finest effects achieved in recent American work in colored glass. . . ."

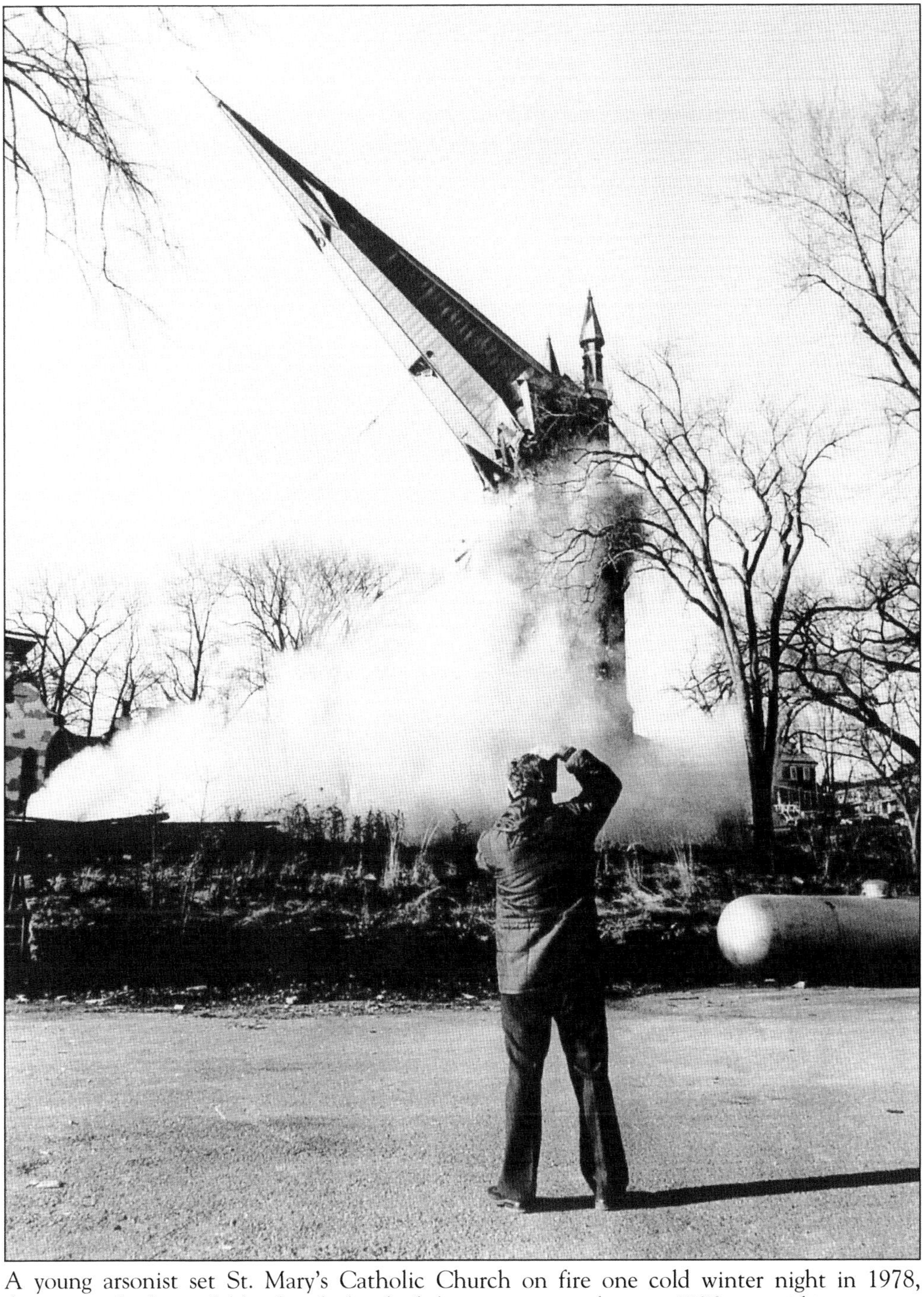

A young arsonist set St. Mary's Catholic Church on fire one cold winter night in 1978, destroying the beautiful landmark that had thrown open its doors in 1873 to parishioners west of the Kenduskeag Stream. The badly gutted building, including the 180-foot spire (shown here being photographed by Dan Maher), was taken down when it was determined it could not be saved. Part of the old building lives on, however, in the new St. Mary's on Ohio Street, which incorporated the old stained glass in its own windows.

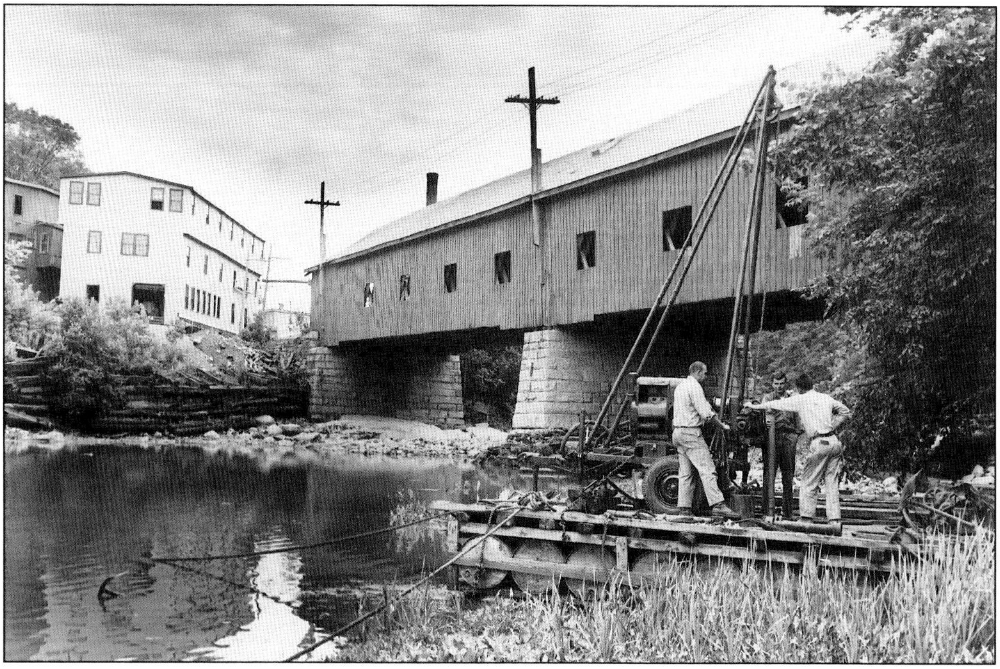

Engineers take the soundings in the Kenduskeag Stream for the new Valley Avenue bridge, July 1960. The men were not able to keep the 1882 Morse Covered Bridge in its original location. Efforts to relocate it upstream within sight of the Interstate 95 overpass were rejected by Maine Department of Transportation officials who cited highway hazards from motorists above who might stop their cars in busy traffic to photograph the bridge.

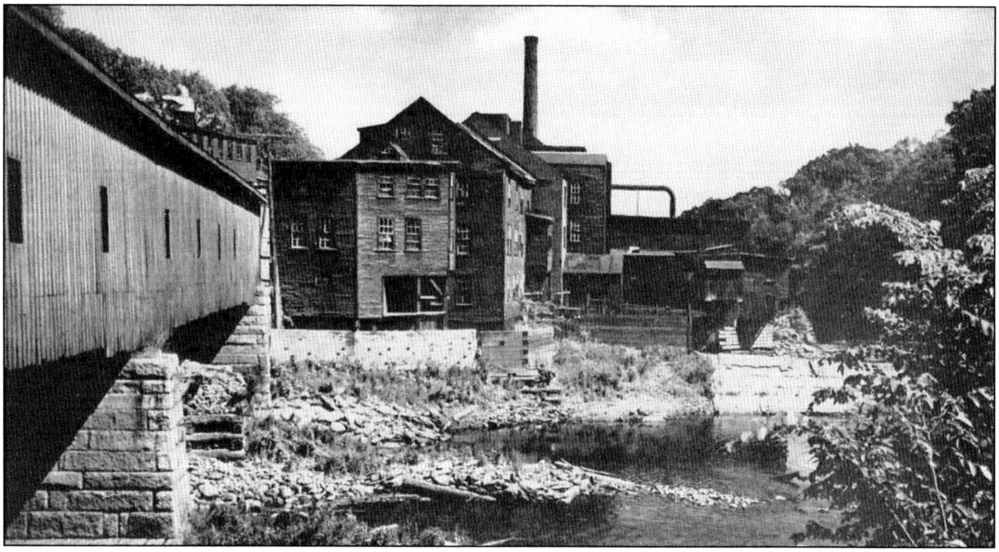

This scene from the 1940s, taken by Marion J. Bradshaw, shows the bridge and the Morse's Mill for which it was named. At one time it was the only covered bridge located within the boundaries of an American city. The old mill is gone along with the bridge. A minor preservation battle in the 1970s failed to save a remaining building on the property and it was razed to construct a parking lot. In the late nineteenth and early twentieth centuries, this was a very busy section of Bangor since another mill, the S.A. Maxfield Tannery Company, was located down the road.

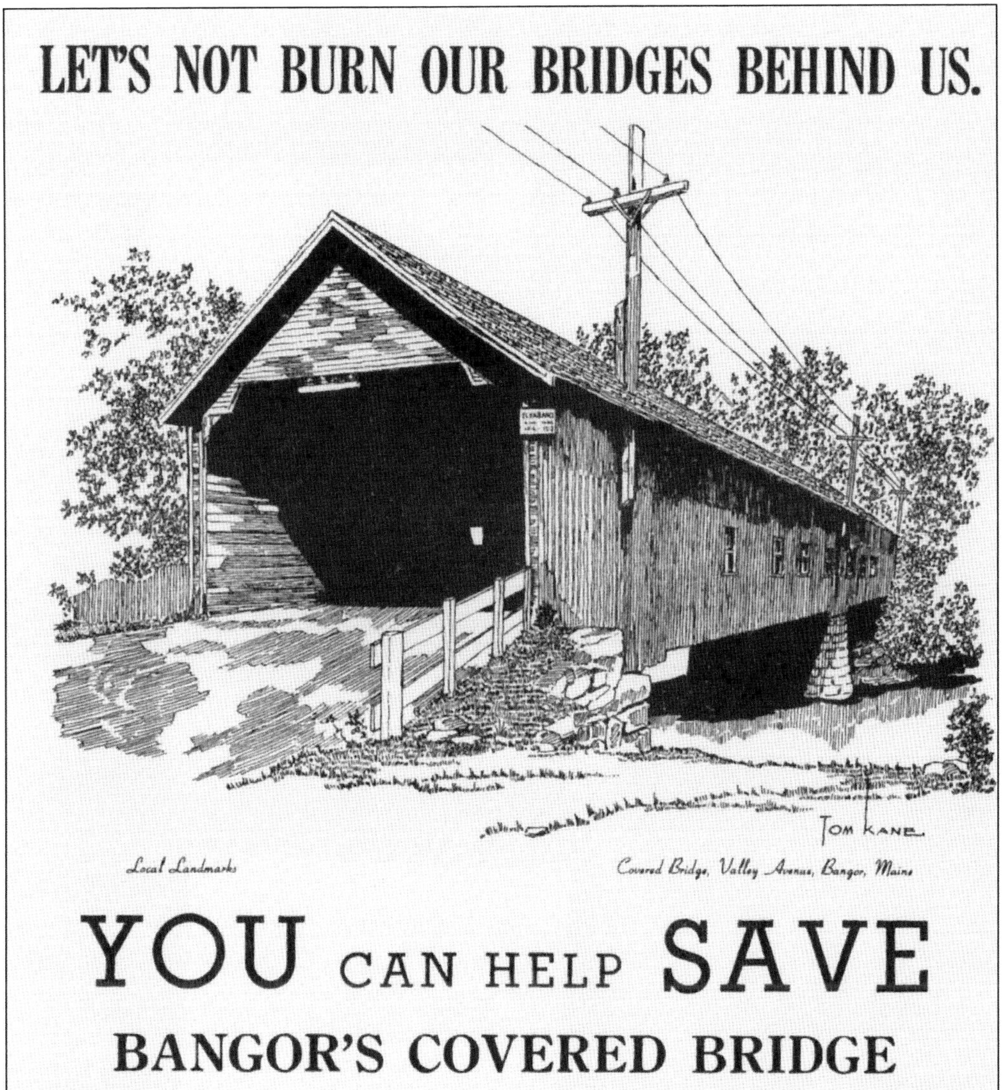

An early preservation effort eventually went awry, but it wasn't the fault of Dr. Bill Shubert and other civic-minded residents who worked to save the old Morse Covered Bridge from oblivion. Private donations and money raised from the sale of plates, notepaper, and other items saved the Valley Avenue landmark from destruction. Plans for the landmark included band concerts, art exhibits, and tourist activities. But its obscure relocation behind buildings on Harlow Street was undesirable, and eventually an arsonist burned the bridge others had tried so hard to preserve.

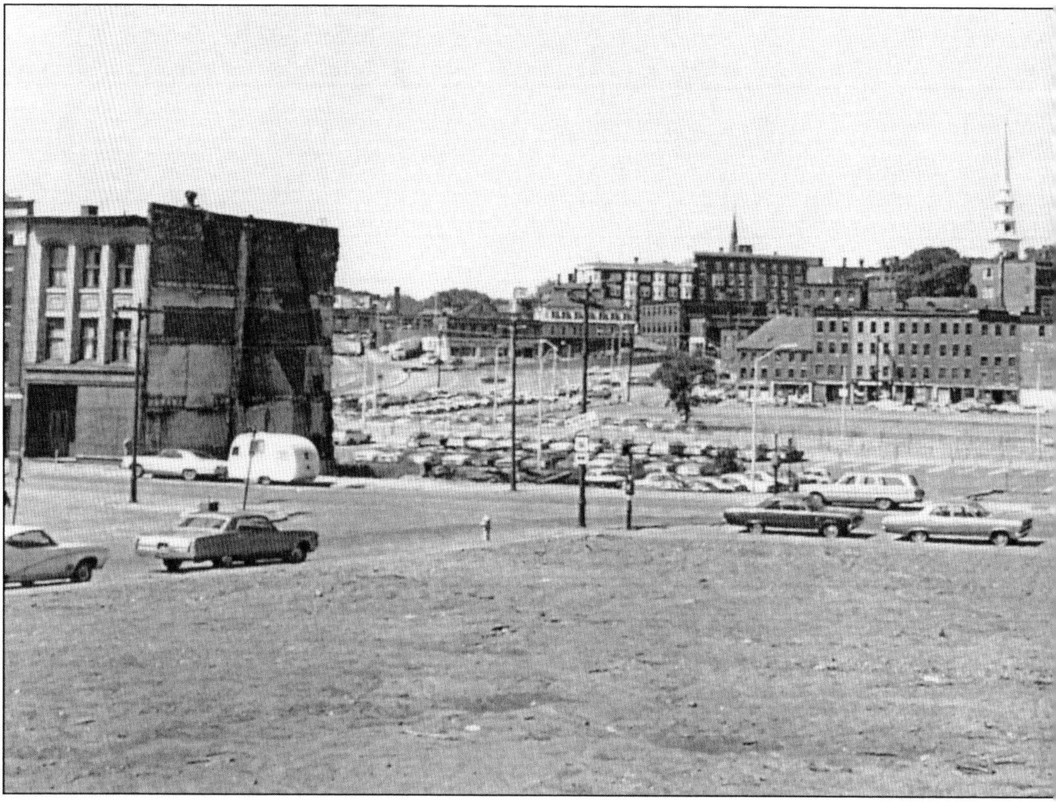

What is wrong with this picture? For a time, nothing seemed wrong with cutting out Bangor's urban blight and planning for a cleaner, more modern downtown. But this photograph was taken five years after voters in 1964 authorized the Urban Renewal Authority to disburse a $5.5 million grant to clean up the city. The problem, in the opinion of many critics, was that much historically valuable property was razed along with the bad. Eventually both sides of Exchange

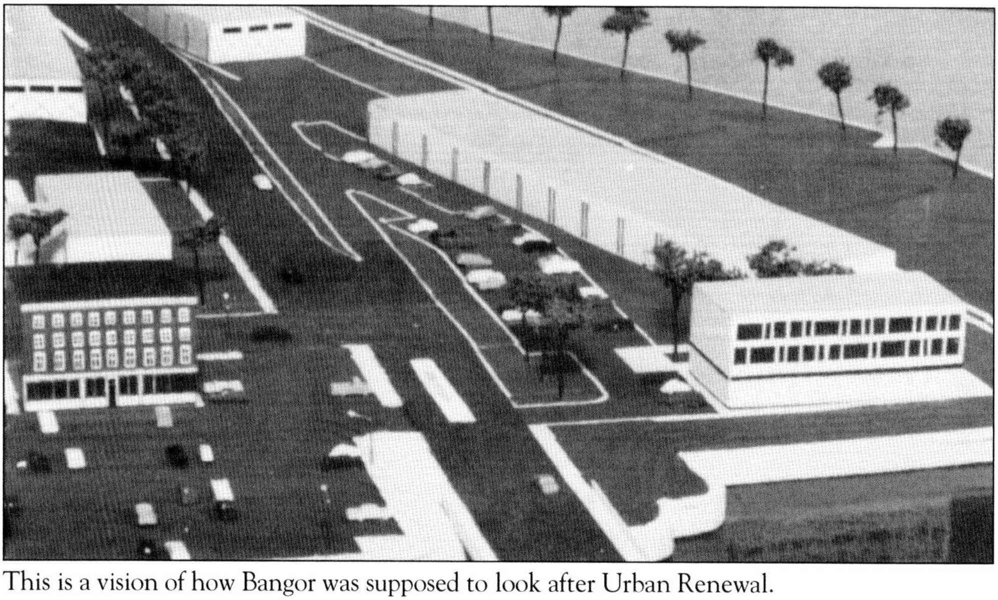

This is a vision of how Bangor was supposed to look after Urban Renewal.

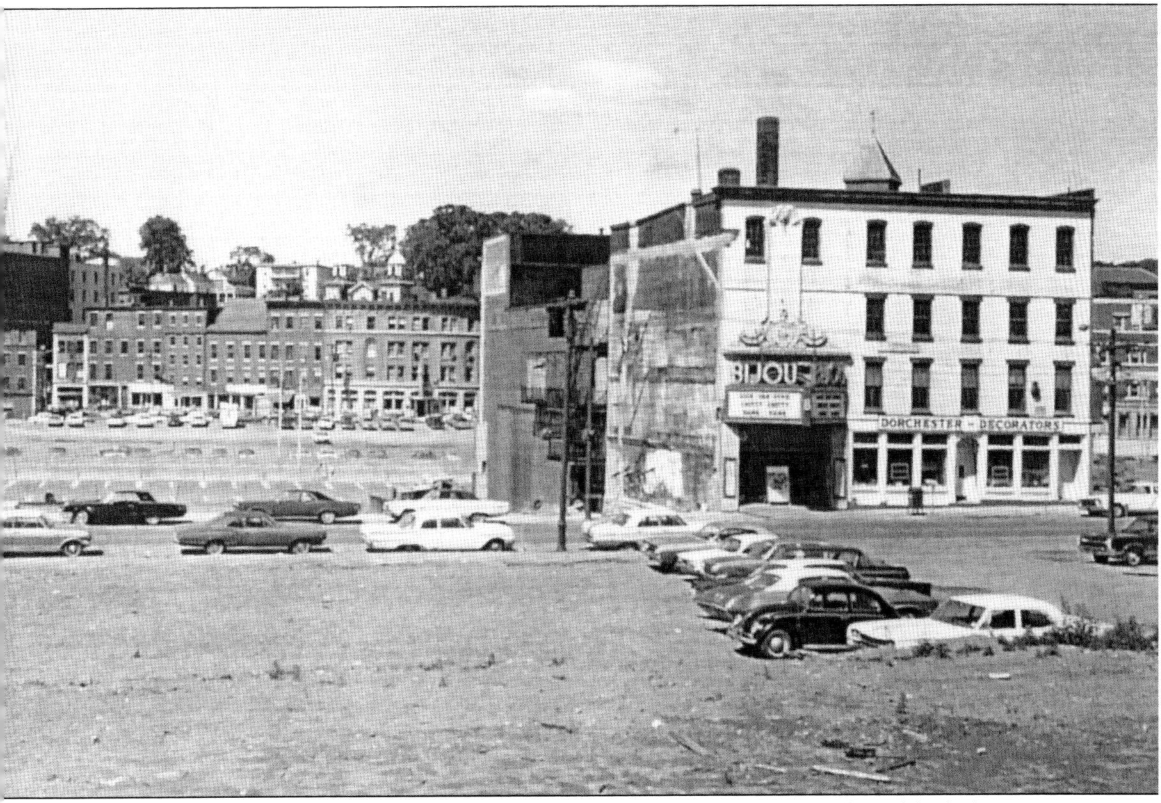

Street (shown here) would be leveled from York to Washington Streets, a three-block distance (the Bijou Theater at the far right was one of the last to be demolished). The heart of one of the city's oldest, most historic districts had been cut out and it would be many years before substantial new construction would fill in the holes. The Urban Renewal promise that new building would soon occur appeared to have been broken.

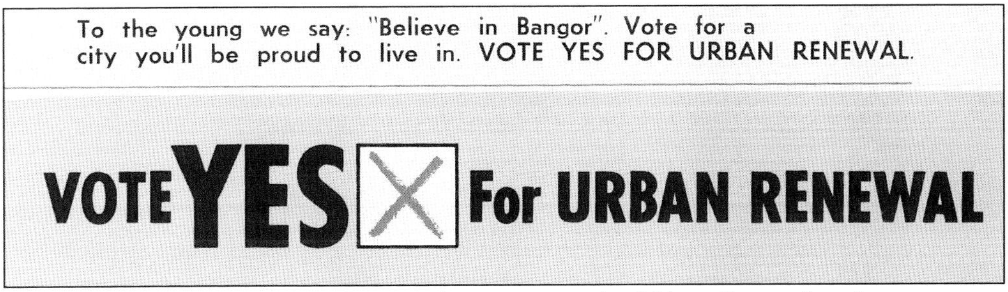
To the young we say: "Believe in Bangor". Vote for a city you'll be proud to live in. VOTE YES FOR URBAN RENEWAL.

VOTE YES ☒ For URBAN RENEWAL

Promotional pamphlets persuading residents to vote for Urban Renewal make interesting reading many years after the fact. Especially ironic is this statement: "Bangor's business district can rise once again to become the vital trading center of northeastern Maine provided its citizens recognize the urgency of the problem and accept this opportunity to correct it by voting in favor of Urban Renewal."

The plan covered a 52-acre area. Included were 200 buildings housing approximately 300 separate business firms; 106 buildings were scheduled for demolition. The assessed valuation of real estate to be acquired was $4.2 million. One of the few promises not seen as empty today was the statement that the plan would provide 150,000 to 200,000 square feet of new and replacement space in the next five years. Vacant downtown space proved it.

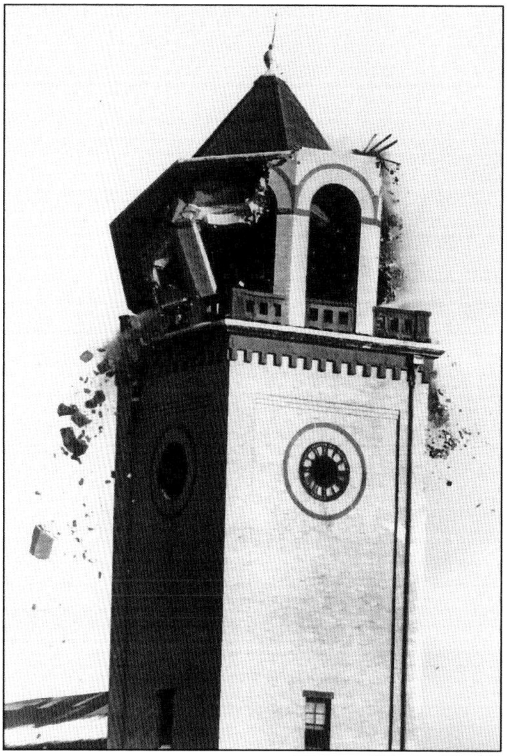

What was there left to say as spectators watched in horror the dynamiting of Union Station tower in 1961? No longer would people set their watches to the huge illuminated clock. No longer could the eye follow Exchange Street to the end and fall upon this beautiful old building's presence. Its loss is widely lamented as the most profound of the Urban Renwal era. No other building touched the public's emotions quite like Union Station.

The station's graceful lines was a feast for the eyes. Inside was a dining room finished in green enamel tile. A barber shop had a white marble floor, gray marble walls, numerous chairs, and many mirrors. An adjacent train shed was very large, being covered with a steel and glass canopy.

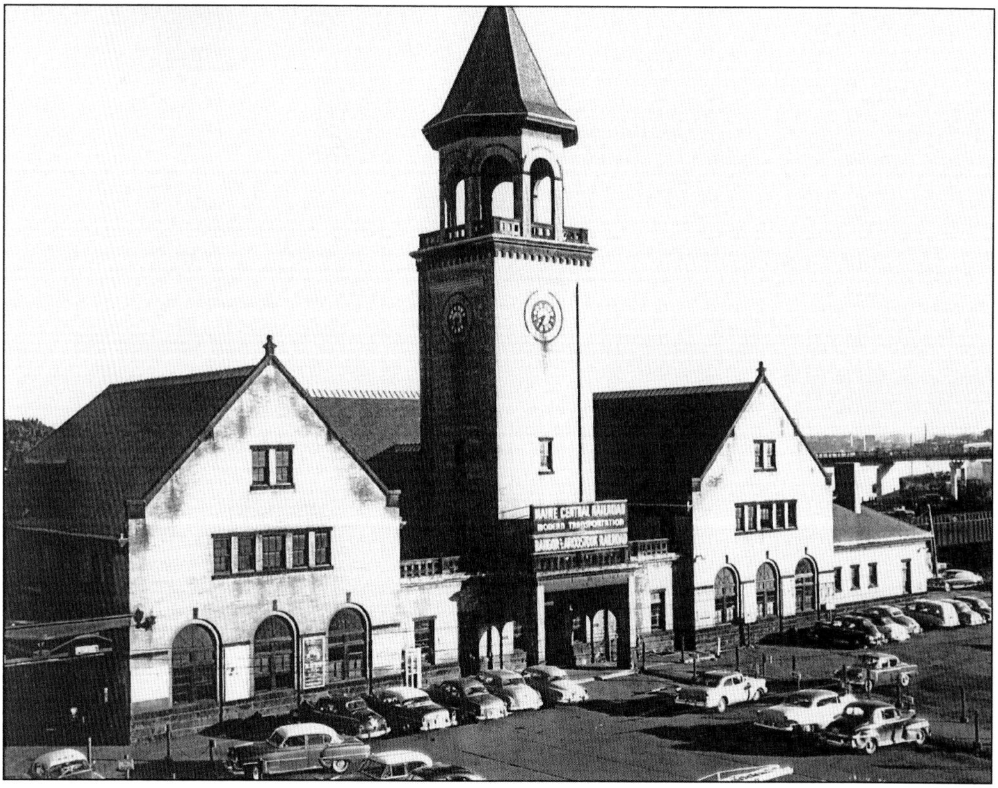

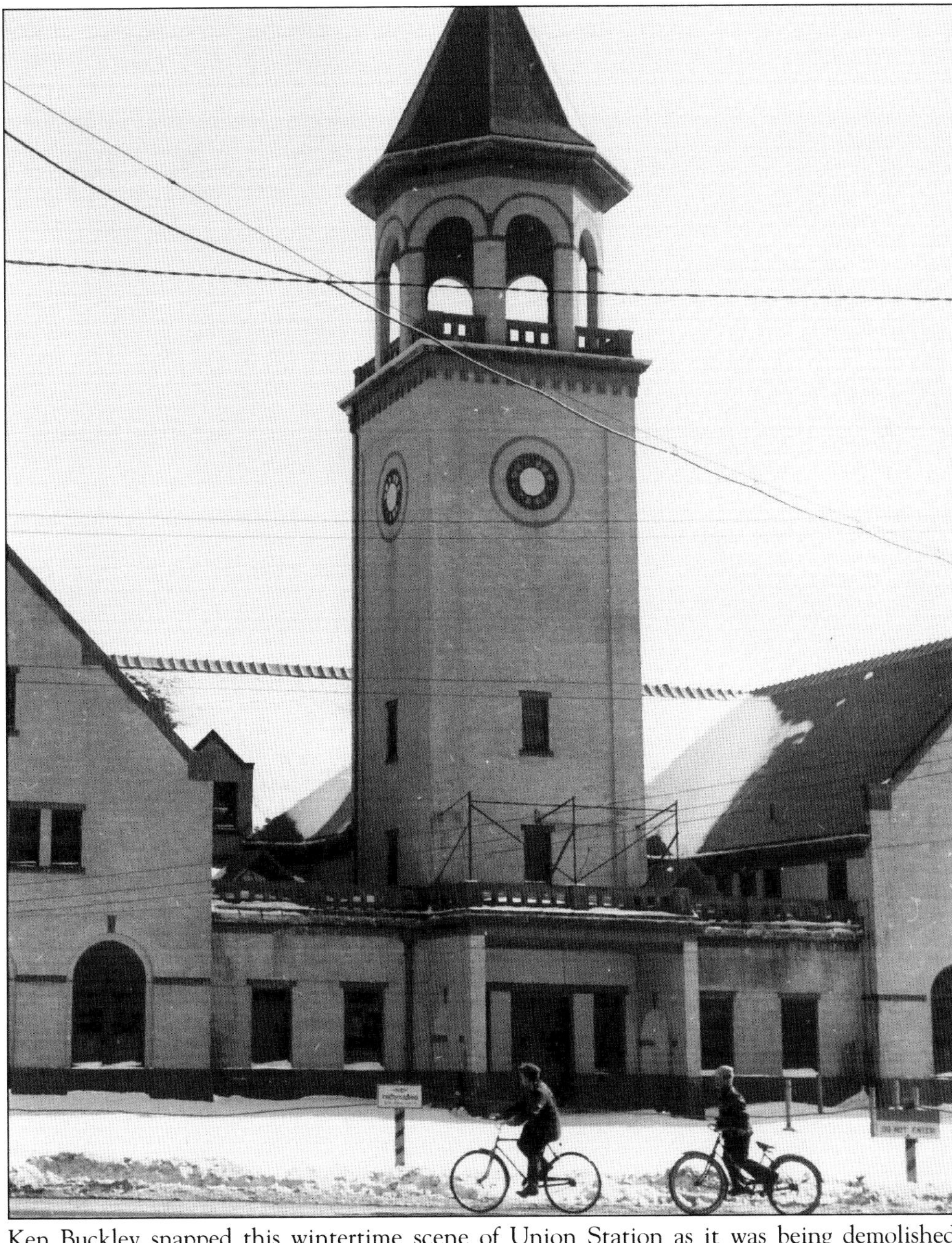

Ken Buckley snapped this wintertime scene of Union Station as it was being demolished. Notice that the hands of the big clock had been removed. Henry B. Fletcher, the architect of the Romanesque Revival treasure, might have wept to see a wrecking ball knocking it down a mere fifty-four years after completion. Today, a nondescript shopping center occupies this site on Washington Street.

Acknowledgments

I hope you've enjoyed this informal look back at Bangor in the twentieth century and will return to it when you want to laugh, learn, or maybe shed a tear over people, places, and good times gone. Even though some of the photographs were selected from my own private collection, I'd be negligent if I didn't credit the other sources of all these wonderful visual images. Many helped out with the first volume of Bangor pictures I compiled for Arcadia in 1994, coming forth again with new photographs to complement those already published. Richard J. Warren, publisher of the *Bangor Daily News*, loaned me the extensive Dan Maher collection, an invaluable help. Charles Campo, the newspaper's head librarian, and fellow librarians Jill Marston and Mary-Anne Saxl answered my questions patiently and dug into the newspaper files to locate rare views of John F. Kennedy and others worth seeing again. Pierre Dumont graciously allowed me to republish a number of fine photographs from his annual historical magazine, *Paper Talks*. Bangor's leading historian, James B. Vickery, again was helpful with historical details, anecdotes, and old images. Mildred N. Thayer let me borrow many pictures from her photographer father's collection; she also spent several afternoons with me adding perspective on the city and its people, and, of course, the Penobscot River. Paul E. Tower shared pictures of fires and firemen and showed me around the Hose No. 5 Museum on State Street. Fred Bryant, the curator of the Bangor police museum on Court Street, turned over fine pictures, including the ones of Eleanor Roosevelt, Teddy Roosevelt, and Jack Benny. Thanks also to the following people: Earle G. Shettleworth Jr. (Maine Historic Preservation Commission); Barbara Rice McDade (Bangor Public Library) and her reference staff; Patricia and Carroll Pickard; Jack and Muriel Lafountain; photographers Scott Haskell, Bob DeLong, Michael York, Jack Loftus, Tom Hindman, Marc Blanchette; the late Spike Webb, Carroll Hall, and Dan Maher; Helen F. Parker; Pat Denner; Peter Bradshaw; Ryan King; Wanda and Eddie Owen; Ken Buckley; Kalil Ayoob; Joe G. Eaton; George and Mary Danby; Steve Robbins; Rick Bronson; Charles Libby; and the Bangor Historical Society. The following books were helpful resources: *Woodsmen and Whigs*, by Abigail Zelz and Marilyn Zoidis; *An Illustrated History of Bangor, Maine, 1769–1976*, by James B. Vickery; and *Bangor, Maine: 1769–1914, An Architectural History*, by Deborah Thompson.